IS YOUR TEEN
STRESSED *or* DEPRESSED?

A Practical and Inspirational Guide
for Parents of Hurting Teens

Dr. Archibald D. Hart
Dr. Catherine Hart Weber

THOMAS NELSON
Since 1798

NASHVILLE   DALLAS   MEXICO CITY   RIO DE JANEIRO   BEIJING

© 2005 by Archibald D. Hart and Catherine Hart Weber
Previously published as STRESSED OR DEPRESSED

All rights reserved. No portion of this book may be reproduced, stored in a retrieval system, or transmitted in any form or by any means—electronic, mechanical, photocopy, recording, scanning, or other—except for brief quotations in critical reviews or articles, without the prior written permission of the publisher.

Published in Nashville, Tennessee, by Thomas Nelson. Thomas Nelson is a registered trademark of Thomas Nelson, Inc.

Thomas Nelson, Inc., titles may be purchased in bulk for educational, business, fund-raising, or sales promotional use. For information, please e-mail SpecialMarkets@ThomasNelson.com.

Unless otherwise indicated, Scripture quotations are taken from the Holy Bible, New Century Version®. © 2005 by Thomas Nelson, Inc. Used by permission. All rights reserved.

Other Scripture quotations are taken from the following sources:
The New King James Version (NKJV). © 1982 by Thomas Nelson, Inc. Used by permission. All rights reserved.

The Holy Bible, New International Version® (NIV). © 1973, 1978, 1984 by International Bible Society. Used by permission of Zondervan Publishing House. All rights reserved.

Library of Congress Cataloging-in-Publication Data

Hart, Archibald D.
  [Stressed or depressed]
  Is your teen stressed or depressed? : a practical and inspirational guide for parents of hurting teens / Archibald D. Hart, Catherine Hart Weber.
      p. cm.
  Originally published: Stressed or depressed. Brentwood, TN : Integrity Publishers, c2005.
  Includes bibliographical references.
  ISBN 978-0-7852-8940-1
  1. Parent and teenager–Religious aspects–Christianity. 2. Adolescent psychology. 3. Stress in adolescence–Religious aspects–Christianity. 4. Depression in adolescence. I. Weber, Catherine Hart, 1957- II. Title.
  BV4529.H345 2008
  248.8'45–dc22

                                                        2008005754

Printed in the United States of America
08 09 10 11 12 RRD 6 5 4 3 2 1

This book is dedicated to
Nicole, Caitlan, and Ashley,
the lovely teen girls of our family and the next generation of adults.
We are honored to be your safe place and to journey alongside you.
Our prayer is that you all come to know God's purposeful love and
that you embrace His hope for your future. May you move through
life's challenges with fortitude, strengthened by God's Spirit to
become a blessing to others. We love you dearly.

And to
Dr. Beth Fletcher Brokaw
on the occasion of your Jubilee Celebration. Your courage, fortitude,
and steadfastness in the face of overwhelming life challenges is an
inspiration to us all. May God be praised for His loving-kindness.

With gratitude to
Kathleen Hart (Arch's wife), whose constant love and intercession
for the family is greatly cherished; Rick Weber (Catherine's husband), for being fabulously enduring, supportive, and enjoyable
along the grand adventure of parenting; Joseph Paul (Sr. Vice
President, Integrity Publishers), whose perceptive vision for a need
enabled this book to be available for parents of today; Laura
Minchew (Sr. Vice President and Publisher, Integrity Family) for
partnering with us and helping to refine and shape the heart of this
book; and Marcus Yoars (Editor) for being painstakingly patient
and giving us his editorial best, even at the expense of sleep!
We so appreciate all your help.

CONTENTS

When to Consider Counseling
Counseling Provides Healing Through Talking and Listening
Types of Counseling
Types of Therapy Pursuing Counseling Help for Your Teen
What Can You Expect from a Counselor?
Finding a Therapist for Your Teen
What to Say During Your Initial Call
Evaluating the Counselor and the Therapy
Understanding the Therapeutic Process
Crisis First
Knowing When to Let Go
Treatment Goals
How Long Will Treatment Last?
What If the Therapy Interventions Aren't Working?
Get the Help Your Teen Needs

Parents Must Stay Informed
Start with a Medical Evaluation
Consider Counseling
How Do Antidepressants Work?
Antidepressants Take Time to Work
Maximum Dose for Maximum Results
Common Fears About Antidepressant Medication
Types of Antidepressant Medications
Side Effects
Questions to Ask
What About Integrative and Herbal Medicines?
Getting Well Takes More Than a Pill a Day

Strategies for Living Well
Building a Wellness Action Plan
Prevention and Restoration

FOREWORD

I (Catherine) began writing this book nearly three years ago. After completing *Unveiling Depression in Women* with my dad, Dr. Archibald D. Hart, we received a great deal of feedback begging for a Judeo-Christian based book to help parents and counselors respond to the rising epidemics of stress and depression among teens, especially in girls. In my own practice as a counselor, I also noticed more teens needing therapy guidance through turbulent times of stress and depression. And so I set out to write.

However, God had a greater plan for this book. No sooner had I begun to write than my family and I went through our own turbulent journey—one that has become a "living testimony" of what the Lord intended for me to write. The result is a more comprehensive book than originally planned, written as both an experienced professional counselor in partnership with my father's years of expertise on these topics and, equally as important, as a parent of teenage daughters. Although I counsel, write, and teach on stress, anxiety, and depression professionally, this resource comes to you fresh out of my personal crucible and empowered with the grace and comfort God has shown me.

I offer this guide as a beacon of encouragement and hope to those of you on a similar journey of parenting teens. Combining my own story with those of others, I pray you are inspired, encouraged, comforted, and filled with the hope of God's mercy and love.

Is Your Teen Stressed or Depressed? is a practical guide for parents, and role models for teens who are struggling in life, in deep waters, or suffering through some form of pain. But this book is also for those wondering if their teen is going through normal growth pains and challenges, or if he is at risk for more serious problems of stress, anxiety, depression, and related challenges and needs professional help.

Parenting teens who are stressed, anxious, depressed, or experiencing other related emotional problems is a challenging, adventurous journey. They are hurting. They live in a confusing, secret world of pain. They are searching for their own ways to deal with their pain yet longing for adults to connect with, understand, love, and accept them. It is our God-given responsibility to provide the help and direction they need.

As a parent, you do everything possible to give your children the greatest protection and opportunity for their success in life. But despite your finest efforts to raise them, you will make mistakes. There is no way to predict when the challenges, twists, and turns on the way will occur. These "suddenlys" of life are always unforeseeable surprises.

When they come unexpectedly, it is easy to surrender to despair as you feel your precious children slipping through your fingers. They can become like strangers and break your heart. Dealing with the complexity and urgency of their survival can seem too much. But here is the truth: no matter how disappointing or overwhelming your situation may be, God is able to use each adversity as an opportunity to learn and grow. There is always hope when you look to God as your source of help and guidance. He offers hope when you are feeling desperate and needing answers and encouragement. And when your children feel they are out of control, you can become a hope giver to them.

Don't try to venture on this journey alone. You may need to call in professional help, and you will certainly need to surround yourself with support from family, friends, and others who can relate. Parenting kids who are struggling with stress, anxiety, depression, and other related challenges will demand that you become intentional in your perspective, focus, and parenting style. Your full attention will be required as you connect and become a safe place for healing and growth. Your character will be challenged, and your own growth will be mandatory. The ups and downs, disappointment, and deep emotional turmoil will necessitate extreme self-care and grueling endurance to the end. But the reward of your teen's healthiness is worth every sacrifice.

As you begin this book, you may feel bewildered, desperately wanting to understand your teen's struggles. Or you may be at your wit's end. I (Arch) pray this book, along with the additional resource suggestions provided, will effectively help you and your teen. But don't try to read it in one sitting. Instead, use this book as an ongoing resource, referring to it frequently and reading the sections most pertinent to you first. And be sure to read the last section. We want to equip you to do your best as you guide your child through this trying season.

Our prayer is that you will be encouraged to find a glimmer of hope and gain a sense of direction. There is a way through these dark hours with our caring Lord as your shepherd, parent, leader, provider, deliverer, protector, forgiver, peace giver, restorer, healer, comforter, and encourager. May the Lord bless you and keep you as you connect with your teen and learn how to parent from the heart of God. As you turn to His strength, wisdom, and courage, may you know His hope and peace through this turbulent journey.

Archibald D. Hart, Ph.D.
Catherine Hart Weber, Ph.D.

part 1

HEARING
HURTING TEENS

1

UNDERSTANDING YOUR TEEN'S WORLD

Those who go to God Most High for safety will be
protected by the Almighty. I will say to the LORD,
"You are my place of safety and protection. You are my
*God and I trust you." —*Psalm 91:1–2

[Parents]. . . put on tender mercies, kindness, humility,
meekness, long suffering, bearing with one another, and
*forgiving one another. —*Colossians 3:12–13 NKJV

I (CATHERINE) RESOLVED TO BE A LOT MORE ATTENTIVE AFTER
recently sitting in the stands at a local high school football game.
On a previous occasion, when my oldest daughter was one of the
homecoming princesses at her private school, my husband and I sat
in the front row of the grandstand, getting the "royal court" treatment.

Not this time. We were just part of the large crowd watching a
game at a new, large, public school. We had climbed into the stands
incognito, finding seats right in the middle of the student body. I
wanted to experience the world of these teens, to be immersed in
their activities while I listened and watched closely.

Our section was filled with a typical group of teens enjoying
some Friday night action. To the right was a cluster of girls wearing
letterman jackets emblazed with badges. Their entire focus was on

who was watching them while they exaggerated every motion and conversation in hopes of being seen. Next to them was a group of visibly awkward students trying to stay low-key, despite having taken special efforts to ensure they looked good. Other teens superficially worked the scene, trying to fit in. To the left of me was a group of teen couples engaged in quite a bit of PDA (Public Display of Affection), as were others scattered around the crowds. As I scanned through the stands, I thought about the difference between these teens' generation and those of the past. Juvenile crime is down. High school seniors drink less alcohol and smoke fewer cigarettes than in the 1970s. In fact, teens nowadays are less likely to smoke than their parents.[1] Fathers are becoming more involved, and many teens are being nurtured and cared for. They are motivated to do well and get ahead, and they show resilience to the many challenges they face in the culture and in the home. A recent Gallup Youth Survey, for example, indicates that teens now show increased interest in helping people less fortunate and have contributed to a society that is less racist, less sexist, less polluted, and more peace loving.

HOPE FOR HURTING TEENS

While there is optimism that many of our teens are journeying to adulthood mostly unscathed, there are others who are hurting and struggling through troubled times, despite their outward appearance of doing well. And as I looked around the stands at the football game, I wondered who would go home later that night, let down the happy facade, and fall into bed in despair because they weren't "attractive" or popular or cool enough. Which ones were grieving a deep loss for which they had no words to express? How many were battling the inner turmoil of stressed lives?

My heart was filled with compassion and empathy as I realized that one in five of these outwardly happy faces were vulnerable or at risk for experiencing depression. Many were under tremendous stress, a major cause of anxiety and depression. I wondered who would be the next to start having panic attacks. Who would become yet another homicide and suicide victim simply being overweight or consumed with materialism? (Both risk factors have contributed to the sharp increase in homicide and suicide rates compared to a few decades ago.)

Teens today are growing up in a different world than we did, facing challenges at a younger age and having more severe troubles with stress, depression, and related problems. They are more readily diagnosed with psychological problems than their parents were as teens. But here is the good news: scientific research has made great strides in helping us understand and treat these problems, meaning that teens can more easily overcome, get well, and stay living well. Of course, there are no miracle cures or magic pills. Still, parents can learn practical strategies and apply biblical principles to make a difference and help their teens get better.

This book purposes to do exactly that. It's important to know that, as a parent, you are not alone. You can find hope, healing, and practical help for your teen. These pages can help you respond to your teen's struggles as you partner with her to get help, get better, and stay well. Your teen can flourish in her journey from childhood to adulthood, and you can become a safe place for her to overcome adversity.

We will begin this journey by helping you enter into your teen's world to understand what she is up against. What fears does she encounter on a daily basis? Who around her gets stressed or depressed? How does she react to this? By recognizing your teen's surroundings, your approach and perspective can impact the relationship you have with her while making you aware of problematic areas in her life. As a result, you can become a caring, safe place for her, which is absolutely crucial in this venture.

Remember, as parents, you matter more than you realize. You are the most important, influential adult in your child's life, despite the masked facades and mixed messages she may give.

TURBULENT TIMES FOR TROUBLED TEENS

I (Arch) grew up in South Africa. I remember taking my future wife, Kathleen, for dates on my bicycle when movies were only twenty-five cents. And when I (Catherine) was young, a "rubber" was just an eraser and drive-ins were a great place for a family outing. Sundays were for going to church, visiting with family and friends, and taking naps. Woolworth's served a great grilled-cheese sandwich and strawberry milk-shake at the takeout counter. The neighborhood was safe enough for kids to hang out all day. The media didn't dominate our lives by telling us how to look and what to buy. Phony "reality" shows didn't exist. In fact, I didn't even see a TV until my early teens when we moved to the United States.

Sure, we had other challenges, just as you may have had. However, with every generation come greater and greater challenges. Today, teens deal with Internet pornography and online predators. Cutting is becoming a major concern. Suicide is becoming the second greatest killer of teens. One in three girls and one in six boys will be sexually abused by the age of eighteen. The age of a teen's first drink used to be fourteen; now it is twelve.

The tumultuous journey of transitioning from childhood to adulthood has never been easy. But what this current generation of teens—and those to follow—is facing will likely be even more challenging than the past. We can already see how major issues are arising sooner in life for today's teens. Future teens will have to overcome monumental hurdles at even younger ages. Their deep pain will be different from what we felt in our high school days. Their internal struggles will complicate the carefree teen years that are supposed to be "the best time of your life."

Health professionals are seeing an increase in the rates of stress, anxiety, depression, and other related disorders such as substance abuse and suicide. There is also a rise in attention deficit and conduct disorders. Extensive empirical research by the Commission on Children at Risk found that large and growing numbers of U.S. children and adolescents are failing to flourish. In particular, more and more young people are suffering from mental illness, emotional distress, and behavioral problems.[2] The mental health and medical communities are now considering these disorders national epidemics with serious consequences to the next generation of adults.

Increasingly, the greatest threat to harming or killing our teens today is mental illness, emotional distress, and the consequent behavioral problems. During the last fifty years, depression has increased at an astonishing rate. About twenty times more people suffer from depression today than in 1955, with greater stress being the predominant cause. Within the past thirty years, the average age of depression onset has dropped from twenty-nine to between fourteen and fifteen! Depression has now become a "teenage disorder" accompanied by such other problems as anxiety, eating disorders, cutting, and substance abuse.

WHO SUFFERS?

Even the most stellar teens face difficult times that can shake up their world. A teen may have been an absolute joy when young, until suddenly, out of the blue, things don't seem quite right anymore. Others never seem to get off to a good start. They may have struggled as soon as they hit the teen years and have accumulated the effects of a secret life of pain and frustration.

It can happen to the best of them—academic achievers, star athletes, homecoming princesses, those from solid, caring Judeo-Christian homes. It can also happen to those who don't feel they fit in, who plunge into low self-esteem, who don't like who they are and become who they don't want to be. Add to this list those whose worlds are being turned upside-down by fragmentation of their family structure, by illness or a sudden loss, and who feel a deep sense of meaninglessness or disconnection. The lonely and abandoned are not exempt. It happens to those lured by peer pressure into smoking, substance use and abuse, sexual promiscuity, violence, or other dangerous, high-risk behavior.

Some are wounded; others suffer consequences of poor choices. Some are born with a genetic predisposition that puts them at risk for stress, depression, and related disorders. Those who grow up in an environment that negatively impacted their early development are especially at risk. Some are born with a vulnerable personality,

U.S. TEEN STATS AT A GLANCE

· Twenty-one percent of children ages nine to seventeen have a diagnosable mental or addictive disorder associated with at least minimum impairment.

· Young people today are more likely to be depressed and anxious than their parents, leading to an increase in suicide attempts, alcohol use, and a wide variety of physical ailments including asthma, heart disease, irritable bowel syndrome, and ulcers.

· Youth are experiencing an increase in mental illness, stress, and emotional problems while also suffering from high rates of related behavioral problems such as substance abuse, school dropout, interpersonal violence, premature sexual intercourse, and teenage pregnancy.

· Among college students, the number of students being treated for depression has doubled in the last thirteen years, while the number of suicidal students has tripled. The number of students treated after a sexual assault has quadrupled.

(Adapted from "A Report for the Nation from the Commission on Children at Risk" by the Institute for American Values. Hardwired to Connect [2003])

learning challenge, or a lower tolerance for stress or brain chemistry that makes them vulnerable to moodiness and pessimism. Others lack close connection with a parent, causing low self-esteem or feelings of abandonment. Parent styles that are harsh, too pressured, or too lenient can also lead to teen problems.

Regardless of the cause, the epidemic of stress and depression has motivated many research scientists and helping professionals to look for explanations and solutions. The good news is that we are making progress in our understanding of teen depression. And it is this good news that motivates us to write this book. Teenagers can be helped through their difficult times.

FINDING HOPE AND PRACTICAL HELP

The parents of stressed and depressed teens share a similar experience: they all feel frustrated and overwhelmed, and they are desperately looking for guidance. They have questions they need answered: *What is normal for a teen? What is wrong with my teen? How do I parent a hurting teen? Never mind my teenager, how do I get through this myself?* Parents realize that unless they are able to successfully survive the trials of their troubled teen, their teen won't survive either!

You and your family might be in such a crisis. It may be why you picked up this book. The world around and beneath you has been shaken like an earthquake, and the effects have been disastrous to your lives, leaving you in what a tsunami survivor described as "the land of walking wounded." Teens can easily crumble in the face of a sudden emotional tsunami, where they are overtaken by giant waves of unexpected turmoil. They can easily be swept off their feet.

Our desire in writing this book is to help you recognize when this is happening and develop a plan to intervene. We wrote this book out of the heart and experience of many strained parents, from our own experience, and based on the practical, proven interventions available in the mental health world. We pray this book offers hope to all your family while providing you with a practical resource guide to:

- *Inspire you* to turn your heart toward your teen, to listen with renewed love, understanding, and perspective. In helping your teen through the turbulent journey into adulthood, you must enter into her world, discovering her need as you partner with her to grow, heal, and flourish.
- *Equip you* to be aware of signs, symptoms, and triggers of stress and depression. It's crucial for you to know how to respond to your teen's struggles and pain, and

how to get help. You can learn how to help her recover from stress and overcome depression practically on a daily basis, while also creating a safe place for her to get well and stay well.

- *Encourage you* along the way. Parenting a hurting, stressed, anxious, or depressed teen can be extremely stressful, tiring, and emotionally exhausting.

In the process, we pray that hope will be ignited so you can in turn become a hope giver; that you will receive comfort to be a comforter for others; that you will persevere in prayer, counting your blessings and refusing to give up; and that you will discover meaning and purpose in your struggle so you can pass on the grace and mercy God grants you.

SAFE-PLACE PARENTING FOR HURTING TEENS

As much as we try to protect our children from the dangers and influences in the world, many teens still run into trouble. The key to surviving their struggle is universal: become a *shelter* for your teen. That doesn't mean you should shelter him in the sense of being overprotective. Teens are crying out for a safe place of hope. You can be that place. No matter where you are in your struggle, it is never too late to provide a safe haven for your teen and make a difference.

In doing so, it is important to understand some of the fundamental truths you will encounter as you enter into your teen's world of stress and depression. For each challenge, you can become a "safe-place parent," a parent who creates a home environment and a personal relationship that is emotionally safe and who establishes the essential foundation of resiliency to help a teen overcome depression.

1. Hurting teens *live in two worlds*: life on the surface and life beneath the surface.

On the surface, an average high-schooler can appear carefree, game for the latest social event, and completely cool in his designer clothes. Yet for the hurting teen, this appearance is often a mask that hides internal pain and fears.

Hurting teens' outward facades don't match their inner reality. On the surface they are bombarded with the challenges of school, pressures to perform, the influence and acceptance of peers, partying, drugs, drinking, sex, and family problems. Yet deep inside they may be struggling with stress, confusion, low self-image, loneliness, turmoil, insecurity, sadness, and despair.

Because they don't always feel safe turning to adults for help, they take matters into their own hands, turning to negative influences for ways of numbing, escaping, soothing, or self-medicating. Alcohol, smoking, cutting, eating disorders, pornography, sexual promiscuity, problems at school, sadness, irritability, and loss of interest in activities are all early indicators that a teen is masking a deeper issue. And they are usually the first signs that your teen may be in trouble.

Safe-place parents *look beneath the surface* to the heart of their teen.

Studies consistently show that an overwhelming majority of teens have friends and acquaintances that have experienced depression, drug and alcohol exploration, and sexual activity. Yet most often, teens say they wish they could discuss these issues in-depth not just with their friends but with their parents and other adults. Teens are letting out a primal scream of fear, anger, confusion, and hurt. Many have deep needs that are not being met, and your teen may be one of them. They want to be trusted, understood, and loved. They need to feel safe and secure, and they long for a life of meaning and purpose. They want to be listened to and heard, to be appreciated and valued, and to be supported in their efforts. They long for genuine connection and meaningful relationships based on real love.[3]

To begin the process of helping your teen, you must first discover exactly what he is facing. What's really going on beneath the surface?

2. Hurting teens tend to keep secrets, longing to be understood and loved.

This can apply to everyday events, but especially for teens who experience traumas such as rape, physical abuse, or overwhelming stress. Teens tend to keep hurtful and stressful things to themselves and internalize their pain. They don't yet know what to do with their painful feelings or where to go for help, so they keep these struggles hidden. Teenagers don't always understand the reality of what is happening to them, how to make sense of their strong emotions, or how to communicate their feelings.

Deep down they wish they could just go to their parents or other adults for support, but few actually do. Most think that parents and adults in general are not available to talk to, or if they were they wouldn't really understand — and tragically, their fears about sharing with adults are often justified. Teens who are in desperate trouble truly believe that there is nowhere to turn for help.

This means your teen could be going through desperate times of struggle and pain right under your own roof, and you either don't know it or are completely misinterpreting the emotional and behavioral signals. Unless you are intentionally observant of the deceptive exteriors and question the subtle changes you might see, you will be totally unaware of what your teen is hiding deep inside.

Because teens generally don't give clear signals of distress to adults, they end up not getting the help they desperately need. And a teen who stays secretively alone in pain will only spiral to much bigger and more severe problems.

A feature on CBS's *The Early Show* highlighted the current rise of teen suicides on college campuses, which is now the second leading cause of death among teenagers, second only to accidents. A few parents who had lost their teens to suicide were interviewed as part of their campaign to raise awareness among other parents and the general public. They all had a similar message: they never saw the signs, and their teens never said anything about the extent of their pain or went to get help. The suicides came out of the blue, with absolutely no outward signs whatsoever.

HOW WELL DO YOU KNOW YOUR TEENAGER?

What is going on inside your teen's world? Ask yourself the following questions:

1. Who are your teen's friends? Why does he hang around them? What does he like about them?
2. What does your teen worry about? What specifically is on his mind?
3. How do God and spiritual matters fit into his life?
4. What does he enjoy doing in his spare time?
5. What is important to him? Ask him to share some of his music, video games, or whatever is important to him with you. Listen, be interested, and temper your own reaction.
6. What adults does your teen admire? Why?
7. What drama or crisis has recently occurred at school among his friends or with any of the groups he is associated? How has that impacted him?
8. What does your teen long for? What does he need and want from you right now?

One son had been a star basketball player who, after getting injured, had lost his position on the team. He never told his parents, apparently afraid of disappointing them, yet he grew more discouraged over time. The first sign that anything was wrong was when they got a call one night informing them that their son had shot himself. He had kept his deep pain secretly locked up inside until it became unbearable and he couldn't take it anymore. And his parents didn't have a clue! Looking back, they could see how they might have been more aware—but it's too late now. As a result, they have committed themselves to helping other parents detect the early warning signs of teenage despair.

Safe-place parents *venture inside their hurting teen's world* with empathy and respect.

As you observe and listen to your teen's world, you will begin to discern the deep emotions and longings that lie behind the big talk, the exaggerations, the makeup and trendy clothes, and the smiling masks they wear. You have to look beyond the surface behavior and outward appearance with a questioning, inquisitive, from-his-perspective point of view. By placing yourself in his shoes, you can become empathic and compassionate toward his life experience and emotional turmoil.

Ask yourself questions like:

- What does he really feel about himself, and how does he overcome being so insecure?
- How does he fit in, connect, and belong in the subculture in which he lives?
- How does he deal with the tension of pushing you away as a parent while still needing to feel secure, knowing he has a safe place he can return to, a place where he feels he is loved unconditionally?

The point of entering into your teen's world is to understand him better, empathize with his pain, and be aware of his struggles and often harsh environment. But be warned. Many parents go in and come out sick to their stomachs, heartbroken, disappointed, and devastated. The reality is that many teens are drinking, using drugs, cutting themselves, vandalizing, or victimizing the innocent. Others are "hooking up" for sexual experimentation, attending wild parties, viewing pornography on the Internet, meeting older predators through instant messaging or chat rooms, or acting out violent crimes. Even realizing that your teen has a mental health disorder can be a rude awakening.

But be assured, this discovery is just the beginning of healing. Your disappointments and even tragedies may be the very means God chooses to show His love, grace, and transforming power. Wholeness and restoration is always possible after brokenness.

WATCH YOUR INITIAL REACTION

The initial shock of discovering what goes on in your teen's life can be alarming and can cause an array of painful emotional reactions for parents. Some parents are totally devastated. Some experience spiritual confusion, feeling betrayed by God. *Why is He allowing this to happen to our family? I live to please God. If I love my son so much and don't want him to suffer, why would God allow this to happen to us? What have we done to deserve this? Where did I go wrong?*

Grieving parents wrestle with anger, embarrassment, guilt, and self-blame. These are all normal initial reactions. But for their children's sake, parents have to get beyond their reactions and move toward taking constructive steps to deal with the problem facing them.

In doing so, it is crucial to use "parental self-control." This involves initially calming yourself down. Don't lash out at your teen from a place of pain and anger. Your unfiltered initial response is to overreact and judge him as a delinquent, a disappointment, or simply unlovable. Such an overreaction will greatly hurt your relationship with him, and you will lose the most valuable resource you have for transformation and maturity: your connection and relationship with him.

Instead, calm down, choose your words carefully, and be patient. Ask the Lord to comfort you, give you wisdom, and lead you through your grieving process. Pray for Him to transform you into a safe place and to put you into the position where you can intentionally and purposefully parent your teen through these struggles as he journeys into adulthood.

3. Hurting teens *push and pull as they become their own person.*
Teens live between two worlds; they are partially adultlike and partially childlike, and they often fluctuate between the two. It's reflected

in their attitude: "It's my life, I can do what I want to." Part of parenting involves simultaneously letting teens go while also keeping them close and engaging in the battle for their souls. Teens need to be supported and freed to be their own person, but parents must also maintain an open heart and door, keeping a vigilant wartime lookout for danger.

Teens go through several developmental changes as they grow, moving in and out of being a child while experimenting with being an adult. This push-and-pull can be a terrifying process for parents, especially when a child is going through challenges that complicate it. Teens need parents to understand the developmental process, to be patient, and to be flexible to love both the growing child and support the emerging adult.

The battle between being a child and an emerging adult, however, can become fierce for you as a parent. Your negative responses can be easily triggered, bringing out your protective, emotional dragons. *What is my daughter thinking? Doesn't she know better? Didn't she listen to anything I taught her?*

The truth is that hurting teens can be clumsy and out of control with their moods and attitude. Their thinking can become distorted. They can become physically weak and easily trade their joy in for sorrow. Their brain chemistry seems to derail them to a state that can only be described as temporary insanity. Something inside them can shut down, and they can easily move into isolation. God can seem unreachable and rejecting to them. In public they can look and act appalling, causing great concern and embarrassment. And wouldn't you know it: this is when they actually need triple doses of your love!

Safe-place parents *change and grow, being flexible* in their parenting style.

Because teens go through several developmental stages on their journey from childhood to adulthood, both the style and process of parenting have to change as the needs of each stage emerge. A parent cannot be locked into any one style of parenting the whole way through adolescence. The needs of teenagers will change as they develop. Some will develop faster than others, often putting them out of step with their peers. Some might be physically or emotionally older than a peer, or vice versa. This discrepancy can be challenging for parents who have just settled comfortably into one style of parenting, only to discover that they have to change again. You will need to maintain a flexible attitude in your parenting style that takes into account your teen's maturing and individuating.

4. Hurting teens' *symptoms of distress look different from adults,* often causing them to delay getting the help they need.
One of the main reasons parents and the medical community overlook or downplay disorders of stress, depression, and anxiety in teens is because the symptoms of these disorders can be tricky to identify. "Normal" teen development can be confused with emerging difficulties. There is no one symptom that clearly indicates a serious problem. Some teens do not show a dramatic drop in grades or change in personality, but instead operate as if nothing has changed on the surface.

Fortunately, there are ways to detect indications of a problem when parents pay attention. (We'll expand on this in the following chapters.) Teens can manifest subtle signs of changes in appearance, a change of friends, or the type of music they listen to. They can isolate themselves behind closed doors or appear unusually sullen. We often take for granted that easygoing children will always be that way, even if they still seem somewhat disturbed. But every parent of a teen needs to keep his eyes and ears open all the time. When things don't seem to make sense, if you suspect your teen is lying or you intuitively have concerns, assume that there might be things that aren't right. Go against your false guilt or fears of not trusting her and consider that something else might be going on. Question her attitude, behavior, and mood if something naturally doesn't make sense.

Many parents, in retrospect, lament what they could have done earlier to intervene in a troubled teen's life. They are plagued by questions such as: *What were the signs I should have seen? How could I have done a better job to get help?* The advice of parents who have gone down this road before is that it's better to have your suspicions lead to nothing than to be sorry you didn't listen to your gut feelings — the still, small nagging voice inside — and follow the subtle clues.

Safe-place parents *become aware and learn* to recognize and respond to the signs, symptoms, and triggers of distress.
Teenage depression doesn't always manifest itself like adult depression. There are more acting-out behaviors linked to teenage depression than most parents realize. This means that as parents you cannot just leave it to the professionals to figure out when your teen needs help. You need to be knowledgeable enough to initiate this help yourself.

Your teen may need professional help to get better. The sooner she gets help, the sooner she will get well and the less severe her depression will become — decreasing the chances of her having other related problems or recurring episodes.

5. Hurting teens can *become depressed and anxious when stressed.*
Stress is the culprit for many other teenage problems, putting teens at high risk for all sorts of substance abuses. Because of excess or prolonged stress, a teen's entire life is affected. Teens' brains get overwhelmed and distracted, so they don't do as well in school. Their immune system is lowered, making them more vulnerable to illness. Stress makes teens psychologically and physically sick!

I (Catherine) recently counseled a bright teen girl who had gone off to a prestigious college after high school, only to come back after her first semester an anxious wreck. She began experiencing panic attacks and social phobia out of the blue and couldn't function well enough to stay in school. Her parents brought her back home and sent her to counseling with me. As it turns out, the dear girl was loaded with pressure and stress. Her brain and body just couldn't keep up with the demands in her life. As a result, she became anxious and depressed.

Through her awareness of the effects of stress in our counseling process, she learned ways to deal with expectations and adjust her lifestyle to recover from these stressors. Today she lives life with a lot less damaging stress. Her example is proof that understanding the dangers of teen stress is crucial for parents helping their teens journey well through the adolescent years.

Safe-place parents *help teens recover from stress and overcome depression* **while implementing a practical lifestyle.**
Once you recognize the signs and symptoms of stress and depression in your teen, it is essential to consider the importance of effective professional intervention and treatment from a doctor, counselor, or psychiatrist. Along with these conventional treatments, she needs to learn practical skills and strategies for recovering from stress and growing through hardships in life.

Daily lifestyle habits such as what she eats, how much she exercises, and the amount of sleep she gets is crucial to enhancing her journey. You can learn how to infuse her life with positive factors while reducing negative ones, which will greatly increase her chances of overcoming depression and preventing relapse. Along with this, she can learn how to be more attentive to her strengths, emotions, and relationships that will undergird her efforts to prevail over adversity.

6. Hurting teens can feel *disconnected, lonely, and abandoned.*
The concept of teens lacking close connections has appeared throughout recent research. In fact, the Commission on Children at Risk discovered that, for the most part, the cause of the deteriorating mental, emotional, and behavioral health of teens in America today is a lack of connectedness. This is strongly verified by Robert D. Putnam's research, published in *Bowling Alone*[4] and *Better Together,*[5] in which he shows how the decline in our culture has led us to become increasingly disconnected from family, friends, neighbors and other important structures.

Teens feel disconnected from family and society. During the past few decades, there has been a general decline in close connections to other people, and with it, a deep disconnectedness to moral and spiritual meaning as well. Other studies on current trends in the youth world have also found that many teens report a feeling of abandonment by their busy parents and disconnection from society in general.[6]

In *The Disconnected Generation*, Josh McDowell states that an intimate bond with teens is essential to providing their needed sense of authenticity, importance, security, significance, lovability, and responsibility. We must become a safe place for our teens while helping them renew and build communities of connection. These "communities" include people who are committed to one another over time, who model good values, and provide nurturing and direction. Family, church, neighborhood, school, sports teams, groups of interest, work place, non-profit organizations, government—all are places that play a role in positively impacting teens lives.[7]

Safe-place parents *build a safe, connecting relationship* so their teens can flourish and heal.

Hurting teens in crisis want help and answers. Parents need to be in relationship. Surveys clearly show that most teens want their parents' input. Parents are the healing heart of the home. That means you need to turn your heart toward home, being available to learn, listen, and know how to respond in effective, hopeful ways to your teen. You set the tone for your teen's healing and well-being. There are three major ways you can establish this environment for an impacting relationship with your teen.

Create a safe place. We are absolutely convinced—and research supports it—that if you create a home that is a safe place for your teenager, you will be providing him with the best environment in which to thrive and cope with stressors. It won't prevent all problems in life, but it will provide a stronger foundation for overcoming challenges and adjusting to change.

Hurting teens need a safe place to be, become, and belong. It is essential for their development and healing. When you create a secure, protected place and make a strong connection with your teen, he will be more likely to come to you in times of need and risk sharing his pain and joys. Without this heart connection, you will not have the same level of influence to speak into his life or earn the right to have access. No matter if you are divorced, a single parent, or a caregiver, the relationship you have with a hurting teen can make a big difference.

This is so important that we outline some essential principles for building such a connection with your teen in chapter 12. These include: giving unconditional love, offering and creating trust, being emotionally available, and being responsive.

Become a hope giver. Hurting teens need hope. They need to feel that there is a future with purpose and opportunity. Without hope, their spirit will despair.

"The people who have impacted me the most were those who told me that what is right with me is more powerful than anything that is wrong with me."

This quote from a teenager is profound. In everything you say to your teen, start with affirming the positive, speaking encouragement—even if you can only think of one thing. Express genuine concern for your teen, assuring her that you want to listen and be there with her through these difficult times. When you do this, you give her hope!

Ask your teen to share with you what she is feeling and experiencing—and *listen*. Ask how you can be a better parent to her, and what would be helpful—and *listen*. Assure her that she can overcome these challenges and that you will find help and partner with her during this difficult season. Apologize and ask for forgiveness for any ways that you have dismissed her and been insensitive to her experience, perspective, and longings. Let her know that you want her words to challenge and captivate your heart, so that the change in you will bring a more effective change in her. And finally, tell her you want to be a safe place for her.

Take it to the Lord in prayer. As a parent of a hurting teen, you may frequently be driven to pray out of desperation. The good news is that is absolutely the best place you can go. And thank God, that is where He wants us—to turn to Him, to trust in Him, and to discover that He does answer prayer. If at this moment your desperation and struggle as a parent of a hurting teen is too overwhelming, then turn to chapter 13 on prayer and start looking over some of the prayer guidelines we offer as you pray for practical direction and the healing of your child. Ask for God's wisdom, guidance, strength, and endurance for the long haul. Pray for the Holy Spirit to open your heart with renewed love and perspective and practical application. Pray for your teenager's particular hurts, struggles, and needs. Pray for breakthrough, healing, wholeness, and peace for your child.

Invite God to partner with you in all you do to fulfill your assignment of parenting and loving your teenager. You can pray something similar to the following prayer right now:

Lord, forgive me where I have not been sensitive to my teen's hurt and need for nurture, protection, care, and guidance. I come to You in utter desperation, fear, and longing for my child. Help me deal with my emotional reactions and confusion so I will do no harm. Open my heart toward the heart of my child, to be objectively sensitive to his needs and pain. Give me insight into the reality of the world my teen lives in, and what he has to encounter daily. I submit myself to You, embracing faith, hope, and love for the assignment of being a parent to this child. Amen.

2

WHAT IS NORMAL AND WHAT IS NOT: A HEALTHY JOURNEY THROUGH THE TEEN YEARS

Despite all the new scientific research . . . there is a consensus among experts that the most beneficial thing for teenagers is good relationships with their parents . . . With all the science and with all the advances, the best advice we can give is . . . to spend loving, quality time with our children. —"Inside the Teenage Brain," *Frontline*, PBS

THE TIME FROM CHILDHOOD TO ADULTHOOD IS ONE OF change, growth, and development. Getting through to adulthood poses some of the most adventurous yet difficult years for families. Teens are eager to arrive, yet they face many changes internally and externally along the way. It can make for a frustrating journey. Teens may feel that no one understands their feelings, thoughts, and struggles, and as a result they can become angry, feel alone, and become confused while they face the complex issues of their changing bodies, brains, and identity. To add to the equation, they also face difficult social issues such as sex, drugs, drinking, and the party scene.

As we discussed in the previous chapter, all these elements can contribute to teens becoming stressed, depressed, or anxious. And those conditions can subsequently delay or interfere with their mental and emotional health into adulthood. In this chapter, we will discuss normal teen development and how you can partner with your teen to help him be aware of pitfalls, overcome obstacles, and flourish into adulthood.

A TIME OF TRANSITION

Believe it or not, the terms *adolescent* and *teen* are relatively new to our society. The journey from childhood to adulthood used to be relatively swift, with a much briefer "in-be-t(w)een" phase than today. But recent and significant changes in this phase have ushered in the potential for stress, anxiety, and depression sooner than ever before. There are a couple of reasons for this phenomenon.

1. Children are starting puberty at a younger age.

There's no definitive explanation why—whether it's the growth hormones in food, the toxins in the environment, or subtle genetic shifts—but the onset age of puberty is lowering, especially in girls. There is an increase in children ages eleven and twelve who are physically beginning the phase of puberty and the emerging journey into adolescence. A hundred years ago, the age of puberty was closer to seventeen, and immediately afterward a person was ready for marriage. As a result, many did marry young. But teenagers today wait longer, which can be stressful and lead to depression.

2. The phase of adolescence is becoming longer.

While children are starting puberty younger, adolescence is ending later—as late as age twenty-nine or thirty, according to some sociologists. One of the reasons for this is the extended education needed to fit into the workforce and the high cost of leaving the nest egg; hence a prolonged financial dependence on parents. The result is that the transition into independent adulthood has been prolonged, resulting in a growing group of parents of adult dependents. This is especially true for teens who have been depressed.

PERSONAL DEVELOPMENT OF A TEEN

Teens are developing in every aspect of their life. They are growing in who they are as an emerging adult by gaining a strong sense of identity and self-worth, and a measure of control over their goals, values, and destiny in life.

The following section and chart list the primary changes and developments that typically occur during the teen years and include how stress and depression can impact each area of your teen's life. You may want to photocopy this to help you keep track of his progress over the years and better understand the areas on which you can focus as a parent. You can also use it to accompany the suggestions from chapter 13 regarding how to pray purposely for your teen.

1. Physical changes
Parents can help teens deal with the challenges of body changes that put them at risk for problems. For the early bloomers, especially girls, watch for the "pursuit of thinness." Build authentic self-esteem to counter inner conflict and poor body image. Protect them and set boundaries, especially when they are around older boys.

The late bloomers (usually boys), on the other hand, are often picked on by peers who developed earlier and have advanced muscles and body build. Show empathy and find activities in which they can succeed that will foster a sense of competency and self-confidence.

2. Mental changes
Early teens tend to think in all-or-nothing, black-and-white extremes. Their rationalizing is concrete. As they mature, their thinking becomes more abstract, equipping them to better handle relationships and gain a healthy perspective.

Hurting teens also tend to struggle with negative self-talk and distorted thinking, and they are less able to see the bigger picture using their abstract thinking skills. Often, they will fluctuate between their concrete and abstract ways of thinking. Expect this, and be patient.

HELP YOUR TEEN EXPERIENCE
AND EXPRESS EMOTIONS

Few teens are able to accurately convey their inner feelings, much less identify them. Here are some tips to help you aid your teen in learning how to express what's inside.

1. *Provide feedback.*

Reflect back to your teen what you think he might be feeling underneath his surface reaction. By giving honest feedback about what you see him feeling, you can help increase his emotional awareness.

2. *Model emotional maturity.*

Set an example for your teen through your everyday interactions with people and circumstances. By showing emotional maturity in your own life, you teach them how to process and handle emotions rather than simply react to them.

3. *Display self-control.*

Refrain from overreacting. There's nothing wrong with having feelings of anger; the sin is always in the behavior of anger, not in the feelings. If you totally blow it, take responsibility, be real, and apologize.

Stress and depression also interferes with cognitive functioning by causing problems with concentration and memory. These result in problems with school, work, sports, and relationships. But keep academic performance in perspective. For a stressed or depressed teen, the priority should be getting better. Once his brain and emotions are restored and balanced, everything else will fall into place.

3. Emotional maturity

Success in life is more than good grades and what college you attend, although these are important. It's about who you are becoming as a person, how you are able to understand and manage your own emotions and motivations, and how you respond and relate with others. Teens are developing well when they become more self-aware, are able to identify a vast array of complex and subtle feelings in themselves and in others, and can share in meaningful connections with others. All three of these aspects impact their emotional life. As teens understand how their emotions are linked to their motivations and actions, life will be more fulfilling and successful.

Hurting teens don't always know what they are feeling. They might be flooded with surface emotions (secondary) such as anger and spite yet remain unable to identify their deeper underlying emotion (primary). Help your teen become aware of or express what she is really feeling underneath—emotions such as fear, rejection, shame, or loss.

4. Emerging identity and autonomy

As teens become more comfortable with who they are, their true identities flourish. But being able to make their own choices, rather than being told what to do all the time, and to be their own unique person is a slow-building process during these tumultuous years— one that involves several factors.

Throughout your teen's journey, she slowly separates from you to gain her own identity, independence, and autonomy. This is a challenge for parents who desperately want to protect their teens from risks and poor decisions.

Your teen is also on the journey of *individuating* from you in order to establish her own identity, uniqueness, interests, and point of view. It can be hard to accept and watch your teen disregard the beliefs and manners in which she was raised in an attempt to find herself.

Your role as a parent is to teach, guide, and prepare your teen to become a mature, responsible adult who loves God and can contribute to society. This isn't easy when your teen often vacillates between a desire for independence and a need to still be somewhat dependent.

ASPECTS OF TEEN DEVELOPMENT

Indicate where your teen is doing well (W), struggling (S), needs to grow and mature (G).

BEING

Physical Self

__ Developing a healthy body image, self-respect, and good physical boundaries

__ Practicing a healthy lifestyle in diet, exercise, sleep, hygiene, etc.

Mental Changes

__ Adjusting well to increased demands at school; learning new study habits

__ Expanding verbal skills and abstract thinking; seeing things in a broader way

Personal Identity

__ Developing a capacity for enjoyment and fulfillment in life

__ Discovering a sense of self: Who am I? What are my skills, gifts, and talents? What are my strengths and weaknesses? How can I grow in these?

__ Establishing a sense of worth as a person; becoming accomplished in individual strengths; building authentic self-esteem

Behavior Maturity

__ Decreasing behaviors that place teen at risk physically, socially, and educationally

__ Developing a set of behavioral self-controls that are more acceptable for adulthood

__ Learning to turn away from temptation and make good choices; gaining self-control

___ Constructing a conscious plan for maturing in areas of weakness; avoiding mistakes already made

Personal Values and Spiritual Beliefs

___ Assessing parental and childhood values during conflicts with the values expressed by peers and other segments of society

___ Restructuring and developing personal beliefs and values; an outlook on life based on what is important, right, and proper

___ Making informed, thoughtful choices that apply a foundation of biblical and moral values

___ Connecting spiritually; growing in relationship with God and other believers

BECOMING

Sense of the Future

___ Preparing for a career by increasing vocational goals and skills, or considering, "What do I want to be when I grow up?"

___ Discovering individual gifts, talents, and interests; considering how to serve and make a lasting impact

___ Developing purpose, goals, and vision for life—and living with these in mind rather than simply drifting through life; having a sense of direction; finding guidance, hope, and promise for the future

Responsibility and Self-Sufficiency

___ Establishing emotional and psychological independence; becoming a unique individual

___ Developing an affectionate, safe, secure connection with parents without full dependence on them

___ Gaining a sense of responsibility and control over personal direction and destiny in life

(continued)

__ Growing in decision-making skills
__ Learning to abide by rules and boundaries; being considerate of others
__ Doing well in school, at work, and with extracurricular activities

BELONGING
Preparation for Marriage and Family
__ Incorporating into individual identity what it means to be male/female
__ Developing values about sexual behavior; setting good sexual boundaries; differentiating between sexual impulses and genuine intimacy
__ Maintaining healthy friendships and dating relationships with the opposite sex
__ Experiencing healing, redemption, and restoration from mistakes, violations, or abuse
__ Gaining basic knowledge for home management, relationship skills, and child-rearing

Peer Connectedness
__ Finding a valued place of belonging in a constructive group
__ Keeping a sense of self and maintaining good boundaries
__ Learning how to get along with boys and girls; improving communication skills
__ Acting more mature in adult relationships
__ Finding a way to be useful to others; learning to work with others for a common purpose
__ Becoming socially responsible toward family, friends, and community

As a parent of a hurting teen, you may find it difficult to keep the balance of progressively letting your teen become her own person, allowing her to take risks, and yet monitoring and doing damage control. But take comfort: God uses an infinite number of ways in a teen's life to sculpt maturity of character and responsibility. He will give you practical wisdom and endurance. And, if your teen won't heed to your rules and advice, she is bound to hear it again through school, authority figures, doctors or counselors, and even through friends and dating relationships. She will also learn from natural and logical consequences in life.

5. Relationship connections

The teen years are no different than any other stage of life: above everything, it comes down to relationships. Keep in mind the following.

Connections matter most. Research has repeatedly proven that both boys and girls need healthy, secure attachments to know that they have meaningful connections not only with their peers, but also with their parents and other family members. Having an anchor at home gives teens the courage to explore the world beyond, knowing they have a safe connection that will be there when they hit hard times. They need this most to survive peer pressure and the stresses and struggles along their journey. (We'll explore this further in chapter 9.)

Being disconnected causes problems. If your teen is withdrawn, isolated, or struggling to find a connection with friends at school, this is a warning sign and a risk factor for challenges. Research shows that balanced friendships and connections with groups are important factors in preventing and recovering from depression. One study focused on significant risk and protective factors that caused depression among college students. The study found that two conditions were most instrumental in protecting students from mental illness: *parent-family connectedness* and *connectedness at school.* Connected students are the least depressed, have the highest self-esteem, feel most comfortable with their families, are the most positive about their education, use the least drugs or alcohol, feel the least stress, and have the highest grade point averages.[1]

Bad connections cause problems. Positive connections are protective, preventive, and essential to healthy development; bad influences, on the other hand, can undermine every attempt to build a healthier teenager.

If your teen is struggling and cannot connect with solid friends, he can become lonely and experience low self-esteem. At that point, it's easy for him to associate with kids (often older) who will take him in. These friends—who are usually struggling, hurting teens themselves—may be nonjudgmental and accommodating, offering solace through their own alternative solutions. Talk with your teen honestly and openly about the influence of the people in his life, and support him in other positive social connections. You may have to consider making drastic changes to remove negative influence friends. After the depression starts lifting, and stress is dealt with, they will naturally gravitate toward friends with a healthier influence.

Teens are grappling with their sexuality. A recent teen magazine survey reported the obvious: teens think a lot about sex. This is a normal part of development. Talk openly with your teen and make biblical resources available about sexual values, birth control, unprotected sex, STDs, oral sex, "hooking up," same-sex exploration, and the value of abstinence until marriage.[2]

Hurting teens have a higher likelihood of sexual exploration and promiscuity as they seek escape, comfort, and distraction through these relationships. Direct your teen to people and resources that can provide the necessary intervention and guidance as she integrates her sexuality into her life in a healthy way.

6. Spiritual development

Although your teen is establishing his own personal faith and conclusions, you as a parent still have an incredible opportunity to coach and shepherd him to make sense of his daily troubles and failures. How can you use these situations to be in constant conversa-

---

THE GROWING AND CHANGING TEEN BRAIN

Physiological changes in the brain first begin occurring around age 11 or 12, with the more complex developments taking place from 13 to 19. This transformation is evident in shifts of problem solving and regulating emotion.

· *Frontal cortex*

This part of the brain recognizes anything new or foreign and decides if it is important to act quickly. Because this process can be slower for teens, they tend to simply react.

· *Corpus Callosum*

This cable of nerves connects the two hemispheres of the brain. It grows significantly during the teen years.

· *Amygdala*

This is an important area of the brain associated with emotional gut responses. Teens use this reactive part of the brain more than the "thinking" region (frontal cortex). This may be why teens have trouble modulating their emotional responses.

· *Cerebellum*

This part of the brain is involved with the coordination of muscles and physical movement and the thinking process. It also undergoes dynamic growth during the teen years.

---

tion, helping your teen become aware of such things as his own strengths and weaknesses, rebellion and sin, and God's redemption and healing? How can he learn to integrate practical, biblical, moral principles into the situations in his life?

Teach him the truth. Reflect a positive mirror of who God is and who your teen is as a spiritual being. Practice more, preach less. Live the Christian faith. As St. Francis of Assisi said, preach the gospel at all times, using words only when necessary.

THE DEVELOPING BRAIN

Why does your teen act the way she does, taking dangerous risks without thinking? Why does she often react so differently according to the situation, as if she were two different people? Why is everything such a drama with her? Why is she so prone to get stressed and depressed?

We are now discovering that the reason for teens' erratic behavior is mostly in their head—their developing brain, not just their raging hormones. This doesn't explain everything or provide all the answers. However, it helps parents understand how this crucial aspect of development has implications for helping teens through difficult times and how to apply the science to effective parenting.

1. I want what I want and I want it now.

Two of the main developments of the brain during the teen years are gaining the ability to fight impulsiveness and learning delayed gratification. (Some of us are still learning these!) The amygdala—the emotional, reaction-based area—is the dominant part of the teen brain (other parts are not as developed) and is what can be dangerous to a stressed or depressed teen.

Today's teens are often described as "overindulged." They are reaping the benefits of the baby boomers, getting what they want sooner and in bigger quantities than any other generation. As you might expect, that's not always a good thing. Consumerism has become top dog in the teen world, creating the necessity for brand labels and keeping up with the hottest trends. Parents are too lenient and, despite good intentions, too indulgent—both of which put teens at risk for not learning delayed gratification, self-control, a good work ethic, and other important qualities to succeed in society. Because of this "instant" mentality, some teens are more likely to fail in future marriages as a result of becoming more stressed, disappointed, and depressed.

Not only does this generation of teens thrive on immediate gratification, but it also has developed an over stimulated pleasure center. It takes more to entertain them or give them a high out of life. The music has to be louder, movies more shocking and impressive, video games more graphic and challenging, and schedules busier.

Finding pleasure in life isn't all bad. But it seems this concept has gotten a little off balance for today's developing teens. As a parent, it's important for you to help your teen enjoy the simple things in life, not just the big thrills. Teach them that life isn't about just satisfaction in the moment but also about keeping a bigger, long-term perspective.

2. Teens go for the thrill, live on the edge, and take dangerous risks.
The key players in this teen typical phenomenon are the prefrontal cortex and the neurotransmitter dopamine. Dopamine modulates the other transmitters in the brain and interacts primarily with the prefrontal cortex. Interestingly enough, dopamine increases with increased stress. During the teen years, the level of dopamine declines from the peak levels of childhood. Maturing teens therefore tend to be dopamine depleted in their reward system. To compensate, they seek more stimulating activities as they subconsciously try new things to get the same "kick" of dopamine release to adult levels. Teens tend to be risk takers anyway, but anhedonia (diminished sense of pleasure) drives them to seek new stimulating activities to a higher level.

3. The teen brain needs a high.
Depending on their level of dopamine, some teens will be higher risk takers and more vulnerable to choosing drugs to boost their dopamine. One of the reasons they do these things is to stabilize their brain chemistry. For instance, while under the influence of alcohol, teens experience increased levels of dopamine. Science has now discovered that both addicts and children of addicts demonstrate decreased levels of dopamine and serotonin in specific areas of the brain. Addictive behavior seems to be an attempt to normalize brain function. However, these transmitters are also key contributors to

depression. The truth is that drugs and alcohol actually damage the very brain cells that produce dopamine and serotonin—and at a much higher rate in teens than adults. The thrill teens seek through substances can actually set them up for serious brain imbalance and depression.

Can teens be stimulated by safer alternatives and satisfy their risk-taking thrills in more pro-social ways? I (Arch) am old enough to remember adolescence from a very different era, a time when there was no television, when you passed the time by inventing outdoor games, and when summer vacations were filled with long, eventless days at the public swimming pool. My teen years were even boring at times because there was not a lot of pressure. We hung around the soda fountains and drank lots of malted milkshakes, or we just sat around and watched girls. In retrospect, my brain had a much easier time developing than my grandchildren's brains.

Teens these days have a different standard for thrills. Taking a cue from the litany of foolish daredevil and prank shows on MTV, they film themselves jumping from heights, trying to catch dangerous animals, hotwiring golf carts to ride around at night, having punching matches in the dark, or crashing hotel parties. All for a dopamine boost.

Teens need clean, adventurous outlets for fun. Your teen may need to experience a boost of excitement and adventure. Ask him what he would like to do on the next family vacation. What camps, mission trips, concerts, or similar activities could you encourage for him? What new adventures could you allow him to try, or even try with him? Extreme adventures and sports, traveling, and discovering new things are all great options.

AN ENTRYWAY FOR STRESS

The teenage years are some of the toughest years in life. Not only is his body in a state of continual change, but a teen's mind and emotions are severely effected by raging hormones. Add to this his sexual, spiritual, and identity development—all occurring simultaneously—and it can often make for a stressful time, both for teens and parents. For a hurting teen, these transitions are magnified.

It is at this stage when stress enters the picture for many teens, as they become overwhelmed with the combination of new pressures and continual changes. In the next chapter, we will discuss how to recognize various symptoms of stress in your teen—and if he is already struggling, how you can help him overcome it.

3

TAMING TEENAGE STRESS HORMONES

*Depression also has firm roots in adolescence, with rates
starting their most dramatic climb during the teen years. . . .
There's no doubt stress plays a part. . . . Some evidence
suggests that adolescents overall are more reactive to stress.*
— Barbara Strauch, *The Primal Teen*

THERE'S NOTHING LIKE CHEERING FOR YOUR TEAM WHEN the game goes down to the wire. Or rushing to the grand opening of a new wing at the mall, with all your favorite shops and incredible sales. Or discovering your favorite artist is coming to town and you have a chance at front-row seats.

Each of these cases can cause an adrenaline and cortisol rush. Teens love that flowing through their veins. Think of life without those stressful situations. How many teens would actually get a paper done or study for a test if they didn't have a looming deadline? How many would aim for good grades if there weren't any rewards? Would they experience the anxiety of lost privileges if there were no consequences for failing a class? The fact is that not all stress is bad. As parents, we are especially grateful to the stress response when our teens are driving late at night and are alert enough to slam on their brakes to avoid a tragic accident.

The stress response, at its best, is what adds to the excitement and spice of life. It keeps our teens motivated to be creative and accomplish things. It is the body's way of rising to a challenge, mobilizing us to take action. And it protects us in tough or dangerous situations. For teens, it gives the focus and strength they need to perform well under pressure.

God even uses times of stressful difficulty and adversity to stretch and change our teens, helping them grow and develop character.

WHEN STRESS TURNS BAD

However, not all stress is beneficial. The television show *7th Heaven* provided an excellent example of this. A bright seventeen-year-old named Simon was driving in his neighborhood one day. As he turned the corner, a boy skated out of nowhere and, without looking, crossed straight into the car's path. The boy hit the car and was thrown hard to the ground. Because he wasn't wearing a helmet, the boy's head injuries eventually led to his death. From that day on, Simon's life as a high-schooler was never the same. He started having nightmares, reliving the situation, wondering what he could have done differently. *I looked both ways, I swear!* he told himself. Or was his mind playing tricks on him?

Things gradually became more difficult for Simon. The brother of the deceased boy went to Simon's school and began to make life unbearable for him. So Simon left that school. His behavior began to change. He stopped talking about the incident. When confronted, he'd say he was just fine. "It wasn't your fault, Simon," his consoling parents would say. "The inquest showed that the skater boy was high on drugs. He was responsible for his dangerous behavior." But Simon dove deeper into his pain until it became too much for him. His methods of escaping finally caught up with him, and he broke down. It was then that he realized he needed counseling.

Acute, short-lived stress keeps teens alert to the protective response, equipping them to deal with challenges. However, if it is too traumatizing, as it was for Simon, the stress response causes damage. Intense stress can go so far as to trigger the onset of depression and anxiety disorders, which are increasingly becoming serious problems for teens.

WHEN STRESS IS INTENSE AND PROLONGED

When any stress—good or bad—is prolonged, excessive, and intense, a teen is at risk for problems. In fact, severe stress can become damaging as soon as two weeks after its onset. Samantha was a perfect case of this. She entered high school with a bang, deciding to sign up for a number of honor classes, join the cross-country team, and run for class president.

It wasn't long before the days grew longer and the nights got shorter. Samantha was in charge of designing and coordinating the class homecoming skit and set. It left her little time to study for tests, and the lack of sleep left her physically exhausted. On the weekends (which is when most teens' adrenaline drops), she started having crying spells. She was also now in constant conflict with her parents because of her irritability and sassy attitude. Noticing that she was mentally and emotionally overwhelmed, her parents knew she was slipping into a danger zone. It was time for her to learn how to prioritize her schedule and recover from the stress damage to her system.

Teens unable to recover from stress or remove themselves from their stressful environment transition into *distress* (early stress disease). The overactivity of the stress response system, when it is not managed, can cause not only exhaustion and general fatigue but a high level of circulating cortisol, which, as the cousin of adrenaline, upsets the delicate chemical balance in the brain and triggers anxiety and depression. It is a physical manifestation of a guiding principle that every parent needs to grasp: We are designed only for short periods of extreme stress.

Both adrenaline and cortisol turn against the body when their elevation is prolonged. About fifty percent of teens who are depressed have overactivity of the stress hormone response, evidenced by the fact that their adrenal glands have engaged to accommodate the high stress demands of their lives. A teen's body, mind, and emotions are simply unable to handle the ongoing levels of modern-day chronic stress. We were designed for camel travel, not cyberspace travel! And while short bursts of high-octane living may be tolerated, perpetually pushing ourselves will cause the human body and mind to fall apart. This is the primary reason for the epidemic of depression we are seeing in our teens today, and the great challenge of helping them live balanced lives in a world that is now pushing us outside the limits of God's design.

WHAT IS STRESS, AND WHAT DOES IT DO?

So how does the stress response work, and how has excess stress become the root cause of anxiety and depression epidemics? A brief review will help you as a parent understand the importance of stress management in protecting your teen.

The stress response system starts in the brain, where "higher" levels look out on our world and evaluate anything that is dangerous or demanding. When a stressor is detected (and it can be a thrill or a threat), the *amygdala* (fear response), *hypothalamus* (emotional evaluation), and *pituitary gland* (emergency signaling) trigger the stress response—also called the "fight or flight" response.

There are two phases to this response. In phase one, a nerve signal to the inner part of the adrenal glands (one above each kidney) releases the first group of hormones, of which adrenaline (also called *epinephrine*) is the best known. Adrenaline gives us a feeling of enhanced well-being, which is why we can become addicted to it. As these hormones are released, the *sympathetic nervous system* is activated, increasing our heart rate, blood pressure, and breathing, to help us fight or flee.

The body also responds by increasing the flow of blood to muscles in the arms and legs (to run faster), or cold or clammy hands and feet (so we can hold on to things better). This also accounts for increased cholesterol levels, which is a part of the stress response. If left unchecked, it is this reaction that can cause cardiovascular disease.

Phase one lasts about ten days if the stressor stays around. If the crisis is not resolved by then, phase two is triggered. At this point, a chemical messenger (that's what hormones are) is sent to the outer layer of the adrenal glands in case the nerve pathway has been severed. This messenger tells the adrenal glands to release another group of stress hormones needed to fight long-term stress. Two of the main hormones involved here are cortisol and cortisone, which both help to fight inflammation and get energy stored in the fat out to where it is needed.

If these emergency hormones were the only ones to contend with, matters wouldn't be so bad. But mixed in with all the other adrenal hormones are the raging rushes of the sex hormones. Together they make a powerful and disruptive mix!

The outpouring of stress hormones impacts virtually every system of the body, top to bottom. Five main systems respond to stress (adrenaline and cortisol mainly) and can be severely compromised by prolonged stress:

1. **The cardiovascular system.** Increased blood pressure and cholesterol make us prone to heart disease.
2. **The immune system.** Reduced immune system activity makes us more susceptible to viral and other infections.
3. **The pain killing system.** Reduced endorphins increase our experience of pain.
4. **The tranquilizing system.** Lower number of the brain's natural tranquilizers makes us more prone to anxiety disorders, especially panic attacks.
5. **The "happiness" system.** Interference with neurotransmitters makes us prone to depression.

There are other systems also affected by stress: the endocrine system, digestive system, and respiratory system. Eventually, when the brain decides that the situation is no longer dangerous, the state of emergency passes, and the body begins to relax and calm down as levels of the stress hormones drop. This can be facilitated by the "relaxation response." Learning ways to lower the stress hormones is key to recovering from stress, as well as most depression and anxiety disorders.

WHY ARE TEENS SO STRESSED?

The consensus among many experts is that teens these days are extraordinarily stressed. At any time, many are on the verge of going over the edge and crossing into the depressed realm, due to a stressor. Too much too soon with too many places to go! Just going through adolescence is stressful. Transitioning into adulthood is now more perilous and prolonged, and the result is that parents of high school and college-age kids are facing the disastrous fallout. Why? Let's examine a few of the important contributing factors.

1. Most teens feel that they have too many *pressures and demands* being placed on them.

The push to succeed is especially burdensome for most of them. These pressures include social pressures and activities, the demands of school, and the need to get good grades so they can go to a decent college. Then they also have to financially keep up with their peers, finish their daily homework, and perform at peak competitive levels in athletics. This can push some teens into the danger zone.

They also might not feel equipped to handle all the rapid changes into adulthood. It can become overwhelming. The perils of peer interactions—being accepted or rejected—are constant sources of stress and depression. Then there is the peer pressure to explore outlets of partying, drinking, smoking, drugs, or sex. Is your teen wrestling with any of these pressures?

As a parent, it is important to be aware of your part in contributing to these pressures and demands. Do you set reasonable expectations and manageable goals in academic and extracurricular activities? Or does your teen complain that you are unreasonable and unfair? Does your teen lose sleep worrying about academic and social pressures and problems? Is he moody, irritable, fidgety, and anxious about life in general? Is he afraid to come to you with the truth about what's going on in his life while secretly feeling burdened with unresolved problems and alone in his pain? These are possible signs that stress is having a negative effect.

2. Teens also complain of the general *strain of life challenges as they are developing.*
As a teen recently said, "I just couldn't deal with a stressful crisis this week. My schedule is already full, and I already feel maxed out! It won't take much to push me over the edge." Teens have a lot of pressure going through the developmental journey from childhood to adulthood. Some experience an identity crisis as they figure out who they are. This is stressful. Some find it difficult to cope with instability at home while individuating and becoming connected to their peer group.

If you are experiencing difficulty in your marriage or other personal problems, don't burden your teen with the details. Be aware of how the changes and conflict may be impacting them. She needs stability and a safe place in relationship with you. Remember to compliment her and encourage her as much as possible as she experiences her own life challenges.

3. Other teens say they are just way too *busy.*
They grumble of overloaded schedules, with not enough time to get everything done. As a result they are mostly irritable and frazzled. Does your daughter eat and put on makeup while driving to school, running out the door hurried and hassled? Is your son's room a pigpen because he has no time to order his private world? By the time most teens reach late high school, they want more money and take on a part-time job, which raises the busyness factor. A teen who works more than twenty hours a week adds significantly more stress to his life, which can often result in lower grades and possibly push

him toward dealing with stress in damaging ways such as smoking or using alcohol and drugs.

4. Most teens are *tired*, even to the point of exhaustion.

Teens are just too busy for their own good. You might be tired too, having to parent at the speed of a teen these days! A major contributor to teens' tiredness is their lack of a full night's sleep. Sleep research shows that normal adults should get at least eight and a half to nine hours sleep a night. But teens need more—up to two hours more—for their brains to function normally. Recent studies across the nation have clearly shown that the more sleep teens get, the lower their stress levels and vulnerability to related stress disorders, not to mention an improvement in grades.

Teens need enough sleep, rest, and recovery time ("recuperation," as my daughter would say), as it is essential to reverse the damage done to the body and soul by excess stress. Emotional energy expended to deal with confusion and conflict can also be exhausting. They also need time to relax and dream, allowing the inner swirling to get sorted out.

THE STRESS, DEPRESSION, AND ANXIETY LINK

Depression and anxiety can put down firm roots in a stressed adolescent. We are now seeing a dramatic climb in teen depression. Why? As we discussed in the previous chapter, there's no doubt that the sharp increase in teen stress plays a major part. Depression happens when the stress response system continuously stays on alert and doesn't get time to relax. There are four important elements regarding stress that parents should know.

1. Teens need recovery time from stress.

They need down time to just "be" and recuperate. The dramatic increase in depression and anxiety cases is mainly due to lack of recovery time for the adrenal system. This is not just from the high level of modern-day stress. People in past times had to contend with much harder living conditions, greater threat of illness with few medical interventions, and a shorter life span. But what they had that we don't is a more leisurely lifestyle and time to interact with people — both of which afford the emergency systems plenty of time for recovery. During the day, people weren't distracted by media or instant anything, nor were they caught up in a fast pace of living. Going to sleep when it became dark provided lots of rest time. Physical work helped to burn off surplus adrenaline and facilitated restful sleep. Even traveling from village to village involved plenty of down time.

Today teens have lengthened their day by staying up later, so they don't get enough sleep. They may live more exciting lives, but it comes at the expense of their overall quality of life.

2. Stress overload can trigger depression.

This is especially true if your teen is at risk for depression, which we will discuss in the next chapter. And once a teen's brain has experienced a depressive episode, it becomes more susceptible the next time around (called the "kindling" effect). Stress then can have a more negative effect and is one of the main triggers to watch for in recurring depressions. The main culprits in modern-day depression and anxiety are excess levels of the stress hormones of adrenaline and cortisol. Whereas fifty years ago genetic factors had a greater influence on causing depression, today stress eclipses the gene factor. Stress gets to the teen brain before the stress gene even has a chance to express itself!

Once a child or teen is exposed to severe or prolonged stress such as the loss of a parent or child abuse, he is at even higher risk for depression, anxiety, impulsive behavior, and substance abuse in adolescence and adulthood. The reason for this is called neural plasticity, which means that the brain is shaped by early experiences and becomes "hard-wired" for depression. This also proves the need to start treating childhood depression and equipping them with the necessary skills as soon as possible after it shows itself. Early intervention and treatment gives a child's brain the best chance for avoiding depression later.

3. Stress can make teens sick.

Chronic low or high levels of stress can keep the glucocorticoids and catecholemaines (stress hormones) continuously in high circulation, causing a host of other problems—notably fatigue and exhaustion problems and drug and alcohol use, which we discuss in chapter 5. It lowers the immune system, causing vulnerability to colds, the flu bug, or whatever is going around. The body also forms free radicals that are associated with all sorts of disease and illness. Stress causes damage to brain functioning, causing teens to be forgetful, confused, and unable to concentrate. Stress can also result in severe weight gain for teens (especially girls), causing the body to hold on to fat around the stomach, especially for those who compensate for stress by overeating.

4. Teens can recover from stress damage.

So far, we've outlined the seriousness of stress, not to create despair but to point out that it is a problem within our capacity to correct. Your teen can learn to take control over some stressors that can be changed and learn to better live better manage the givens. However, teens don't necessarily have the capacity and skills to deal with stress. There are resources that can help him recover from the damage done by excess stress. He can learn to change and control both his perceptions and his reactions to stress. Risk for anxiety, depression, and other problems can be reduced and even prevented. We cover some of these practical resources at the end of this chapter and in chapter 9.

EVALUATING YOUR TEEN'S STRESS LEVEL

Just about anything in life that causes emotional distress is stressful. But what is stressful for your teen? To help you evaluate your teen's stress level, we have compiled an inventory of possible stressors she might be experiencing. It is important to know what stressors she is dealing with.

Our goal in presenting the following checklist is to sensitize

DOES YOUR TEEN SHOW SYMPTOMS OF DISTRESS?

Before we can turn to ways for remedying the problem, we need to help you determine just how much stress is a problem in your teen's life. No two teens will have the same stress profile, nor will they have the same coping skills. As a parent, you need to customize an intervention that fits both the severity of the stress problem in your teen's life, as well as the level of coping skills that already exist.

The following are signs and symptoms of stress. Do you recognize any of these in your teen? If so, place a check in the box to the left:

☐ Anxiety or panic attack symptoms, fearful behavior
☐ Feelings of being under constant pressure, hassled, and hurried
☐ Irritable and moody, outbursts of anger or aggression
☐ More fidgety or jumpy than usual (shaking leg, biting nails, or picking at skin)
☐ Frequent physical aches and pains such as stomach problems, headaches, even chest pain
☐ Immune system vulnerability such as frequent colds and coughs
☐ Allergic reactions such as eczema or asthma
☐ Sleep problems, can't fall asleep, or can't stay asleep
☐ Self-medicating by drinking alcohol, smoking, or doing drugs
☐ Overeating and weight gain
☐ Sadness, emotional outbursts, or crying spells
☐ Difficulty in concentrating, forgetfulness, memory loss, lowering school grades
☐ Opposition to rules, refusing to comply

☐ Lack of enjoyment in normally enjoyable activities
☐ Physical or emotional exhaustion

While the only valid way to diagnose stress is to consult a professional, the following scoring of your results from above can guide you in assessing your teen's level of stress:

· Three or fewer may be within normal limits for a teen
· Four to six may indicate some mild to moderate stress
· Seven or more checked items clearly indicates that the stress is serious and your teen needs help

Generally speaking, the greater the number of items checked, the greater the level of stress your teen is experiencing.

you to the possible causes of stress in your teen's life, so as to help you develop greater empathy with her struggles. We've divided the stressors into two categories: external stressors (those that come from the world around her) and internal stressors (those she is imposing on herself).

HOW DOES YOUR TEEN DEAL WITH STRESS?

After failing a test, why will one teen go out back and smoke a cigarette, while another will simply brush it off as a learning experience and resolve to try harder next time? When not making the basketball team, why will one teen work through the disappointment and become excited to pursue another area of interest, yet another teen will actually kill himself over it? After a relationship breakup, why will one teen girl grieve her losses yet move on in hopes of meeting someone else, yet another girl might start cutting herself and go into depression?

Teens deal with their stress in a variety of ways. They can act out and take out their stress on others by becoming angry or violent.

IDENTIFYING YOUR TEEN'S STRESSORS

Go through this list and place a check next to the ones you think may apply to your teen. Then have a discussion with her about how these stressors are impacting her life. You might be surprised by her response.

External Stressors

__ Physical conditions (pain, illness, a chronic illness)

__ Conflict in close relationships (friends, dating)

__ Difficulties with peer relationships, social affiliation, status

__ Physical, sexual, or emotional abuse

__ Loss or death of a loved one

__ Unpredictable events

__ Major changes such as moving, starting a new school

__ Pressures of school, work, performance activities

__ Ongoing problems at school—learning disabilities, ADHD

__ Problems at home (parents divorcing or separating, conflict with parents or siblings)

__ Financial problems

__ Relationship stress—relationship breakups, friendship rift

__ Being bullied or made fun of

__ Exposure to violence or physical injury

__ Pressures that are too intense or last too long

__ Crammed schedule (no time to rest and relax)

__ High expectations from family

__ Feeling let down after achieving a goal

__ Facing consequences to poor choices, lack of boundaries, rebellious or defiant behavior

__ Others:

Internal Stressors

__ Physical changes, infections, inflammation

__ Changes in hormones (menstrual problems) and brain chemistry

__ Depression

__ Poor eating habits (excessive dieting, eating disorder)

__ Intense worry (excessive anxiety or panic attacks)

__ Low self-esteem

__ Major life decisions

__ Emotional turmoil due to family and relationship problems

__ Feeling disconnected, lonely, not belonging

__ Feeling empty, lack of purpose and meaning

__ Feelings of failure or disappointment

__ Irresponsible behavior and consequences

__ Unrealistic expectations

__ Self-rejecting thoughts and attitudes, negative feelings about self

__ Perfectionism, pessimism, negativity

__ Trying to do too much

__ Trying to keep everyone pleased, happy, or not disappointed

__ Others:

This is usually what guys do. Girls, on the other hand, tend to internalize their stress by developing eating disorders or turning to substances and promiscuity to escape from their problems and numb their feelings.

The following sidebar provides you with a simple test to determine whether your teen is dealing with stress in a healthy way or not. Any one of these behaviors indicates that his stress is not being managed well.

These differing responses to stress are determined by a combination of factors.

MALADAPTIVE PATTERNS IN RESPONSE TO STRESS

Is your teen using any of these unhealthy ways to deal with stress?

· Misuse of food as an escape, as a "filler," or as a protector
· Misuse of relationships (overdependence on others)
· Self-medicating or escaping by using substances (see chapter 5)
· Stimulating the pleasure center with risk-taking behaviors
· Sexual acting out
· Self-destructive behavior such as cutting
· Relieving or releasing the pain through unhealthy ways
· Escaping/avoiding pain (social withdrawal, isolation, avoiding friends)
· Use of pornography for self-gratification
· Use of violence (on self, others, or animals, etc.)
Other ways you have noticed:

_____

_____

_____

_____

_____

_____

1. Stress tolerance level

Each teen has a different physiological stress tolerance level. Teens differ in how their bodies release stress hormones. Some recover more slowly than others, and there is actually a differing amount of stress hormones in each person. For some, it is all about genetic inheritance; for others, it is how they have learned from the past to tolerate stress. Studies in children show that early experience (even in the womb) can have an impact on both the stress response toler-ance and ability to regulate emotions later in life.

Research shows that a specific gene, called 5-HTT, helps regu-late a brain chemical, called serotonin, in the brain. Those without this gene are more vulnerable to depression when experiencing stressful times, while those with it seem to cope better and move on. They physiologically have different levels of stress and brain hor-mone chemistry regulation. Teens without 5-HTT face the chal-lenge of learning to work around their disposition.

Although teens overall are more reactive to stress, the stress response is different for every teen. Some teens are better equipped to handle some forms of stress than others. One teen's stress is another's challenge.

A good example of this differential in stress tolerance is how teens differ in their response to the horror movies that are unfortu-nately becoming so popular. While some may be able to separate reality from fantasy in these gory movies, others won't even go near them. These differences in individual responses exist not only in how a teen can handle horror movies, but also in how he responds to stress.

2. Personality

Personality also determines how a teen perceives stressful situations. Does he immediately have a negative response, feeling it is the end of life as he knows it? Or is he able to be more objective and posi-tive, not putting so much pressure on himself? Does he go to a place of fearing that he won't be good enough and become an utter fail-ure? Or does he not take things so seriously by keeping an optimistic attitude? Some teens refuse to take any responsibility and blame others for all their woes.

How teens react to stress and are able to adjust has to do in part with their traits and their defenses (see sidebar on personality traits in the next chapter). This does not mean your teen is doomed. The good news is that he can change his perceptions of stressors and learn strategies to build on his strengths and strengthen his weakness.

Is he aware of his personality pros and cons? What does he believe are his own strengths? How effective is he at coping in difficult times? How resilient has he been in responding to previous challenging experiences? In chapter 9 you will learn more about this and how you can parent him to increase his skills for overcoming and growing through difficulties.

3. Environment
Another influence on how a teen reacts to stress comes from the environment in which she is raised. If your teen is experiencing stressors such as demanding expectations, fighting, anger, money problems, fear, and neglect, then she will live with continuing higher levels of stress hormones being released in her body. Is she feeling excess pressure to perform at school or in sports? Is she treated badly, ridiculed, or put down at home? Are there others in your home struggling with mental illness or other disabling problems? All of this can put your teen at risk for damaging consequences such as disease, illness, depression, and other related disorders. Alternatively, if the home environment is a physically and emotionally safe place for your teen, this will serve as a healing place where she can learn and grow through hard times. (Refer to chapter 11 for details.)

4. Stress inoculation
Recent literature on stress uses the term *stress inoculation*. As the name implies, it is possible for your teen to become immunized against the negative effects of stress. Small victories and lessons learned during challenging times help build up a teen's inner resources, strengthening him for the ability to get through future hard times. By allowing him to fight his own battles, he will learn to struggle through a certain amount of stress and will gradually increase his ability and capacity to deal with it. However, if you constantly run interference for him as an overprotective parent, you take away the opportunity for him to learn how to cope in a stress-filled world. Just don't let him sink alone for too long without help.

HOW PARENTS CAN HELP THEIR TEEN DE-STRESS

De-stressing is the term used to describe what a teen does to wind down the high adrenaline arousal associated with life's stressors. Often there is not much that can be done to remove the stressors in a teen's life. She has to go to school, make good grades, and deal with difficult teachers, bullies, and the social scene. So breaking the connection between high stressors and the consequent stressful effect on her body and mind is an important skill to learn.

Many factors contribute to the stressors that can cause emotional and physical damage to teens. But it's not stress itself that kills teens; it's how they react to it. Their sense of helplessness in the face of stress (feeling hopeless and out of control), the duration of the stress (the longer it lasts, the more damaging it is), the timing and frequency of stressors (continuous "little" stress is more damaging than infrequent "big"), the lack of recovery (time to allow the body to recover) from stress hormone damage—these are all factors that combine to aggravate a teen's stress-related problems.

You can help your teen learn how to manage her reactive emotions and cope with stress in more constructive ways. Teach and coach her to manage the stress in her life and to build in time for recovery in her everyday life. This is an essential part of her emotional maturity and protection against anxiety and depression. Become aware of the additional stress she may be experiencing from the pressure or challenges at home.

The following are some of the most practical and effective strategies for dealing with stress in teens. (These will work in your life as well!). Don't be overwhelmed. They may not all be appropriate for your teen. Pick and choose the ones that seem to fit her best.

1. Take your teen for a complete physical exam.
Make sure that it includes a complete blood workup to rule out any physical illness or complications. If you suspect any substance abuse or any other disorder, mention this to your doctor. There may be additional special tests he can request. If there is indication that

stress is causing your teen's problems, get a recommendation for professional counseling. Sign a release for your doctor to work with your counselor or psychiatrist if necessary.

2. Observe and try to understand the underlying causes of stress.
What stressors are impacting your teen's health, behavior, thoughts, or feelings? Listen to what your teen tells you is stressful. Use the checklists provided earlier. Help him understand the nature of the underlying causes of his stress. Prompt him with statements such as: What is your body and mind trying to tell you? What is causing you stress? How are you alleviating and recovering from stress? What can you not change but learn to live with better? What can you change to gain a stronger sense of control?

3. Keep stress under control by setting limits for your teen.
Don't be afraid to step in and establish limits. For example, if your teen seems to be taking on too much extra work or activities, or is out and about too much, talk about the necessity for boundaries against over-scheduling. Be aware if she is headed for overload. Learn to detect what triggers stress for her. If she has unresolved problems, discuss ways to solve them with her.

The little annoyances and unresolved challenges of growing up are what can be extremely stressful to teens. Help keep your teen's goals and expectations realistic. Help her make lists, keeping a planner updated with all events and deadlines. This allows her mind to not get bogged down or overwhelmed, as well as lets her know when assignments are due and managing her time accordingly.

4. Evaluate your teen's response to stress and get help where needed.
The most telling signs of overstress can be seen in your teen's symptoms. Physically, these can come as: headaches (especially those that come on later in the day), general aches and pains, excessive muscle tension, sleep problems (either difficulty in falling asleep or waking up too early), stomach problems, and high blood pressure (usually

reveals itself in dizzy spells). Emotionally, a stressed teen can have an extremely short fuse or be continually irritable, angry, and frustrated. And spiritually, your teen may begin to avoid going to church or participating in family activities surrounding church. Although, these may be due to normal development, they could be an indicator of stress, which must be dealt with. Help implement some of the helpful resources throughout this book, but also provide other help for your teen such as counseling, so they can learn ways to build their capacity to deal with stress and resolve the underlying causes.

5. Support your teen's involvement in stress-reducing activities. This includes both *passive and active* stress-reducing activities. Your

---

REDUCING THE STRESS RESPONSE
AND RECOVERING FROM STRESS

There are two main ways of recovering from stress: passive and active.

Passive recovery is all about lowering the stress response in the body—getting the adrenal glands to calm down and not pump an overload of stress hormones, which can cause depression. This can be done through biofeedback, progressive relaxation, meditation, massage, a hot bath with soft music and candles, or simply escaping into a fun movie. Journaling, art projects, or just "hanging out" are also ways to relax and lower the stress response system. The goal is to get that rush of adrenaline and cortisol down.

Active recovery is done through exercise. When the heart rate is up, the body is stressed to build muscle, pumping blood through the heart until you sweat and are a little breathless. When your body recovers from the workout, it also recovers from the stress damage.

teen should participate regularly in activities for relaxation as much as for fun.

6. Promote physical activity.
Physical activity is excellent as a stress reducer because it helps burn off stress hormones. This can come via sports, healthy social interaction, hobbies, or other positive lifestyle choices. Exercise also is an active approach to overcome depression because it releases feel-good hormones in the brain.

7. Help your teen eat well.
Balanced mini meals eaten regularly throughout the day—rather than heavy meals far apart—can help lower stress. It's important to pay attention to good nutrition since your teen will most likely prefer junk food. In particular, avoid pseudo stressors and stimulants such as caffeine, sugar, and processed foods. These either raise stress or increase adrenaline stimulation, which is why caffeine-based drinks are so popular in a stressed-out culture! Discourage your teen from using caffeine (coffee or sodas) late at night to help him stay awake while doing homework or studying for a test. Stress can deplete nutrients in the body, so provide your teen with a high-quality vitamin and mineral supplement. Add extra B-complex vitamins if he is particularly stressed, as these get depleted the most.

8. Make sure your teen gets enough sleep, rest, and recuperation.
Sleep is important in sorting out the emotional and mental turmoil from the day. It also helps the body recover from the damage of stress hormones flooding throughout the body. Recent studies have found that those who listen to soft, slow music before going to bed experience physical changes, such as lowered heart and respiratory rates that help in getting restful sleep.

9. Discourage the use of illegal drugs, alcohol, and tobacco.
If your teen is using substances, these will greatly interfere with the brain chemistry and stress hormone levels. It is critical that he seek

treatment for substance abuse in order to get well. If he is using substances as a means to deal with stress, then resolving the underlying
causes and learning healthy, more productive stress management
skills are essential. It might also require not hanging out with peers
who reinforce the lifestyle.

10. Use over-the-counter medications or calming herbs.
Use herbs such as Kava Kava (if your physician permits) for milder
symptoms of pain, headaches, stomachaches, tension, and insomnia. Unfortunately there is no "chill pill" to reduce stress (yet). This
is accomplished by dealing with underlying causes, lifestyle
changes, and learning stress reduction and management skills. But
for some of the more uncomfortable symptoms, your teen can get
temporary relief through natural substances and over-the-counter
treatments for such things as pain and inflammation. Make sure you
ask your doctor first to ensure there isn't danger in mixing substances, or if there are any side effects you should be aware of.

11. Encourage optimism and a sense of control.
As a parent, you are your teen's greatest encourager, comforter, and
fan. What comes out of your teen's mouth reflects what she's thinking. Help your teen decrease the negative self-talk and increase biblically based, hopeful-reality thinking. Stress can motivate her to
take positive action rather than devastate her and cause her to feel
trapped. Help your teen think of change as a challenging and normal part of life. You can help change her perception and response
to stress in the following ways:

- View setbacks and problems as temporary and solvable.
- Believe that you will succeed if you keep working
  toward your goals.
- Learn to think of challenges as opportunities and
  stressors as temporary problems, not disasters.
- Laugh a lot. Humor is like internal jogging. Seeing the
  funny or brighter side of a situation can help reduce

HOW TO GET A GOOD NIGHT'S SLEEP

Research shows that teens these days are increasingly sleep-deprived. The consequences can be extremely detrimental, especially for stressed teens. Here are some tips to help your teen get enough sleep.

1. *Go to bed at the same time and get up at the same time.* There is an important clock in the brain that is reset by the sleep cycle. By not going to bed at the same time every night, you confuse the brain. It's as if you're experiencing a daylight savings time change every day!

2. *Create a comfortable sleeping environment.*
   Light—Keep your bedroom as dark as possible. You might even consider wearing an eye mask, because darkness helps the brain to produce melatonin, the "hibernation" hormone that puts you to sleep.
   Noise—Less noise means more sleep. To reduce noise levels, try using earplugs, background white noise such as a fan, or soothing music.
   Function—Try not to use the bedroom for work activities. Make it a stress-free zone.
   Temperature and other comforts—For most people, slightly cooler is better than hot. And a good mattress can improve the quality of sleep.

3. *Create relaxing bedtime routines.* Establish bedtime rituals such as a snack, calming herbal tea, warm bath, watching a calm television program, reading a book, or listening to soothing music. The body will associate these stimuli with sleep, which will help it de-stress.

4. *Journal and make notes.* Just before lying down, write a note to remind you of what you must do the next day. If any other thoughts are bothering you, write them down so your brain won't keep reminding you or keep you awake ruminating.

5. *Exercise regularly, but do not exercise vigorously before going to bed.* That also includes reducing other stimulating activity or work (especially on the computer) within a couple of hours of going to bed. Being active prior to sleeping simply revitalizes your adrenal system.

6. *Avoid heavy meals, spicy foods, stimulating substances (caffeine, chocolate), alcohol, and nicotine close to bedtime.* If hungry, a light snack of a small turkey sandwich with a glass of milk or nuts, sunflower, or pumpkin seeds may prevent hunger pangs and help your teen get a better night's sleep.

the negative or helpless thoughts that fuel the stress response in the brain.

(Note: we discuss these in more detail in chapters 8 and 9.)

12. Express and deal with difficult emotions.

When stressed teens have a hard time emotionally, they often hold it in and keep it to themselves, not knowing how to process their feelings. This emotional turmoil is very stressful. Every teen needs an outlet for expressing and resolving these deeply confusing emotional challenges. Encourage conversations that will draw your teen to express what he is thinking and feeling. Listen and empathize, helping him sort through his self-talk and feelings. Suggest healthy emotional outlets such as journaling, talking with friends, drawing, music, or having a good cry. If that seems too difficult for your teen, then counseling might be the right "safe place" for him to work through the emotional stressors he is experiencing.

13. Urge your teen to talk and interact with others.
When your teen is stressed out, she has many confusing thoughts and feelings to sort through. Being alone in her struggle will only cause her to become more frustrated and at greater risk for depression. Encourage your teen to utilize her support system and ask for help. Talking with a friend, family member, teacher, or counselor can help her see her problems in a different light. Counseling can help her identify sources of stress, change her priorities, change her perceptions and response to stress, and find ways to manage her stress.

14. Teach your teen stress-management and relaxation skills.
If your teen is stressed, it is imperative that you learn strategies for preventing his stress response system from pumping out those damaging excess stress hormones. It's all about stress management and learning relaxation skills. Model them to your teen in your lifestyle choices. (Gain additional tools by reading *Adrenaline and Stress*[1] and *Stress and Your Child*[2] by Dr. Archibald D. Hart.)

The body can't be both relaxed and tense at the same time. By learning strategies to manage stress, your teen can infuse a sense of control over the stress response, which counteracts helplessness and hopelessness. Your teen can learn some of these on his own, while others require some additional tutoring and instruction. Refer to the last chapter and additional resource section for further details on these:

- Deep-breathing exercises
- Prayer and Christian meditation
- Biofeedback
- Journaling to express thoughts, emotions
- Progressive muscle relaxations (see *The Anxiety Cure*[3] for tips on this, or go to www.archibaldhart.com)
- Relaxing lifestyle rituals (as suggested in the "Reducing the Stress Response and Recovering from Stress" sidebar on p. 48).

- Massage therapy—this is one of the most effective ways to get relief of stress in the body. (Unfortunately, some states won't allow non-medical massages to teens younger than sixteen or eighteen.)

Teens can also benefit by learning other stress-reducing skills such as problem solving. Encourage your teen to ask others for help and guidance rather than letting the stress build up. This may include developing assertiveness skills, so she can be better equipped to handle stressful situations.

4

BEATING BACK
TEEN DEPRESSION

*Depression is a disorder of the ability to regulate stress,
something adolescents have a lot of.*
—Dr. Harold Koplewicz, *More Than Moody*

T HE WORLD A TEEN GROWS UP IN TODAY IS VERY DIFFERENT
from what it was fifty years ago, and it is not going to get any easier as we head into an even more stressful future. Depression is on the
rise. Today's teens and young adults are at higher risk than any generation before them. Though depression used to be an adult disorder, it
is increasingly becoming the second-leading cause of death among
teens from the suicides and accidents it provokes.

Depression is increasingly becoming a part of many of our lives.
If you or your teen does "walk through the valley of this shadow,"
don't be afraid. As painful as it is, you are in good company.
Millions of other families are learning to grow through and overcome depression as well. We have advanced tremendously in our
understanding of stress and depression.

But research and science aren't the only things that help. Many can attest that God will be with you in the darkest times of life. He will lead you and comfort you, as He has done for others for thousands of years. Depression is miserable and debilitating, but it is usually treatable and can be overcome. We hope to give you, as a parent, some reassurance that treatment research findings are valid.

A BASIC UNDERSTANDING OF DEPRESSION

Every parent of a depressed teen must be willing to understand and empathize with her pain. To do this, it is important to understand several basic facts about depression.

1. God has designed us with the capacity for depression.

Depression is a part of the human condition. This is true for both psychological and biological depression. Emotionally, whenever we experience a significant loss we can become depressed. God designed us to experience pain when we lose a loved one or precious belonging. This pain is to prompt us toward the process of grieving. Ecclesiastes 3:4 tells us that there is "a time to weep, and a time to laugh; a time to mourn, and a time to dance" (NKJV). Grief is a form of depression and is built into us as a way for us to come to terms with our losses. Whenever something goes wrong with the brain's mood hormones, we become physically depressed. This is part of God's phenomenal creation and, in the final analysis, a form of protection.

But don't think of depression only in terms of disturbed brain chemicals. As we will see shortly, there are many causes of depression, from everyday life pressures to major, stressful events. What's important to realize is that we were all created with the capacity for depression. It is a natural response to what is happening—good or bad—in our minds and bodies. By grasping this purposeful nature of depression, we can empathize with those who suffer from this affliction.

TEEN DEPRESSION STATS

- Between 20% and 50% of depressed kids and teens have a family history of depression (U.S. Surgeon General Survey, 1999).
- An estimated 10% to 20% of children worldwide have one or more mental health or behavioral problems (World Health Organization).
- Research indicates that depression onset is occurring earlier in life today than in past decades.
- Each year up to 8.3% of the teen population in the United States suffer from depression.
- One in five high school students in the United States has thoughts of suicide.
- One in five teenagers reports having had a major depressive episode that went untreated.
- Only about a third of those who are depressed get adequate treatment, and those who are untreated have a higher chance of experiencing a recurrence of depression.
- Depression in young people often occurs with other mental disorders, most commonly anxiety, disruptive behavior, or substance abuse disorders, and with physical illnesses, such as diabetes.
- Depression is the most common psychiatric disorder—the number one mental health epidemic—next to stress and anxiety, which tend to be interrelated.
- Women (especially young women) are three times more likely (one in five) than men (one in ten) to get depressed.

U.S. Surgeon General Survey, 1999[1]

2. Like physical pain, the emotional pain of depression is a messenger you need to heed.

Imagine that your daughter is having a hard time getting up for school one morning. She's lollygagging around while you fuss and nag. You seem to be the only one who cares if she gets to school on time. In fact, she doesn't even seem fazed by the possibility of her getting another tardy. When she comes home from school later that day, she's tired, doesn't feel like doing anything, and goes straight to bed.

It's become a pattern. Her shades are always down; her room is constantly a mess. Nothing seems to cheer her up, and she's decided she's done playing high school sports and singing in the choir. In fact, there doesn't seem to be much she's interested in or involved with. She even refuses to take phone calls from her friends and just wants to be left alone in her room. Conversations with her always end up in a fight because she's usually irritable—and even when she's not, the most you get in response are mumbles.

What is going on? Is this normal? Maybe, but maybe not—you're not sure. As confusing as all this can be, these are actually signs telling you that something is not right, messengers drawing your attention to a crisis. The symptoms of depression could be indicators alerting you that things are not right in your daughter's life. They must be attended to because there is never depression without a reason, just as there is no pain without a cause.

Physical pain is highly correlated with depression because the biology of depression parallels some of the same systems that cause pain. This is why depressed people actually feel physical pain more intensely. In a study done at Kaiser Permanente, more than 80 percent of those who complained of a variety of aches and pains at the emergency room or in a physician's office met the criteria for clinical depression. Children and teens will often complain of various physical symptoms, and many times these can be linked to depression. Listen to your teen's signals. What is the stomachache saying? What is causing the fatigue and the headaches? What are these signs telling you?

3. Depression is on the rise for teens, especially girls.

Not only is teen depression now epidemic, but it is also appearing at earlier ages than ever before. Although the specific stats vary slightly, of the more than forty million Americans who suffer from depression, nearly four million are children and teens. This means that about 10 percent to 15 percent of the child and teen population have some indications of depression. In any given year, 8.3 percent (and rising) of the teen population will show signs of depression, compared to 5.3 percent of adults. While these are some of the hard facts, we know that in reality the percentage must be much higher than this.

Some feel that the reason for this increase in child and teen depression is that doctors are now more adept at diagnosing the condition. We doubt if this is the sole reason. From what we know is happening to the teenage brain today, it is almost certain that the marked rise of depression is the consequence of stress.

Despite the evidence that teenage depression is on the rise, teens are, by and large, still not diagnosed early enough with depression. Consequently, intervention is not started early enough to prevent long-term damage. This is where the alertness of parents and others close to teens can be so important. Gaining a better understanding of the signs of depression can go a long way to avoiding a lifelong struggle.

Although the likelihood of becoming clinically depressed rises with age, teens—especially teen girls—and college students are experiencing the greatest increase nationwide.[2] Between the ages of ten and thirteen, studies have shown rates of major depression for boys and girls are about the same: nine percent. But at puberty, the depression rate suddenly doubles for girls, while the rate for boys remains the same. And the risk for girls is at its highest in the turbulent late teens. At age fifteen, females are twice as likely to experience depression as males. At about eighteen or nineteen, when they leave high school and transition into the college years, the incidence of depression is the highest.

It is at this time that teens experience major developmental changes and stresses. They are forming an identity, their sexuality is emerging, and they are separating from parents and making their own decisions for the first time. Meanwhile, they are still experiencing physical, mental, and hormonal changes.

This transition into adulthood is experienced differently for boys and girls. Studies show that female high school students have higher rates of depression, anxiety, and eating and adjustment disorders. Male students, on the other hand, have higher rates of risky and disruptive behaviors. Boys, like men, manifest depression more in acting-out behavior rather than through feelings or sadness. Anger, violence, irritability, and fantasies of revenge for injustice are typical reactions for them. Boys tend to mask their depression either by becoming over involved in activities or by withdrawing from everything and with sulking in isolation.

4. Depression is often underdiagnosed, misdiagnosed, and untreated.

Of teens who experience depression, only about one-third seek treatment. Many teens probably don't get proper treatment due to lack of a competent diagnosis, not getting access to help, or because professional intervention costs too much. Depression can often be subtle and tricky to recognize in teens. Most depression is diagnosed by a general practitioner, and he usually just prescribes a drug.

The symptoms of depression usually start out slowly and are, to the parent, simply awkward and irritating. But then—*boom!*— before you know it, the symptoms are all over the place and you're in a crisis of sorts. At this stage, a major situation could develop, which can easily become overwhelming.

Misdiagnosis and not getting proper treatment are serious concerns for teens, not only because of the negative impact depression can have on their crucial stage of development, but also because if untreated, there is a much higher chance of depression recurring in adulthood. One in five adults reports that they had a major depression that went untreated while they were a teen, which could easily explain why so many adults suffer from long-term depression. Getting the right diagnosis of the specific type of depression and other related disorders is important because it determines the course of depression later in life.

5. Depression is associated with other disorders.

Whenever you see depression, there is a strong possibility that you will find other problems as well. The most common is anxiety (more than 50 percent of depressed teens can also suffer with anxiety), but other conditions include substance abuse, self injury (such as cutting), eating disorders, ADD, learning disorders, and fatigue problems. Many of these conditions are also caused by excessive stress.

A study published in 2003 of females ages eight to twenty-two found that the most common reason for engaging in substance abuse was that it "relieved their stress." This was particularly true of those who were depressed or had been abused.[3] Each issue needs to be treated separately, in addition to the depression.

TREAT THE DEPRESSION, NOT JUST THE SYMPTOMS

The good news is that there is treatment for depression; however, teens must get help to get well. We are increasingly learning more about depression and refining the important issues in prevention and treatment. Still, we need to be careful that we don't get so focused on treating the symptoms of the depression that we neglect to address the underlying causes. Remember, depression is always a sign that something else is wrong! And although there is a need for more trained healthcare providers specializing with teens, there is an even greater need for helping parents deal with the causes of depression in teens.

Teens need more than just treatment for their depression. They need help in coping with the stresses of life. While the treatment of the depression may be the most pressing need initially, the issues that create the depression also need attending to.

WHAT IS DEPRESSION?

The commonly understood symptoms of depression are feeling down, sad, grieved, despondent, melancholic, miserable, unhappy, and being in a bad mood. These are all a normal part of the average teen journey. But there is a difference between the normal depressions of everyday life and the clinical depression that is the main focus of this book.

Teens often talk about being "depressed" when they get a bad grade, the store doesn't have pants their size, or the guy they like doesn't like them back. Obviously, they get over these disappointments—they are normal, everyday, short-lived depressions. Most major disappointments that make them sad or angry will eventually lessen with time. Teens are mostly resilient to these stressors and struggles in life, which don't qualify for the more serious clinical or major depressions.

COMMON CAUSES OF REACTIVE DEPRESSION IN TEENS

Young people are extremely sensitive to loss because they have not yet learned how to deal with it. The following is a list of life events that several studies on teens identified as events that could possibly trigger the onset of reactive depression:

- Breakup with boyfriend or girlfriend
- Trouble with brother or sister
- Increased conflicts between parents
- Change in parent's financial status
- Serious illness or injury of family member
- Trouble with classmates
- Inability to fulfill parental expectations
- Pressure at school with teachers, coaches, or grades
- Conflicts involving friendships or peer rejection
- Humiliating experiences resulting in loss of self-esteem
- Major change such as moving to a new location or country
- Unexpected events such as a car accident, loss through a natural disaster, pregnancy, or divorce of parents

What does qualify as clinical depression is a depressed mood that lasts longer than two weeks, limiting the teen's ability to function normally in daily activities. Clinical depression is not a fleeting experience but a strong, pervasive mood involving sadness, discouragement, despair, or hopelessness. The symptoms of depression impact every part of a teen's life—his mind, thoughts, emotions, behaviors, outlook, relationships, body, and lifestyle. He feels different and appears to be engulfed by an internal dark cloud. Some have compared their struggle with depression with having to fight off the attacks of an internal cruel beast or vicious dog.

WHAT TYPE OF DEPRESSION IS IT?

Depression is considered a "mood disorder" in the mental health diagnostic field, because the most prominent symptom usually is the change and dampening of mood. There are several kinds of clinical depression, depending on the causes. In essence, all depressions are either endogenous, meaning that the cause of the depression is from within the body or brain; or they are exogenous (also called "reactive depression"), meaning that the cause is from outside the body—in other words, it is a response to a life situation, usually that of loss. This distinction is somewhat arbitrary since even a profound loss such as is seen in bereavement can produce some internal changes. The endogenous category more accurately refers to depressions in which something serious has gone wrong with the brain's chemistry.

1. Endogenous depression.
Let's first look at the endogenous form of depression. These depressions can be caused by medical illnesses, by genetics, or by the impact of high cortisol as a result of stress. These conditions mainly create a chemical imbalance in the brain. In effect, the neurotransmitters in the brain (either serotonin, norepinephrine, or dopamine) become depleted. In the case of a genetic predisposition, the important cells of the brain are receiving the wrong infor-

mation. In the case of severe stress, the high cortisol levels (stress hormones) are messing up the same systems. Someone with a genetic predisposition may be more prone to depression, but what goes wrong in the brain can be treated with exactly the same medications as someone who is not. Whatever the case, don't waste time trying to figure out whether your teen's depression is stemming from stress or genetics; just get on with the treatment so your teen can get on with life!

2. Reactive depression.

Now a brief look at reactive depression. Since all of life includes loss and change, this form of depression can impact any one of us at any time. A teen may experience not making a varsity sports team, failing a class, a relationship breakup, or parents involved in a messy divorce. There could be physical loss such as an illness, losing a limb, or the losses involved in being raped. Any experience of loss can cause depression, but it is qualitatively different. While exogenous depression can be painful, it doesn't usually produce the extreme fatigue, suicide potential, or loss of interest in normal activities as does endogenous depression.

However, a prolonged reactive depression can itself be very stressful and thus become endogenous over time. Initially the treatment of reactive depression does not usually involve antidepressants, since nothing is wrong with the neurotransmitters. Certain symptoms such as insomnia can be treated, but primarily the healing comes from the grief experience resolving over time. All losses must be grieved. And grief only needs professional help when it gets complicated or becomes prolonged.

In getting help for your hurting teen, the first step is to determine what type of depression she is experiencing. There are several variations to depression, and getting the right treatment, will be determined by the right diagnosis. This is what health professionals will aim to discover at the beginning of treatment, and as a parent, your input, observances, and general information are essential.

DETERMINING THE SOURCE OF DEPRESSION

Here are a couple of examples of how the process of discovering a teen's type of depression works. I (Catherine) recently received a phone call from a mom who was concerned about her 14-year-old daughter and knew she needed help. Immediately, I began to gather facts to get an initial understanding of what type of depression her teen could be experiencing, in order to follow the most effective protocol for treatment. The mother was calling from her cell phone because her daughter had ripped the phone at home out of the wall in a fit of anger. Things had gotten really bad at home, and her parents were at their wit's end.

1. Depression could be genetic.

As I began my initial questioning to gather the information for a sense of what type of depression we might be looking at, I asked her, "How long has this been going on?"

"Oh, for a few months I guess."

"Did something in particular happen that you know of to cause a change in her?"

"Well, not really. She's actually been struggling for years in various ways—since she was a child." (Okay, now I had some crucial information that could lead to a few other questions.)

"Do you have any history in your family of depression or other mental illnesses. Have you ever been depressed?"

"Well, yes. I am currently on an antidepressant, and my mother committed suicide."

There it was. While one could not with total confidence assert that the daughter's depression was genetic, I at least had a helpful initial sense of direction as to what type of depression we were looking at. It had been longstanding, and probably had a genetic or psychological influence because of the family history.

As a counselor walks with you and your teen through this process, the first recommendation will likely be to see a doctor for a complete physical examination and then a psychiatrist for a medication evaluation. Then, during your first few visits with the counselor, he will gather more information on the family history and stress history of events in the teen's life, which will determine the course for her counseling. This can sometimes take awhile, as other crucial factors usually become evident only after being together for several sessions.

2. Depression could be due to stressful life events.

Another phone call I received was from the parents of an eighteen-year-old girl who were concerned about the way she was handling the breakup with her boyfriend. The parents had spent the night with her in her room (where she stays with a roommate at college) because she seemed extremely depressed and even suicidal. She had mentioned to her dad that she didn't think she could live without her boyfriend, so she thought she'd just bleed herself to death.

I asked similar questions of these parents as the previous case, and it was clear that this episode of depression had been triggered by the ending of the relationship. The girl had experienced a similar previous rejection—something that usually sensitizes one to further rejection. Because she had mentioned she wanted to hurt herself physically and even had a plan of how to do it, I spent a little more time with her parents on the phone coming up with a plan and strategy to intervene immediately in the crisis. Obviously, the girl needed some ongoing counseling, not only to help her grieve her current rejection, but also to explore and grieve previous rejections as well. The cumulative effect of repeated losses can make a teen prone to more severe reactive depression.

DIAGNOSTIC CATEGORIES OF DEPRESSION

The current official diagnostic categories of depression in the *Diagnostic and Statistical Manual of Mental Disorders* is somewhat controversial, primarily because the categories are based on the severity of symptoms, not on what is causing the depression. In other words, the same diagnosis of "major depression," for example, can apply to depressions that are biological in origin (endogenous) or psychological (reactive depression). This does not help any professional trying to treat depression, as it is the cause of the depression that guides treatment.

The DSM also "medicalizes" depression too much. There are many depressed teens who are dealing with the losses in their life, so it is no wonder that antidepressants for many of them won't work. What these teens need is help in resolving their losses. They need to be taught how to be resilient and cope with the tragedies of life.

So that you will know the jargon of the professional world and understand what diagnosis your teen may be given, here are the official categories of depression and their associated characteristics.

1. *Major Depressive Disorder (also known as unipolar, in contrast to bipolar depression).* This is what most people refer to as "clinical depression." It is characterized by a persistent sad mood and the inability to feel pleasure or happiness. Teens experiencing this usually feel depressed for most of the day almost every day.

2. *Dysthymia Disorder.* This is a milder form of smoldering depression that has lasted for a long time. Dysthymia has many of the symptoms of major depression, except in a milder form, like an ongoing low-grade depression. Untreated dysthymia lasts for many years, which means that it usually starts in childhood or early teens. Many depressed adults could have spent virtually their entire teen years depressed.

3. *Double Depression.* This is a combination of major depression and dysthymia. It can be both serious and chronic.

4. *Adjustment Disorder with Depressed Mood.* This type of depression parallels the reactive depression previously mentioned (a reaction to a specific life event such as loss, divorce, or death). It implies that the adjustment to loss and change is taking longer than the average time expected and interferes with the teen's daily activities. This is the most common diagnosis for mild to moderate depression as a result of a stressor or challenging life event.

5. *Bipolar Depression.* Also known as "manic depression," this is

a very serious disorder marked by episodes of depression (low mood, sadness, and hopelessness) with a high-energy, bizarre manic condition (excessive manic activity with irritability and explosive outbursts). It can be drug-induced but is mainly a genetically induced disorder. It comes in two forms: Type I and Type II. Type I involves severe manic episodes, while Type II may only have a period of hypomania (energetic but not bizarre). Unfortunately, there is currently a trend to diagnose almost anyone who is depressed as bipolar, thus trivializing true bipolar disorder.

A teen with bipolar disorder can go back and forth between dramatic swings of mood and energy over time. When he is depressed, he may feel sad and hopeless and live with a low level of energy. When he is manic, he can swing to the opposite extreme, with a high energy level and acting happy, angry, or irritable. These cycles can happen as rapidly as once a day or several times a year. It may feel like riding a roller coaster of highs and lows.

There are several other forms of depression, and we will only mention them briefly here, as they are not the primary focus of this book. It is important to note, however, that severe stress will aggravate every one of them.

6. *Premenstrual Dysphoric Disorder (PMDD)*. This is the depression associated with a milder disorder called "pre-menstrual depression or disorder."

7. *Seasonal Affective Disorder (SAD)*. Those who live in northern regions where there are long, dark winters do not get enough sunlight to turn off the melatonin daily and are prone to SAD. The prevention and actual treatment involves spending time in specially designed "light rooms" that help to simulate sunlight on a daily basis.

8. *Cyclothymic Disorder*. This is a mild form of bipolar disorder (though there is usually no link between the two) in which a person seems to be up and energetic for a brief period of time and then goes into a low mood or becomes mildly depressed. It should not be confused with the personality style of being up and down, or the Type A person who has bursts of high energy. Cyclothymia

seems to have more of a biochemical cause, as it responds to medication treatment.

9. *Substance-Induced Mood Disorder.* This can be depressive or manic. It is the direct result of substances, including prescription medications, as well as illegal drugs. In teens who suddenly manifest either depression or mania, substance induction needs to be ruled out.

WHAT CAUSES DEPRESSION?

Along with determining the type of depression and identifying the symptoms and severity, it is crucial for successful treatment to discover the underlying causes. As you might expect, these can be complex and multifaceted. There can be many factors in life that

---

MOST COMMON RISK FACTORS
FOR TEEN DEPRESSION

· Biological influences (genetics, illness, and learning disabilities)
· Family factors (chaotic family environment, depressed family member, disruptive family structure)
· Children with depressed mothers (they are twice as likely to have depression)
· Stress and life events (change, loss, abuse, trauma, sexual assault)
· Patterns and styles of thinking (pessimism, self-degradation, rumination)
· Personality styles (shyness, perfectionism, poor boundaries)
· Behavioral influences (substance use, promiscuity, defiance)

contribute to your teen's depression, and they can all overlap and interact together. For example, initially there may be what seem to be obvious causes for depression, such as family history or a recent traumatic event. A previous loss or experience can interact with your teen's biological vulnerability to stress or her predisposition to depression, as well as the impact emotionally of the current situation. All these varying aspects overlap and contribute to the overall picture of her current experience. And they are all important to be aware of and address in getting better and staying well.

A few risk factors rank the highest and are usually the first considerations in determining a cause for teen depression.

1. Physiological and pharmaceutical causes

Does your teen have a physical ailment of which you are aware? A learning disability? Anything originating from the body or brain that could cause a side effect of depression? This would include also considering what medication your teen is taking. Is he taking any medicines or herbal supplements? (even allergy medicine can have an effect)? Make an appointment for a checkup and evaluation with his physician, and be sure to mention this to your doctor.

2. Family history of depression

Have you or your husband been depressed? Has anyone in your and your spouse's family line suffered with depression, substance abuse, or any other mental illness or psychological disorder? If you aren't sure, ask those who might know and list those in a place of safekeeping for the rest of your family to know as well. Be sure to mention these as well to the healthcare providers you are receiving treatment from.

3. Significant stressful life experience of change, loss, trauma, or other source of emotional upheaval

The majority of depression is as a result of reacting and adjusting to these stressful life events.

PERSONALITY TRAITS THAT CAUSE PROBLEMS

The following personality traits in your teenager can signal trouble, especially if there has been a dramatic loss or change recently. Primarily, these traits can cause a dramatic increase in the stress levels of teenagers, resulting in depression.

· Aggressive and antisocial behaviors
· Impulsive behaviors, obsessions, or excessive and unreal fears
· Withdrawal, isolation, or detachment from others
· Overachieving or extreme pressure to perform
· Poor social skills caused by excessive shyness or feeling blameworthy, ugly, or inadequate
· Excessive perfectionism—unable to turn in a project on time because it isn't "good enough" or being excessively tidy and organized
· Poor boundaries, unassertiveness, too easy going

TREATMENT DEPENDS ON THE TYPE
AND CAUSE OF DEPRESSION

Identifying these complex causes is important to the treatment process primarily because it determines how the time and focus of the treatment (and your money) is spent. The most important goal of treatment is to come to resolution, develop a strategy, and help your teen move through to complete remission. And in order to do this, all the underlying causes must be addressed. Some of this will unfold over time, as it isn't always initially obvious to your teen, you, or the counselor.

Remember, there isn't going to be perfect resolve for everything. You're not looking for a quick, Band-Aid fix for symptoms either. Your teen must be able to face the underlying cause head-on.

Think of it as you would if she had a physical problem. If you went to a doctor with a festering wound, you'd be upset if all he did was put some ointment and a bandage on it and sent you on your way. You could have done that! You need to have it cleaned out. Disinfected. Maybe have some tests run or X-rays taken. Then possibly you'd be put on antibiotics or other medications. You'd be given a protocol of how to increase healing and recovery.

You'd receive instructions on how to rest, eat properly, and move your body. You'd find out other ways your body could benefit more from medicines and therapy.

The same considerations should be taken when it comes to mental health. At its best, good mental healthcare can and should offer specific ways to guide those who are suffering through their condition.

WHAT DOES TEEN DEPRESSION LOOK LIKE?

So far we have discussed the general aspects of depression and what can cause it. Before we discuss how to identify the symptoms or type of depression, there are a few important considerations to point out. Keep in mind the following points as you consider the behaviors, thoughts, and moods that indicate something is out of the ordinary with your teen:

1. Depression looks different in every teen.

What is it like to be depressed as a teen? Although there is a range of standard and atypical symptoms of depression, depression looks different in everyone. Personality differences will certainly show through. For instance, a teen who is by nature pessimistic will express that trait even more through depression. If your teen has a bad temper, he will appear even angrier.

Just as there are variations among teens of the same age in regard to their development (some mature faster then others), so there is no standard teen when it comes to depression. Two teens of the same age will react differently to being depressed. Avoid stereotyping or comparing your teen with other teens who are more

CAUSES OF DEPRESSION IN TEENS

As you go through this list, put a check next to the ones you think relate to your teen.

__ Physiological causes—illness, medications, hormonal imbalance, nutritional deficiencies (you will need medical testing for this)

__ Family history of depression (a parent in particular)

__ Stressful life event or accumulation of damaging experiences (loss, change, abuse, trauma, sexual assault)

__ Early adversity or negative childhood experiences

__ Anxiety disorder (either currently or as a child)

__ Childhood history of depression

__ Challenges during growth and development of teen years

__ Temperament and emotions

__ Personality disorder

__ Learning disability such as ADD or ADHD

__ Being female (girls are three times more likely than boys to become depressed)

__ Family conflict

__ Lack of parent-child bonding and attachment

__ Ineffective parenting styles and negative use of power

__ Conflict between parents or parents splitting up

__ Feeling disconnected from family, school, friends, and the community

__ Negative and ruminative patterns of thinking or pessimistic attribution styles

__ Substance abuse (smoking, illegal drug or alcohol use)

__ Sexual promiscuity

"mature" than yours. Instead, appreciate him for his unique personality and progress in life.

2. Depressed teens look different to adults.

Your depressed teen may not always look sad, as you might expect an adult to be. She will probably show other signs that could easily be misinterpreted as the teen-typical angst to be expected during the tumultuous journey into adulthood. And she will also fluctuate continually, acting severely down one hour only to be mildly sad the next.

Depressed teens ride an emotional roller coaster that doesn't stop. They can be irritable and grouchy in private, yet act perky and upbeat in a social setting. Then only a short while later, they can go home and fall apart. This "atypical depression," or varying depression, is sometimes seen in adults but is the most common form of depression in teens. It is also known as "masked depression" or "smiling depression." Because teens generally experience and show their depression differently than adults do, it can be trickier to recognize if they're depressed.

IS IT NORMAL OR IS IT DEPRESSION?

Parents, who discover the symptoms of depression in their hurting or stressed teen automatically want to know if their teen is depressed. The truth is, not every nonverbal, cranky, smart-mouthed teen is depressed. Still, these troublesome behaviors that start manifesting in the teen years make us wonder where the boundaries are between normal and officially stressed and potentially depressed.

Unfortunately, it's not so easy to read between the lines. But a parent who really knows her teen and is aware of his usual patterns of behavior is the most valuable contributor to determining the correct diagnosis. Here are some pointers to keep in mind:

1. Look at the bigger picture and the overall patterns of your teen.

Don't just look at one aspect of your teen's behavior to determine if she is depressed. Girls can show patterns of acting irritable, moody, or not wanting to be touched or hugged—but that doesn't necessarily mean they're depressed. It could merely be PMS. Likewise, just because a guy is spending a lot of time alone playing computer games or keeping his door closed and grunting when spoken to doesn't mean he's depressed. It may just be normal teen brain development. All teens go through a period when they want to be alone. Look over all your teen's behaviors for possible signs of depression, and note the frequency and duration of these behaviors.

2. Depression looks different depending on what phase it is in.
Symptoms range from mild depression in the early stage to increasingly moderate to severe. Parents and even professional health caregivers often miss the signs of early depression because they are looking for the more typical "severe" symptoms—what you would expect to see in an adult. It makes it even trickier when teens mask their depression by trying to overachieve or hide themselves in busyness.

The features to look for in children and teens may not be the typical symptoms of sadness or perpetual crying, but those of irritability and anger. Their minds focus on the negative, so they become hopeless and self-critical. They feel worthless and unloved. Small problems get blown out of proportion and seem overwhelming. They feel like giving up and can't see the larger picture. They have poor concentration and frequently space out. While discerning normal behaviors from depressive symptoms, also be alert to physical complaints such as headaches and stomachaches.

3. Don't over pathologize; no one is perfectly healthy.
We all manifest, in some minor way, many of the traits that occur in more serious disorders. We are all a little anxious or down at times. This is especially true in developing teens. They are more emotional, moody, stressed, miserable, and frustrated as they venture through the teen years. This is normal. In times of crisis, it is easy to only see the worst in our teens. We catastrophize most when we are

least prepared to cope with a crisis. If you aren't careful you could easily overpathologize your teen's condition. To avoid this, make sure you talk over your concerns with your spouse, a trusted friend, or a professional counselor.

4. Don't dismiss the signs of depression.

On the other hand, make sure you don't downplay signs of a looming depression. There is a balance between trying not to overpathologize and ignoring the indicators. Parents often see only subtle differences in their teens and can easily dismiss other problems that are in fact serious. This neglect could cause serious problems later on by either allowing the depression to become chronic or causing other ongoing challenges. It's better to be safe than sorry.

The primary set of symptoms to be aware of are continual sadness or emotional turmoil, feeling hopeless and helpless to do anything about it; loss of all positive enjoyment in life, and passivity and lethargy.

GETTING HELP FOR YOUR TEEN

We will discuss more about the counseling process in chapter 6 and talk about the specifics of selecting the right counselor for your teen. But for now, here are some simple reminders on how you can help your teen in the early stages.

1. *Get a complete examination from your teen's doctor.* If depression is suspected, get a referral to a psychiatrist, psychologist, or other counselor.

2. *Find a therapist your teen can start counseling with.* Also consider counseling support for yourself for parenting direction and support.

3. *Get a referral to see a psychiatrist* if the counselor or doctor recommends it.

4. *Get a referral to any other specialty counseling your teen might need.* Groups may include substance abuse, rape trauma, or eating disorder groups.

5. *Stay involved in the process of healing.* Although your teen's counseling is private and confidential, parenting and family therapy sessions allow you to reiterate your availability to her. Convey daily that you want to provide a safe place for her and will make every effort to contribute to her recovery.

6. *Continue to learn about depression, your teen's needs, and how you can contribute to her healing.* The more informed you are, the less powerless you'll feel.

7. *Reach out for support—for yourself and your teen.* You'll need friends, family, professional help, and prayer support to encourage you, give you hope and sustain you through the healing journey.

8. *Build a wellness lifestyle for your teen.* This will naturally increase and enhance recovery.

A PARENT'S CHECKLIST

We have devised a checklist to help parents be aware of their teen's moods and behaviors. Make several photocopies of this list and then review your teen's progress every two weeks, noting any changes that have taken place with him. Keeping a record like this for a period of time will help the psychologist or psychiatrist treating your teen to determine whether progress is being made.

TO USE: Simply check the box next to each behavior if the behavior described is still occurring in your teenager on a regular basis (i.e., more than once a week).

My teen: _____ Date: _____

☐ Does things very slowly
☐ Believes that the future is hopeless, that life isn't worth living

☐ Has negative, pessimistic thinking, talk, and attitude
☐ Thinks about how he might end life by killing himself
☐ Has difficulty concentrating
☐ Has difficulty making decisions; indecisive
☐ Has difficulty remembering things; loses things
☐ Has school problems (low grades, tardy, frequently absent)
☐ Takes no pleasure or joy in anything he does
☐ Has lost interest in things that used to be important
☐ Lacks energy; often feels extremely tired and fatigued
☐ Complains of being bored
☐ Takes great effort to do things
☐ Feels sad or unhappy most of the time, even when good things are happening
☐ Has a persistent anxious or empty mood
☐ Cries at the slightest frustration or disappointment
☐ Hardly ever smiles or laughs
☐ Hates himself and wishes he were someone else
☐ Is extremely sensitive to rejection or failure
☐ Feels he is hateful and that bad things happen to him
☐ Feels hopeless and helpless most of the time; pessimistic
☐ Feels like a failure; low self-worth
☐ Feels worthless; blames himself for what goes wrong and thinks he should be punished
☐ Has problems sleeping (too much or too little); can't fall asleep; nightmares
☐ Is often agitated and keeps moving around; fidgety or restless
☐ Is irritable; loses temper; overreacts
☐ Has aggressive, impulsive, or risky behavior
☐ Speaks of efforts to run away from home
☐ Has problems with appetite and eating; gains or loses weight without dieting

☐ Often complains of physical aches and pains
☐ Is preoccupied with physical problems and illnesses
☐ Has thoughts of suicide or self-destructive behavior
☐ Is unsociable; withdrawn; spends a lot of time alone
☐ Has problems getting along with others
☐ Other:

Other aspects of depression signs and symptoms to be aware of: What part of the day does your teen experience these? For how long have you noticed these changes? How often do you notice them?

MORE THAN DEPRESSION: DEADLY TEEN ISSUES

The younger you are when depression first hits,
the greater the likelihood that it will recur.
And if this isn't bad enough, once a child
becomes depressed, a whole host of other negative
situations arise. . . . Once the depression goes away,
the more intractable problems often remain.

—Karen Reivich, Ph.D., and Andrew Shatte, Ph.D.,
The Resilience Factor

I N THIS CHAPTER, WE WILL EXPLORE SOME OF THE RELATED problems that contribute to depression, as well as some of the most common accompanying problems that can add considerable confusion and risk to depressed teens. In addition to anxiety, the other urgent issues we will discuss are substance abuse, sexual abuse and sexual trauma, and cutting (a form of self-mutilation). Medical conditions can also coexist with teenage depression (such as diabetes or thyroid disorders), but these are outside the scope of our book. Bear in mind, however, when you take your teen to the doctor, it is estimated that about 20 percent to 25 percent of teens with certain medical conditions also have depressive disorders.

ANXIETY

Anxiety in the heart of man causes depression,
but a good word makes it glad. —Proverbs 12:25 (NKJV)

The age we live in has been called the "age of anxiety." Nearly half of depressed patients, including teenagers, have anxiety symptoms, and half of anxiety patients have depressive symptoms. Sometimes you cannot tell anxiety and depression apart! It is rare to see a major depression without also seeing some anxiety, because the same stress that messes with the brain's neurotransmitters also disturbs the delicate balance in the brain's natural tranquilizers. The result is that there is often depletion of both, thus causing depression and anxiety to coexist. This is why the same antidepressants that help to restore a happy mood are also used to treat anxiety disorders long-term.

Children and teens have general anxiety in their lives just as adults do, and they can suffer from serious anxiety disorders, such as panic attacks, in much the same way. This general anxiety is often referred to as teenage angst, and it is what revolves around issues such as the adolescent developmental turmoil and everyday insecurity. Much of this is normal and seldom needs professional help.

The more serious anxiety problems result from severe stressful life events, such as beginning or ending a school year, moving, or the loss of a parent. These can trigger the onset of an anxiety disorder, often complicating an already existing depression. While teens can develop any of the recognized anxiety disorders, some are more common than others. Generalized Anxiety Disorder and Social Anxiety Disorder are more common in middle childhood and adolescence. Panic disorders can occur in adolescence as well, especially in the late teens or when a teenager leaves for college. This is also when teens have a greater chance of getting depressed.

How can you tell if there is any anxiety coexisting with your teen's depression? Look over the brief anxiety questionnaire we've provided as a sidebar.

WHAT ARE THE MAJOR ANXIETY
DISORDERS OF ADOLESCENCE?

Here is a brief overview of the major anxiety disorders that your teen might be struggling with.

1. *Panic Anxiety Disorder.* A sudden, uncontrollable attack of terror that can manifest itself with heart palpitations, dizziness, shortness of breath, and an out-of-control or terribly frightening feeling.

2. *Generalized Anxiety Disorder.* Excessive anxiety and worry that last for at least six months, accompanied by other physical and behavioral problems such as a teen who is jittery, jumpy, sweats, gets dizzy, worries, ruminates, and is constantly on edge.

3. *Social Phobia.* A persistent fear of one or more situations in which the person is exposed to possible scrutiny of others.

4. *Obsessive Compulsive Disorder (OCD).* Repeated, intrusive, and unwanted thoughts that cause anxiety, often accompanied by ritualized behavior that relieves this anxiety.

5. *Post traumatic stress disorder (PTSD).* Caused when someone experiences a severely distressing or traumatic event. Recurring nightmares and/or flashbacks and unprovoked anger are common symptoms.

Contact a psychologist if you suspect any of these conditions. According to the National Institute of Mental Health, 90 percent of people with emotional illnesses such as these will improve or recover if they get early treatment. By their very nature, these disorders don't easily go away by themselves.

Due to space limitations in a book of this sort, we cannot do justice to this important topic and would refer you to Dr. Archibald Hart's book, *The Anxiety Cure*,[1] for further help should your teen be suffering from severe anxiety (especially if it is panic anxiety).

SUBSTANCE ABUSE

A woman was dropping off her kids at the movies one night and noticed a friend's 15-year-old daughter sitting on the sidewalk by the

TEENAGE ANXIETY SCALE

This quiz is designed to measure anxiety in teenagers. You can either have your teenager take the test or respond to it on your own as carefully as possible, making sure your answers reflect how your teenager would answer.

As you read each question, place a number corresponding to each of the following categories in the blank alongside the question:

0 = None of the time   2 = Some of the time
1 = Once in a while   3 = Most of the time

____ I feel tense and nervous, both at school and at home.

____ I have nervous physical habits like body twitches, shaking my leg, or picking my nails or my face.

____ I suddenly feel that something terrible is going to happen, for no reason.

____ I feel that I cannot get enough air to breathe and must get out of the classroom or public place, or to a window or door to get enough air.

____ I worry about the future and what might happen to me.

____ I have thoughts that bother me that I cannot control.

____ I am afraid to leave the house even to go to school.

____ I sometimes feel overwhelmed by panic or am overcome by panic attacks.

____ I am afraid of open spaces or closed spaces like cupboards or the toilets at school.

____ I am afraid that I will faint at school and be humiliated.

____ I don't like traveling to school on buses or trains.

____ I'm afraid of high places, certain animals, or flying on a plane.

_____ I don't like to be left alone or travel by myself, and I
begin to feel panicky when in those situations.
_____ Due to my fears, I avoid social settings.
_____ I am bothered by dizzy spells.

ADD UP the numbers and enter the total here: _____
Scoring: There are 15 questions and the maximum score
possible is 45.

A score below 10 indicates a normal level of anxiety.
Between 16 and 25 reflects some clinical anxiety.
Between 26 and 35, the anxiety level is moderate to high.
Over 35 indicate severe, incapacitating anxiety.

This quiz does not substitute for professional help. If your teen
shows signs of high or elevated anxiety, get professional help.

parking lot with a cigarette in her hand. What was that about? she thought. Very out of character for her. The girl's explanation when questioned? "I was feeling so stressed, and my friend said she smokes to relieve stress. So I thought I'd try it too."

A dad walks into his eighteen-year-old son's room at 10:00 a.m. to find him drinking a beer. "What on earth are you doing? Have you lost your mind?" the dad yells. "Get out and get off my back! I'm in the privacy of my room!" the son snaps back. "I'm stressed out and feel depressed, and I don't need this. I'm trying to relax and feel better before I face the day."

SELF-MEDICATION THROUGH ALCOHOL AND DRUG ABUSE

Although some teens use drugs for pleasure, to experiment, become more popular, help them think better, or be a better athlete, many teens using and abusing substances are really trying to change their own brain chemistry.

When stress is not managed well—and adolescents inherently don't have the skills to cope or recover from stress—teens find their own ways to deal with it. Using alcohol or drugs is a way to self-medicate their stress and troubles, to drown their blues. And very often, this self-medicating takes the form of addictive substances. Unfortunately, substances don't solve problems; they just hide unresolved feelings and hurts. When the drugs wear off, the problems still remain—often getting worse. Substance use and abuse can ruin every aspect of a teen's life.

Research confirms a strong correlation between stress, depression, and drug or alcohol use. Teens with overactive brains—such as those who suffer with a bipolar or manic-depressive disorder, anx-

WHO IS AT GREATER RISK: BOYS OR GIRLS?

Both girls and boys tend to use substances to alleviate a negative mood, increase confidence, reduce stress and tension, cope with problems, lose inhibitions, enhance sex, or lose weight. Boys generally use substances to feel a sensation or for social status. Girls, however, are more vulnerable to substance abuse and addiction, as they get hooked faster.

Recent studies show that girls now drink as much as boys and smoke more than boys. And they use illicit drugs only slightly less. Unfortunately, girls are suffering more damaging consequences than boys. They are using substances at younger ages, with increasing chances of later using heavier substances and developing psychological problems such as brain impairment, depression, and anxiety.

(National Center on Addiction and Substance Abuse at Columbia University. *The Formative Years: Pathways to Substance Abuse among Girls and Young Women Ages 8-22.* February 2003.)

iety disorders, certain forms of depression, or obsessive compulsive disorder—tend to abuse substances that calm the brain, such as marijuana, alcohol, or opiates.

Teens with underactive brains—such as those who have attention deficit disorder—tend to abuse stimulating drugs such as methamphetamine or cocaine. That's why it is essential to treat the underlying problems in order for your teen to heal from the substance abuse.

Because of their developing brains, some teens also tend to be risk takers. When a teen experiences anhedonia (lack of enjoyment and pleasure in life that is a symptom of depression), it can drive him to find ways to boost the pleasure center in the brain. These high-risk takers are more vulnerable to using drugs and are the ones who need to be alerted to, as this can result in destructive consequences. It's crucial that these teens find safer alternatives that can stimulate their brains rather than damage them.

GENERATION RX

I (Catherine) was at the pharmacy recently buying cough medicine for my daughter. Because I hadn't bought any for a while, I decided to take a few options home for her approval. However, I was informed that according to a new California state law, I could only purchase two containers of cough medicine at a time. This made more sense to me a few days later when I read a news report on the concern of teens now becoming Generation Rx.

According to a recent study on substance abuse by the Partnership for a Drug-Free America, today's teens are more likely to raid the medicine cabinet to experiment with getting high on prescription painkillers such as Vicodin, Tylox, and OxyContin; ADD drugs Ritalin/Adderall; and cough medicine. This is a wake-up call for parents to keep their medications locked up and to educate their teens of the dangers of abusing any type of medications. It appears that adolescents are seeing a fuzzier line between drugs that do well for you and drugs that make you feel good.[2]

CLUES TO INDICATE WHETHER
YOUR TEEN IS USING DRUGS

Parents need to know the signs that might point to possible substances abuse. Here are the main behaviors that can alert you to possible abuse.

Physical
Constant and unexpected fatigue, repeated health complaints, red and glazed eyes, a lasting cough, smell of substances in your teen's room or on their personal items, drastic weight loss or gain, sudden sloppy appearance

Emotional
Marked personality change, sudden mood swings, paranoia, anxiety, irritability, irresponsible behavior, overreaction to criticism, rebelliousness, general unhappiness, low self-esteem, poor judgment, depression, constant need for money (drugs are expensive), general lack of interest

Social
Cheating, stealing, problems with the law, sudden change to less conventional styles of dress, connecting with new friends who are less interested in standard home and school activities

Family/Home
Frequent initiation of arguments, disrespect, breaking rules, withdrawing from the family, lying about activities or where he has been, not coming home on time, abusive to family members

School
Decreased interest, negative attitude, drop in grades, many absences, truancy, discipline problems, sleeping in class, attention/memory decrease

Note: Some of these can also be signs of other problems (for instance, clinical depression), so consult with a physician, psychologist, or psychiatrist if you have any reason to suspect that something is wrong.

THE PROBLEM: TEENS DON'T GET HELP EARLY ENOUGH

A teen's developing brain is centrally involved in how she thinks, feels, and acts. When brain chemistry is imbalanced or damaged from abusing hazardous substances, she has trouble being herself, working efficiently, and developing normally. Her brain chemistry affects everything she does. Here are just two of the serious results.

1. Alcohol and drug abuse damages the brain.

It's a well-known fact that's often taken lightly, yet it's as true today as ever. Drug and alcohol abuse tends to cause overall decreased activity in the brain and throws off the balance of neurotransmitters, increasing the chance of depression.

2. Alcohol and drug abuse disrupt development.

Younger, still-developing brains are particularly vulnerable to the damaging effects of substance abuse. When a teenager or young adult starts using drugs or alcohol, he disrupts the brain's natural development, especially in the prefrontal cortex (in the front of the brain) responsible for decision making. He often stops maturing while using substances and has difficulty with judgment as a result of brain damage.

The good news is that there are medications to help stabilize the brain chemistry disturbed by drugs. On top of that, God has created the brain with an incredible ability to heal itself. Once your teen stops using substances, the brain will partially repair itself. The earlier your teen stops, the greater the chance the brain can heal.

WHAT CAN REDUCE SUBSTANCE ABUSE?

1. *Research is clear that the parent-teen relationship matters.* As a parent you are the main point of influence in your teen's life. You mean more to her than you realize. When you convey the seriousness of deterring from drugs and alcohol—and follow that up with meaningful conversation with your teen—she will be, on average, 61 percent less likely to use these substances. If she does use them, you are still the most important advocate for getting her the help she needs and continuing to be a positive influence.

2. *Parents can model, coach, and teach their teen ways to de-stress.* Recovering from stress, building resilience skills, and resolving underlying emotional hurts will determine whether your teen grabs a cigarette or a beer, or heads for the gym!

3. *Teens need to identify their stressors or triggers for depression and find constructive ways of dealing with them.* By learning stress management and how to identify and express their true emotions, teens can avoid turning to drugs and other substances to escape from their stressors.

4. *Religion and spirituality also play a protective role in eliminating substance abuse.* It's proven that the greater importance attached to spirituality and religion, the less substance abuse. And for those who have used substances, spirituality is the key to staying clean.

5. *Extracurricular activities promote school connectedness and involvement.* These activities can build authentic self-esteem and prevent teens from using substances to escape.

6. *Take advantage of prevention and educational programs.* These have been effective in schools reaching fourth through eighth graders, especially when they take a comprehensive approach involving parents, caregivers, and the family. Utilize other drug prevention video resources that can help teens visually see and hear the damage done to others.

HOW PARENTS CAN HELP

- Become a safe place for your teen to be able to communicate openly with you. Avoid panicking and overacting.
- Be aware of warning signs and risk factors that lead to substance use.
- Find out what kinds of drugs your teen is using or has used. Do drug testing if necessary.
- Educate yourself on the substances your teen is using and possible effective treatments.
- Monitor your teen's activities. Be aware of friends who may be using substances or activities where they may be going to participate.
- Get professional help and treatment intervention for substance use. Find a help group that matches your teen's needs.
- Get counseling and treatment specifically to address the reasons that your teen is turning to substances (stress, depression, anxiety, relationships). Remember, he will need to remain in treatment for at least three months or longer.
- Teach more constructive life skills to deal with problems. As stated before, tools such as stress management, identifying and expressing deep emotions, and problem solving better equip your teen to find resolve.
- Seek medical treatment. Antidepressants and selected vitamins, minerals and amino acids are necessary to stimulate the brain and repair damage. Substances mess with the brain and body chemistry, which will need to be rebalanced and repaired. Talk to a substance abuse recovery counselor regarding what medicines your teen may need.

SEXUAL ABUSE AND ASSAULT

- A woman is raped every forty-five seconds in the United States.
- One in three girls and one in six boys will be sexually abused by the age of eighteen.
- One out of every two women will become a victim of sexual assault in her lifetime.[3]

These statistics are mind-boggling. Acts of sexual violence are going on all around us. And girls mostly—but boys as well—are suffering profound injuries to their entire body and being, impacting their whole life from such human cruelty. The psychological impact of sexual assault can be severe and long-lasting. Girls who are violated suffer devastating losses. Because they are young and still growing, however, these innocent victims can find hope and healing. The teen years are the best time to make permanent life transformations. Many young women and men have found healing. God does redeem and restore the brokenhearted and downtrodden.

1. Teen sexual assault

Teen girls are at a higher risk for sexual violence than any other age group. This is mostly due to the large number of date/acquaintance rapes that occur at this age. A girl has a four times greater chance of being raped by someone she knows than by a stranger.[4]

Along with these statistics is the fact that many teen girls are the victims of sexual abuse and incest, even by close relatives or other people they trusted. Teens who have gone through these experiences are more likely than nonabused peers to have problems with depression, substance abuse, cutting, attempted suicide, school problems, conflict with authority, early sexual promiscuity, and eating problems.

Those who experienced life-threatening, sexually violent situations may develop Posttraumatic Stress Disorder (PTSD), which is an anxiety disorder and often includes depression or Rape Trauma

Syndrome (RTS), which is a form of PTSD that often affects rape survivors. They can also suffer from Acute Stress Disorder, due to the highly stressful (but not life-threatening) nature of the assault. These girls are especially vulnerable to relieving their stress and pain through substance abuse and sexual promiscuity.[5]

(Note: Zoloft is the selective serotonin reuptake inhibitor [SSRI] that has been approved as effective for treating teens with PTSD and related disorders.)

2. Rape trauma symptoms and characteristics
Each teen will be impacted differently from the trauma of rape, depending on the particular circumstances. Generally though, teens will experience impact in a three-stage process, which could last from two years to a lifetime.

Phase 1—Acute Phase
This happens immediately, within hours and up to six weeks.
Physical reactions:
- disorganization
- sleep disturbance
- eating problems
- symptoms specific to the focus of attack
- slitting of wrists to relieve pain
- cutting
- attempting suicide

Emotional reactions:
- shock and disbelief
- fear
- frequently remembering rape situation and what it felt like
- intense and conflicting emotions
- anger, desire for revenge
- guilt, shame, self-blame
- confusion, denial
- grief

- feelings of betrayal, disgust, bitterness
- rapid, inexplicable mood changes
- paranoia
- nausea
- numbness
- disassociation
- feeling dirty
- nervousness and worry
- easily upset
- feeling different from other people
- not sure how to relate to others
- signs of depression and anxiety
- want to get better and feel whole again

Phase II—Reorganization Phase
This lasts from six weeks to six months or more.
Readjustment to normal life:
- Changes in lifestyle—changing friends, phone number, school, turning to support of close family and friends
- Need and desire to talk about the experience, no matter how painful
- Questioning who she is and where life will take her
- Physical problems such as nausea, headaches, nightmares
- Phobias such as being alone, fear of men, fear of specifics to the trauma, paranoia
- Mood swings, anger, depression, flashbacks, denial, anxiety

Phase III—Resolution Phase
This begins at about six months and can continue indefinitely.
Integration: Teen integrates the bad event into her life as just another adversity to overcome.

Resolution: Teen resolves the traumatic event and the effects it has had on her life.

OVERCOMING SEXUAL ABUSE

Teens who recover well from sexual trauma seem to have several things in common:

1. *They want to get better.* They will talk about what happened and find healing to get on with their lives.

2. *They courageously face and confront their painful, troubling emotions* and use these as an opportunity to grow and heal. They grieve their losses and develop healthy adaptive responses.

3. *They want to learn and explore new things.* They intentionally discover more about themselves, others, and the world around them.

4. *They find comfort in and draw from the support of safe-place friends, caring adults, and family.* A close attachment with their primary caregiver is essential in helping them be resilient in overcoming the trauma.

5. *They learn from and find comfort from others.* They seek help from those who have also gone through a similar experience.

6. *They don't stay isolated and disconnected.* They look for supportive friends and a supportive community of which to be a part.

(Adapted from excerpts of *It Happened to Me: A Teen's Guide to Overcoming Sexual Abuse,* Wm. Lee Carter, Ph.D.)[6]

WHAT TO DO IF YOUR TEEN HAS BEEN SEXUALLY ASSAULTED

1. *Get your teen to a safe place where she will be comfortable to share her experience and get help.* Your teen may not be able to tell you about the sexual trauma she has experienced. That is very common.

2. *Take your teen to a gynecologist or family physician of the same sex for a complete medical evaluation.* Medical treatment is usually the most urgent need immediately after an assault. Encourage her

to be open and honest with the doctor about her current health or any concerns she may have.

3. *Encourage your teen to get counseling.* She will need a safe place to make sense of her thoughts and feelings. Find a respected, trusted woman who has effectively worked with sexually violated young women. Several new therapies have proven highly effective in the treatment of sexual trauma. Teens who receive medical, psychological and spiritual help will recover and overcome the trauma much better than those who struggle to cope alone. In fact, getting competent professional help is the key to being a rape survivor and not a rape victim. Untreated sexual trauma can have serious, long-lasting effects that can interfere with adult mental, emotional, physical, and relationship health.

4. *Utilize helpful resources such as the Internet, workbooks, and rape crisis hotlines and centers.* One option is to call the Rape, Abuse, and Incest National Network (RAINN) at 1-800-656-HOPE. Additional resources are listed at the end of this book.

5. *Provide unconditional support, comfort, love, and grace.* Assure your teen that the sexual abuse wasn't her fault. Regardless of what happened, she is going to be able to move forward and be healthy. Teens often have a hard time sharing personal experiences this deep with parents. At the same time, most parents have a hard time hearing about it and knowing what to do. To make the process easier, help your teen get the help she needs through counseling intervention and support. But never stop expressing your unconditional love for her. She needs you more than ever during this time.

6. *Be patient and kind.* The recovery process will take time and hard work, but in order for your teen to move on with her life, you and she must both allow yourselves time to work through the experience and integrate it into your lives. This is different for each person. Your daughter may struggle with other mental and emotional problems. It may be an uphill battle for her to regain self-respect, self-esteem, self-assurance, and self-control. Whatever the situation, remind her that getting healed quickly isn't the priority—her well-being is.

SELF-INJURY AND CUTTING

Some recent studies indicate that as many as 14 to 39 percent of adolescents engage in self-mutilative behavior. Even more astonishing is that those who self-mutilate do so anywhere from once to 745 times a year.[7] Self-injury, and particularly cutting, has become a disturbing trend among students as young as eleven and twelve years old.

Why are so many teenage girls (and boys now) cutting themselves, hitting themselves with their fists or objects, and bruising themselves or breaking their bones? It's difficult to understand, but when teens are overflowing with emotions like sadness, depression, or anger, and they don't know how to express it, cutting themselves actually makes them feel better. Often, teens who harm themselves feel emotionally distant or abandoned by their parents. Some feel numb, physically dead inside, or unnoticed by their parents. They are full of intense emotional pain but don't know how to relieve it. This tension can become so unbearable that cutting somehow relieves the stress and emotional pain. Harming the body calms them for a short time. It helps them feel temporarily alive and in control of their situation and moods.

1. Paradoxical pleasure

Research suggests a few explanations. Some self-abusers may have been discouraged from expressing emotions as children and don't know how to deal with intense emotion. Others have a history of physical and sexual abuse that may be associated with self-abuse. Teens who cut themselves often have other problems, like eating disorders, bipolar disorder, or drug and alcohol abuse. The cutting is an attempt to numb the pain and avoid the problems behind all their self-destructive behaviors.

Many of these "cutters" are actually depressed. They have low levels of serotonin in the brain, which is linked with depression and anxiety. As stated in a previous chapter, depression can potentially shut down the pleasure center in the brain, a phenomenon called anhedonia (meaning the lack of hedonism or pleasure). Anhedonia is one of the major symptoms of depression in adults, but it is also found in children and teens.

What teenagers and some young adults have discovered is that when one can feel no pleasure from ordinary life, hurting yourself can actually become pleasurable. It sounds strange, but it is true, as every teenager who has ever cut herself will tell you. It allows her to feel something else, and this distracts her from her emotional pain. The fleeting "high" teens feel when self-abusing is a result of endorphins that are secreted into the bloodstream. This "rush" provides a quick numbing or pleasurable sensation and temporarily distracts from the stress she feels.

2. A growing trend

Girls and boys between the ages thirteen and fifteen are the primary group of cutters. Their peers who don't cut see the self-abuse as profoundly disturbing, yet they all know about it. It's viewed more as something shocking, stupid, and even pathetic. Yet hurting teens still recommend it to their hurting friends as something to try that will help them deal with their bad feelings.

These teens don't intend to permanently hurt themselves, but they are at risk every time they cut. They could easily misjudge the depth of the cut. Wounds can become infected. A teen could get HIV or hepatitis if sharing cutting instruments. Self-cutters indicate that suicide is less likely because what they are doing relieves their depression. However, those who cut are more likely to commit suicide if they don't get help. Girls are much more likely to harm themselves than boys. (Boys and young men attempt suicide far less often than girls but succeed far more often; they intend to die whereas the girls are trying to get help.)

3. Noticing the clues to cutting

Often, parents and teachers of teens who cut have no idea what these teens are doing. Since teens can harm themselves in several ways, parents need to be alert to any of the following signs on their teen's body:

- Wearing pants and long-sleeved shirts all the time, even when playing sports and in warm weather
- Cut marks (usually in hidden places)
- Burn marks
- Bruise marks (excused with, "Oh, I just bumped myself there") or unusual markings on the body
- Unexplained or unusual accidents
- Becoming highly distressed and locking herself in her bedroom
- Anorexic or bulimic signs (eating disorders often accompany other forms of self-abuse)
- Overdosing that sends her to the ER

4. What Can Parents Do to Prevent Cutting?

Since it is hard to distinguish between serious cutting and experimenting with cutting, it is better that parents err on the cautious side and seek help right away. The act of cutting is a sign of emotional difficulty that needs to be recognized. Once the underlying causes are addressed, the teen is better able to handle stress more effectively. And when combining this with treatment for depression and subsequent problems, a teen is then able to resume getting pleasure from the normal activities of life.

SUICIDE

Every suicide is a tragedy, and any increase in suicidal thoughts, no matter how small, must be taken seriously. Suicidal behavior is often triggered in a teen by events or challenges that she finds too difficult to tolerate. It is a permanent solution for a seemingly irresolvable temporary situation. Even things that seem minor to an adult can be major to a young person. Teens don't have the life experience to put problems into perspective or to understand that life comes with changes and losses. That's why it's important for depressed teens to have ongoing therapy. Not only can it provide

DEPRESSION AND SUICIDE MANAGEMENT

1. If your teen's suicide seems imminent, it is critical that you seek counseling or crisis intervention. The counselor may ask for her to go voluntarily to the hospital.
2. As her parent, you will be called or asked to take her.
3. If she refuses to go voluntarily and she is deemed dangerous to herself or others, the counselor has an ethical responsibility to provide for her safety. The counselor will then call 911, the police, or PET (Psychiatric Evaluation Team) and have your teen held for 72 hours.
4. If the suicidal thoughts don't seem to be leading to immediate action, then the counselor may suggest that sessions be increased to several times a week.
5. A counselor may arrange for a daily call-in-system.
6. A suicide prevention plan will be drawn up with what your teen is to do when she feels overwhelmed.
7. Together the counselor and your teen will compile a phone list of who to call when she is faced with hard times and what to do.
8. Other strategies may be implemented, such as a letter of encouragement, a list of positives to focus on, or a no-suicide contract your teen agrees to.
9. You and your family will become involved in setting up a support system and perhaps a 24-hour watch to assure your teen's safety.
10. Stay in close contact with your teen. She should not go on a trip by herself or with others or be left alone for long periods of time.
11. A referral may be recommended to a psychiatrist for an evaluation for medication.
12. When starting the medication, make sure your teen takes it regularly as prescribed. Monitor for any side effects, especially the increased possibility of suicide.

guidance through times, a teen is more likely to confide suicidal thoughts with a trusted counselor than with a parent.

1. Risk factors for teen suicide
- Death of a family member or close friend
- Loss of a romantic relationship, a parent through divorce or separation, pet, treasured object, or opportunity such as being on a sports team
- Fear of punishment for failing or doing something wrong
- Physical, sexual, or psychological abuse (suicide attempts are common for girls who have been raped)
- Unwanted pregnancy
- Poor grades, negative changes in school performance or social dynamics
- Fights or arguments with family members or loved ones that seem irresolvable
- Belief one has harmed or brought harm to family or friends
- Embarrassment or humiliation
- Concerns about sexuality
- Suicide of a friend, acquaintance, or celebrity (copycat suicide)
- Inability to cope with change
- Any other devastating loss inability to cope with change

This means that if any of these are present in a teen's life, extra vigilance is needed. Since teen suicide is now a major concern when taking antidepressants, this will be explored further in chapter 7.

2. Warning signs for teen suicide
The following behaviors are warning signs for possible teen suicide:
- He has shown previous suicidal behavior.
- He has a history of depression or substance abuse.
- He has tried to run away.

- He shows unexplained severe, violent, or rebellious behavior.
- There is a history of suicide and mental health disorders in the family.
- There is a history of abuse, violence, or neglect.
- He has lost a parent through death or divorce.
- He has talked about or threatened suicide, even jokingly.
- He frequently creates poems, essays, or drawings that refer to death.
- He often sends hints, such as, "I won't be a problem for much longer."
- He engages in careless risk taking.
- His sad or angry mood doesn't go away.
- He begins to give away his personal possessions or suddenly starts clearing out his belongings and getting them in order.
- He becomes suddenly cheerful without reason after being seriously depressed.

Part II

GETTING HELP
TO GET BETTER

6

FINDING THE RIGHT COUNSELOR

There are different ways to serve but the same Lord to
serve. And there are different ways that God works
through people but the same God. God works in all of us
in everything we do. Something from the Spirit can be
seen in each person, for the common good. . . . One
Spirit, the same Spirit, does all these things, and the
Spirit decides what to give each person. —1 Corinthians
12:5, 7–11

He comforts us every time we have trouble,
so when others have trouble, we can comfort them with
the same comfort God gives us. —2 Corinthians 1:4

IT CAN BE FRUSTRATING, DISCOURAGING, AND OVERWHELMING
for parents to figure out what sort of help to get for their depressed
teenager. And it can be just as scary for teens. Often, they really don't
know what is wrong with them or how to stop feeling badly. When
teens hurt, parents instinctively want to put their protective arms
around them to soothe their pain, help them get better, and become
whole again. But there are times when, instead of giving hugs, parents
try to shake their teens out of it. From their own fear, parents try to
force their teens to heal.

But unlike bad moods that come and go for every teen, clinical depression does not just disappear. Depression is a real disorder with definite symptoms. But the good news is that there are effective treatments for depression. You can help your teen get better and stay well.

HOW IS TEENAGE DEPRESSION COMMONLY TREATED?

The first step in getting your teen well is knowing what type of depression and other conditions are to be treated. Effective treatment intervention depends almost entirely on an accurate diagnosis and ongoing evaluation of the treatment. Because depression is complex and multifaceted, there is no one way to treat every teen. Each treatment plan must be customized specifically for each teen. A girl will be treated differently than a boy, a younger teen differently than an older teen. Finding the right treatment for your teen will depend on the severity of his symptoms, how long he has had symptoms of depression, the underlying causes, his current situation, and other such factors.

Depression symptoms impact every aspect of your teen's being, so interventions will need to consider building resilience and healing in every facet of who he is. We encourage you to think not only in terms of one specific aspect of the treatment, but to focus on the healing of your teen as a whole person. Every part of an effective treatment plan should consider your teen's developing mind, emotions, relationships, body, and spirit.

Strategies for overcoming depression may include physical exercise, healthy nutrition, positive emotional outlets, making healthy connections, and problem-solving skills. We will discuss several of these in the chapters that follow. A comprehensive treatment plan may also include individual counseling, group therapy, family therapy, hospitalization, or a special school, wilderness challenge, or boot camp. If the depression is severe or biologically based, then antidepressant medication will be essential.

Overall, what is important for you to know is that research clearly shows that in treating severe depression, a combined treatment of counseling and medication shows the highest rates of recovery.

Neither counseling nor medication on its own is as effective as the two combined. So if your doctor recommends antidepressant therapy for your teen, make sure your teen receives counseling as well.

FIRST THINGS FIRST

Now that you have a sense from earlier chapters as to whether or not your teen is stressed and or depressed, you may be wondering how to proceed to get help. If your teen seems to have many of the symptoms outlined in the checklists we have offered, then begin by getting your teen a complete physical examination from the doctor. This should include a full panel of testing to rule out possible physiological causes of depression. In particular, test for thyroid disease of any sort. Once all possible physical disorders and illnesses are ruled out and your teen has been given a clean bill of health, the doctor may refer you to a psychiatrist, psychologist, or counselor. These health professionals can help in managing your teen's depression. What is most important is that your teen feels comfortable with all the health professionals involved. If not, explore some alternative resources.

If your teen's symptoms seem rather moderate to severe, the doctor may give you samples of an antidepressant or a prescription for one until your teen can see a professional specially trained in treating child and adolescent depression. Unfortunately, such personnel are limited in some parts of the country. It's possible that you will have to wait awhile before getting an appointment, so don't delay in scheduling one.

You may initially find it difficult to get a mental health professional with whom your teen feels comfortable. If so, try asking a counselor to recommend a psychiatrist. You can also go through your insurance provider to explore all options of counselors and psychiatrists in your area who specialize in working with teens. They can also be helpful in making other recommendations. And don't forget that while looking for help for your teen, you may also want to consider finding support for yourself as a parent and for your family. Depression in one family member can have an emotional impact on the whole family. (Note: Throughout this chapter, we'll be using the terms *counseling*, *therapy*, and *psychotherapy* interchangeably to refer to the broad range of mental health care that is available. While counseling refers to a broader range of mental health caregivers [such as a youth pastor, school counselor, social worker, etc.], therapy—and specifically psychotherapy—involves more in-depth, professionally trained therapists. It includes intervention for more specific and serious problems, such as panic attacks or mental disorders. While a counselor could be trained, a psychotherapist is professionally educated, trained, and licensed.)

WHEN TO CONSIDER COUNSELING

Why is professional counseling important, and how can it be helpful? Remember Simon, the character in the TV show *7th Heaven* who fatally hit a boy with his car? According to the story, Simon isn't able to process the stressful traumatic event, so he starts dealing with it in his own ways—with disastrous results that only create more severe problems. That may just be a story, but the important lessons are true to the norm. When teens experience hard times, they often try to take matters into their own hands, only making it worse.

It is important, therefore, that your teen has access to a knowledgeable, caring adult who can become a safe place where she can talk and receive guidance through her confusion and hurts. Don't take it personally; you may be a wise and knowledgeable parent, but your hurting teen will probably not be initially willing to share all her deep fears or feelings with you.

Here are some clarifying questions to consider if you are wondering whether to take your teen to counseling and whether it will be helpful:

- Does your teen have some of the symptoms outlined in the previous chapters that indicate she is depressed or overly stressed?

- Is she unable to function in life as well as she used to?
- Does your teen seem to be involved in unhealthy "escaping" behaviors that she could be using to deal with her pain?
- Is she having problems in school, at home, or in other settings?
- Does it seem your teen is having difficulty talking about her feelings, behaviors, or other problems she is having?
- Do her struggles seem to be affecting her life, making it difficult to keep up with schoolwork, relationships, and extracurricular activities?

Remember, the longer you wait, the more severe the depression will become and the longer it may take for your teen to recover.

COUNSELING PROVIDES HEALING THROUGH TALKING AND LISTENING

We have talked a lot about the importance of meaningful connections in your teen's life. So it only makes sense then that counseling can be part of God's provision for her healing. Counseling provides the much-needed safe place for your teen to talk about her problems, put them in perspective, and find some resolution.

1. Counseling is a safe place.

The counseling relationship is a safe place for a teen to explore the underlying causes of his depression and how these impact his life and relationships. A good teen counselor is trained to develop a warm, honest, and meaningful connection with a teen. He should be nonjudgmental and offer unconditional acceptance—essential ingredients to emotional growth and healing. Counseling provides reliable, consistent, uninterrupted time for your teen to be heard and valued. This can also reduce stress, because your teen can be relieved in knowing there is a time and place he will get to talk about his problems.

A counselor should not blame or criticize your teen. He should not tell your teen to stop relationships with family or to never discuss with anyone what happens in the sessions. Counselors are not helping if they force your teen to work on areas he isn't ready to address, or if they make him work harder on his wellness faster than he is able. Obviously, a counselor should never betray confidentiality outside of mandated legal reporting. If at any time your teen does not feel safe in the counseling relationship, discontinue and find another therapist. Report that counselor to a licensing board if necessary.

2. Counseling is a growing place.
This is where teens can clarify priorities and values, set goals to change, think through life choices, and become intentional in living them out. Counseling provides an outlet for teens to become aware of their deep emotions and thoughts. It allows them to analyze how these can be transformed and impact their life in a positive way. Remember, a season of depression can be an opportunity to grow by becoming more intentional about strengthening weaknesses, building on strengths, and developing character. Your teen's symptoms are signaling something is wrong or out of order, so if she is open to honest confrontation, God can accomplish deep healing and transformation. Besides curing various problems, the ultimate goal of godly counseling is building Christian character.

3. Counseling is a partnership.
This may be the only place your teen is able to talk constructively about problems and receive guidance, intervention, and a private, safe, healing relationship.

TYPES OF COUNSELING

1. *General physicians and pediatricians* (M.D.) usually see the teen initially for a complete physical evaluation to rule out physical causes of depression. If the doctor is unavailable or decides it is nec-

essary, your teen may see a nurse practitioner who will do the evaluation and make recommendations.

2. *Psychiatrists* (M.D., D.O.) medical doctors who have extra training in mental health and are able to prescribe medication and sometimes offer ongoing counseling. The doctor or counselor may recommend a complete evaluation by a psychiatrist to get more details about your teen's personality and diagnosis, or to be evaluated for antidepressant medication.

3. *Clinical psychologists* (Ph.D., Psy.D.) are trained in mental health care. Some are trained to provide comprehensive intake testing. Others have specialty training in treating adolescents.

4. *Psychotherapists* (M.A., M.F.C.C, M.S.W., L.P.C., Ph.D.) cover a wide range of specialties. Depending on the licensing board of your particular state, counselors with a masters degree or a Ph.D. can be licensed as Social Workers or Marriage and Family Therapists. Many have been trained to work with families and teens.

5. *Mental health counselors* (M.A., M.Ed., Ed.D or Ph.D.) are typically trained to help with areas of career, vocational, and general mental health counseling. Be sure your counselor choice has specialized training and experience in working with teens and depression.

Others who may help you are your teen's teachers, a guidance counselor, or a school psychologist. These people may be the first to notice changes in your teen and may be the first to alert you to problems outside the home. They can help make recommendations and referrals as well as work with you on the treatment plan and goals. Help can also be available through pastoral counseling, crisis centers and crisis hotlines, self-help and support groups, twelve-step groups, and residential programs.

TYPES OF THERAPY

Therapy is learning and growing process in which a mental health professional can help your teen through times of difficulty. This is usually done by talking and listening, referred to as "talk therapy."

When it comes to treating depression, the American Psychological Association has found that the most effective therapeutic treatment for supporting antidepressant medications is action-oriented, problem-solving, goal-oriented, short-term talk therapies. Therapy should be focused and concrete, with the goal of helping your teen deal with specific issues and causes related to the depression. Effective psychotherapy often includes strategic action plans such as journaling, expressive art therapy and homework assignments that can include the teen getting actively involved in taking action to practice what he has learned.

For more seriously disturbed teens, personality disorders, and deeply traumatized adolescents, more long-term, emotion-focused psychotherapies are necessary. It is beyond the scope of our book here to go into details of these approaches, so if your teenager needs more in-depth psychotherapy, consult a clinical psychologist who specializes in these approaches.

Here is a brief overview of the main types of therapy that have proven to be effective in treating depression.

1. Cognitive-Behavioral Therapy (CBT)

This is a therapy that focuses on behaviors and how to change them, as well as mental processes, such as perceiving, remembering, reasoning, decision making, and problem solving. The focus is on what the teen in therapy thinks and does. With this form of therapy, it's less important to understand the past events that led to a specific pattern of thinking and doing. This approach tries to replace self-defeatist expectations ("I can't do anything right") with positive expectations ("I can do this right"). (Refer to chapter 10 for specific application of this theory.)

2. Interpersonal Therapy (IPT)

This therapeutic approach is appealing to depressed teens because it is brief, focused, and oriented to current social and interpersonal problems. A large number of depressions first occur in adolescence, when major life choices in education, friends, values, and family relationships are being made. Interpersonal therapy helps the teen identify and develop more adaptive methods for dealing with these interpersonal issues. It also reveals how these issues are associated with triggering depression and other related problems, and, through this, attempts to prevent recurring episodes.

3. Emotion-focused therapy

This is a relatively new theory that has recently demonstrated great outcomes. The focus is primarily on relationship attachments, emotional injuries, and depression due to loss or relationship hurts. It has also proven helpful in the healing and fostering of healthy relationships for those who have been abused. Emotion-focused therapy is effective for both individual and family therapy because it deals directly with the emotional attachment styles and process between family members, as well as emphasizing the importance of providing a safe place in which children can grow (refer to the "Building a Safe Place" section in chapter 12).[1]

4. Family therapy

Since the entire family is impacted by the depression of a single member, attention may need to be given to how family dynamics are either aggravating or causing depression. For instance, divorce or severe family conflict can be a major source of depression in children and teens. Family therapy, of which there are several approaches, aims to resolve these conflicts, or at least help the teen adjust to them.

5. Support groups

In tandem with individual psychotherapy, support groups are helpful in healing from trauma, loss and grief, substance abuse, or sexual abuse.

PURSUING COUNSELING HELP FOR YOUR TEEN

The process of getting help from a counselor can become frustrating for teens and parents. Though you might be fortunate enough to find someone on your first phone call, that seldom happens. The waiting lists for good therapists are long. There are few truly excellent counselors and psychiatrists who specialize in working with teens and the particular issues they struggle with. But don't lose heart; there is still help out there. Finding it takes a lot of homework and patience to put up with hassles and waiting lists, but your perseverance will pay off when your teen becomes well.

In your search, begin by having a good sense of what you are looking for, and then prioritize what's most important, because you might not get everything you want in one person. You may have to compromise and go with the best option available initially in order to get your teen the right help. Following are some questions and considerations that can help you choose a counselor for your teen.

1. What are your ultimate goals for counseling?

Before selecting a therapist, clarify what your goals are and what sort of help your teen needs. You and your teen won't have all the answers for what is wrong and what you want to change in life. However you must have a general sense of the main issues. Is your teen overly stressed? Has there been a recent relationship breakup or other situation to trigger the depression? Has your teen been depressed for a long time? Besides the depression, are there other issues that need to be considered, such as substance abuse, rape, eating disorders, cutting, school problems, or addiction to pornography? All these considerations, along with other professional input, will determine the treatment plan and goals for counseling.

2. What are you looking for?

• A *man or a woman?* Usually, teens, are most comfortable talking with a same-sex therapist about developmental issues such as sexuality, self-esteem, and other vulnerable topics.

• A *personal connection?* This is crucial for the success of treatment for your teen. There needs to be some rapport with the counselor. In fact, the connecting relationship is more important than the techniques and style of therapy used. This relationship will become the safe place for self-discovery to learn, grow, and develop effective ways of living intentionally. You and your teen should choose someone who you believe shows insight, empathy, and patience.

• A *Christian?* Ultimately, most people of Judeo-Christian faith prefer a counselor who is sensitive to their faith issues. However, if you are limited to insurance referrals, begin by asking if they are aware of another counselor in the group who shares your faith. If not, it is still important that you get treatment for your teen. Remember that competence in treating depression should take priority. Most good therapists will be sensitive to considering your faith issues. Get your teen the help to get better.

• *Personal qualifications?* In finding someone for your teen, consider his subjective preferences. How old is the counselor? What is his cultural background? Does his personal life seem in shambles? If so, go elsewhere. The counselor's interpersonal style and basic personality will matter a lot to your teen. For example, some therapists allow teens to swear in session and may even use a swear word back themselves to bond and relate to the teen. You might not be comfortable with this, but it might capture your teen and be an effective way of bonding. If the therapist seems to genuinely care about your teen, it is often a sign that he has the healing gifts necessary to do good therapy with your teen.

• *Therapeutic style and methods?* A competent, experienced counselor will use a particular therapeutic style or an integrative approach to meet your teen's growth and healing needs. Refer to the previous section on types of counseling so you are familiar with these while talking with the therapist.

• *Background and training?* Regardless of where the counselor went to graduate school, what counts the most is what clinical experience she has in working with your teen's needs such as depression and/or other problems. Be sure that the therapist you choose has been successful in treating other teens and that you are comfortable with her competence to treat depression.

WHAT CAN YOU EXPECT FROM A COUNSELOR?

Here are some considerations as you create your own list of what you hope to see accomplished for your teen during counseling.

- To find out what's wrong with your teen
- To help your teen get over whatever problems he is having: the depression, taking drugs, cutting, eating disorders, etc.
- To be willing to work cooperatively with other doctors
- To work with your family as well as your teen
- To help your teen learn to take good care of himself
- To teach practical strategies and life skills for dealing with stress, anxiety, and depression
- To be responsive during a crisis or to set up a plan set up for emergencies
- To have an open mind regarding integrative healing that uses other methods, besides conventional medications, such as nutrition, lifestyle, and relaxation skills

FINDING A THERAPIST FOR YOUR TEEN

The best way to find a counselor for your teen is by word of mouth. Call around to ask those who know where teens can get help. Here are some sources for getting names of counselors.

- Your health insurance company
- Your doctor or pediatrician
- A local crisis line for teens
- Friends who have been to counseling or know of others who have been
- Other counselors who can give suggestions
- Community- or hospital-based teen clinics
- Local counseling centers
- School guidance counselors

- Your church counseling center or pastoral care office
- A reputable Christian counseling referral service such as Focus on the Family (719-531-3400) or the American Association of Christian Counselors (800-526-8673)

WHAT TO SAY DURING YOUR INITIAL CALL

When you make that first phone call to a counselor, you may only get a secretary or answering machine. Nonetheless, most counselors are willing to talk to you on the phone so you can get a sense of who they are and whether they are suited to your needs. Ask if the counselor can call you back for a personal interview. If you get an answering service, remember that counselors typically check their messages throughout the day and make phone calls at the end of the day or when they have a break between sessions. If it takes a few days, be patient—the best counselors are usually the busiest. Leave your cell phone number or a number where you can be easily reached to ensure maximum opportunity for connecting. If you don't hear back after a few days, leave another message; and if you don't hear back soon after, try contacting someone else. Since this all takes time, don't delay too long.

Here are some initial considerations for your phone conversation:

1. *Briefly describe your teen's situation.* The counselor will want an overview of your teen's situation and will ask questions to clarify. Be prepared to answer honestly and concisely. Having some notes prepared ahead of time will help you to remember important facts.

2. *Ask about fees, insurance coverage, etc.*

3. *Note how you feel when talking to the therapist on the phone.* Is she pleasant? Are you at ease? Are you being treated respectfully? When you left your message, did the counselor get back to you within a reasonable time (even if you played phone tag)? Do you sense she understands your teen's situation and is willing to help? Does she seem confident and trained to treat your teen?

4. *Ask if she is taking new clients.* If the therapist isn't taking any new clients at this time or isn't able to treat your teen, ask her for a

recommendation of another therapist. This will be helpful to add to your list of possible options.

EVALUATING THE COUNSELOR AND THE THERAPY

See your first appointment as an opportunity to get to know the therapist better. Besides theoretical background and training, the personality of the therapist is crucial. Even if you get a great recommendation, your teen might not feel comfortable with her. Talk with your teen about this. What's lacking in their connection? As you help your teen reflect on the therapist, prompt her to think about these questions:

- Do I feel safe and am I comfortable with this counselor?
- Can I trust her with the deep things I am sharing?
- Do I sense that she really listens and understands me?
- Do I believe this counselor can really help me? Is therapy helping me so far? How?

If for some reason the therapist doesn't seem like a good fit, find someone else. Once decided, continue with the therapist for at least three consecutive sessions to decide if this is someone your teen will want to continue seeing.

UNDERSTANDING THE THERAPEUTIC PROCESS

If you haven't been to counseling or therapy before, you might be wondering how it works and what to expect. Because getting help for your teen is so important, we will briefly walk you through the typical process. There will be variations, but hopefully this will prepare you as you proceed and will clarify some of your concerns.

1. The initial interview.
When you first talk to and start meeting with a counselor, they are going to want to get to know your teen (and possibly your family), in

order to best help you. Initially the counselor will discuss counseling policy, how the fee will be paid, and legal and ethical counseling issues. Counselors are ethically bound to clarify all these issues before proceeding. There will be paperwork to fill out and go over. If your teen is seeing the therapist individually (typical of older teens), then you may only be involved in the initial interviewing process. After that, your teen will continue with the therapist alone, unless family sessions are suggested.

The initial interview is the time for you to ask questions and give detailed information on your teen's problems. The therapist will ask for a history of the problem and will want to know what other problems coexist and whether your teen is willing to commit to the counseling on a regular basis.

The therapist will be looking for what particular clinical issues your teen is dealing with and what the possible diagnoses are. What type of depression is your teen experiencing? Is he also anxious? Are there other factors to consider such as substance abuse, eating disorders, or suicidal thoughts? These are all part of the initial and often ongoing assessment process.

The counselor will also want to know about the family history of mental illness. He will be interested in your teen's home life and what his relationships at home are like. How are his relationships with friends and at school? How is he doing at school with grades, activities, and social life? Has he had any stressful or traumatic experiences recently or in his childhood? Is he using substances? How is he currently choosing to deal with his pain, and how has he dealt with it in the past?

Of course, being as honest as possible is the most helpful. That's why your teen might be interviewed separately. There may be some important information the counselor will need to know that your teen isn't comfortable having you know yet. Teens might not be honest at first for fear of being judged or simply because they have kept secrets for a while. Hopefully, as your teen feels safer in the counseling relationship, the important issues will be continually revealed.

2. The first few sessions.

During your first or second visit, you will also make a decision about when to meet on a regular basis. Having the same time and day helps your teen to remember. The first few sessions will often go longer than usual. Typically, counseling is weekly and in hourly sessions (this is actually fifty minutes of therapy and ten minutes to allow the therapist to make notes, do paperwork, etc.). If it seems that things are going well as therapy progresses, the visits might change to every other week, and then to monthly. If your teen is really in crisis, the counselor might suggest double sessions or a few sessions a week. These more frequent sessions are important initially for your teen to get control over the depression and to provide support in dealing with severe life issues.

If after a few visits your teen doesn't feel okay talking to the counselor, have a session yourself with the therapist and then get a referral to another therapist. As stated earlier, it might take a few tries to find a counselor whom your teen likes, so don't give up. Since she will be sharing deep and sensitive issues, she deserves to have a therapist she feels safe and comfortable with, and one with the most beneficial personality and style for her at that time. For example, if your teen has experienced trauma such as rape, she may initially benefit from a therapist who is trained in dealing with trauma. After a while, when your teen is doing better, she might be ready for working with someone who is more directive and strategic in setting goals, journaling, and other practical growth coaching.

CRISIS FIRST

It's unrealistic to think that once therapy and/or medication treatment has begun, everything will get better. In fact, sometimes the therapeutic process can provoke more crises before you see any progression. During this time, it is important to remember the main priority is for your teen to be safe—even from herself. Healing will eventually come, but your concern should be to get any immediate potential harm under control. For example, if your teen has been hurting herself (by cutting, etc.) or is having thoughts of suicide, with or without a specific plan, then these will become major issues and the first focus of counseling. The counselor will assess how imminent the danger is and will then proceed from there. Throughout the counseling, this will be monitored for progress and safety of the teen. All suicidal threats, gestures, or comments must be taken very seriously. (Refer to the suicide section in chapter 5 for more on this.)

KNOWING WHEN TO LET GO

There comes a time for some parents to release their teen to outside intervention, treatment facilities, professional treatment, or residential programs. Others have had to send their teen away to live with trusted family members or friends. Still others have had to call the police on their teen, for their own safety.

So when does it get to this point? When is it right to call the cops on your teen or send him away? Unfortunately, as with all aspects of responding to depression in teens, there are no generic pat answers. It depends on your child, the specifics of his challenges, and your home situation.

1. Seek wisdom from God and others.
Get guidance from a professional counselor, pastor, psychiatrist, and others who are competent in understanding and treating teens, and who are fully aware of the history and dynamics of your teen's situation.

Consider additional intervention and treatment when your hurting teen is:

- unable to abide by reasonable boundaries set at home
- out of control
- unable to communicate or interact with parents
- rebellious, disrespectful, has no regard for parent's property
- repeatedly stealing or breaking things

- violent or aggressive toward you and others
- a harm to himself or a possible danger to others
- disrupting the rest of family life or negatively impacting other siblings in the home
- abusing or addicted to substances that require rehabilitation
- showing an eating disorder that requires hospitalization or inpatient treatment
- involved in behaviors that are clearly dysfunctional and inappropriate in society (such as stealing, sexual violation, harming animals or property, trouble with the law)
- severely depressed or manic or unable to function in normal, everyday living
- involved in self-destructive behavior that is not improving or may become life-threatening
- running away from home and in high-risk situations

This is when it can get extremely stressful. You have to do your homework, praying for God's wisdom and will to be done in your teen's life. You might even get conflicting input, making your decision even more difficult. The psychiatrist might advise you to hospitalize him in a treatment facility, while the therapist is saying for you to put him in a day program and on medication. Still others may be telling you to ship him off to an out-of-state program. The decision comes down to you, the parent. Do your homework and look into all the various options while praying constantly for God's direction.

2. Move forward with what seems the most practical and obvious solution.

Usually the answers you're seeking eventually become clear through the interview process and as you learn more about each alternative. Use wisdom rather than just feelings and emotions. You might really want to send your teenager away for a while, but your intuition tells you he would be better off if he just changed schools, made new friends, and started a new life while going to counseling on a regular basis.

TREATMENT GOALS

Following are a few goals that you and your teen's counselor should keep in mind throughout your child's treatment.

1. To diminish immediate problems

The first goal in counseling is to treat the major problems at hand. If your teen is depressed, the counselor's primary concern is to help alleviate the severity of the symptoms so your teen can start feeling better right away. If her depression seems moderate to severe, the counselor may refer her to a psychiatrist for an assessment and anti-depressant medication. That is standard procedure for counselors.

2. To accomplish lasting wellness

In the next phase, the counselor will begin to partner with the teen to reach the goals of treatment. Remember, the goal of treatment is not just to Band-Aid symptoms temporarily so your teen will look and feel better.

The goal of depression counseling is complete recovery. It is also to help minimize depression symptoms and prevent a recurrence or relapse. Good counseling will help your teen move all the way through his problems and equip him with resilience and coping skills as much as possible. If the depression is not treated to full remission, he will likely have a recurrence in the future.

This is another reason that it is important to not just go to a few sessions of counseling. If you are with a counselor who is doing a good job, allow enough time for your teen to get past simply feeling better and instead become equipped to stay well.

Depending on the counselor's theory, training, and your teen's diagnosis, a variety of methods will be integrated to help your teen get well. He may receive homework assignments and practical interventions to implement daily. He may get help in implement-

KEY COMPONENTS OF TREATMENT
FOR OVERCOMING TEEN DEPRESSION

Effective treatment for your depressed teen will include the following elements:

1. Building Communication Skills
Good counseling should help your teen learn how to express his thoughts and feeling to others in a clear and understandable way. It should also help him develop assertive skills and conflict resolution tactics.

2. Emotional Education
Part of your teen's progress will lie in his ability to label pleasant and unpleasant emotions, and then identify situations where these emotions are most likely to occur. Identifying and understanding the link between these thoughts, emotions, and situations is key. The same goes for developing strategies for resolving emotional attachment issues.

3. Identifying Negative Thinking Patterns
This helps your teen detect established yet harmful thought processes. By learning how to detect irrational thinking, distortions, ruminating, and blaming, he can dispute the destructive thinking and replace it with a realistic perspective.

4. Training in Life Skills
The basic life-coaching skills of goal setting, problem solving, negotiation, and conflict resolution will better equip teens for overcoming the additional challenges of stress, anxiety, and depression. Other skills that develop stronger self-awareness, build on personality strengths, and enhance self-esteem can be accomplished in counseling when developmentally appropriate.

---

5. Antidepressant Medications (If Needed)

In addition to counseling, antidepressant medication could prove to be an effective treatment to consider. SSRIs (selective serotonin reuptake inhibitors) such as Prozac, Zoloft, and Celexa can make a dramatic impact on the treatment of depression and related problems with teens. (Recently, there has been some concern about whether it is safe for teens to take medication or whether these SSRIs contribute to suicide. These issues will be discussed in the following chapter on medication.)

---

ing lifestyle changes—structuring his day, improving eating and exercising, learning relaxation techniques, journaling, and rituals for sleeping better at night.

3. To partner for the sake of progress

Whatever the counselor decides is the best method for guiding your teen toward lasting wellness, it's important that you become a conduit for positive change rather than a hindrance in the process. Your partnership with the counselor—and obviously with your teen—is vital. This can be difficult for some parents who feel in the dark when their teen is receiving individual treatment that remains confidential between that teen and the counselor. Parents naturally want to be involved in their child's healing. Yet part of your teen's journey to wellness includes the shared trust among you, your teen, and his counselor. Don't call the therapist expecting him to divulge secrets about the counseling sessions. Likewise, don't press your teen for information regarding the sessions beyond the agreed-upon boundaries of privacy.

Your job is simply to be a safe place and love your teen no matter what. At the same time, you are not completely out of the picture. Remain vigilant, aware, and informed about the signs and symptoms of depression so you can help the counselor know when new issues arise. Use the checklists in chapter 4 as a guide to notice progress (or relapse), and keep track of the symptoms, noting how you teen is changing and improving. This will aid the counselor in measuring how effective the medicine or treatment is.

Research has shown that parents tend to be less aware of their teenager's mind-set and feelings. They are much better at observing specific behaviors such as sleep, appetite, and social comfort levels. And these observations are the best way for parents to help the clinicians first make the diagnosis and then monitor the effectiveness of treatment.

HOW LONG WILL TREATMENT LAST?

The length of treatment depends on several things: the individual teen, the severity of the depression, the complexity of issues, underlying causes of the depression, and the response to antidepressant medication (which usually requires six to eight weeks to take effect). Depression can last up to three years without treatment. With treatment, this time can be significantly reduced. More importantly, the therapy will help prevent future episodes of depression. So staying under professional care for at least six months may be necessary.

Research at Duke University Medical Center found that parents should consider a commitment to once-a-week therapy for at least three months. After that, biweekly or monthly appointments should be considered for follow-up. It's also been proven that teens who experience major depression have a high chance of battling depression at some later point in their life, which means it's important to take a long-term view when making decisions about treatment.

When will you know counseling is finished and it's time to end therapy? Sometimes teens start skipping, missing, or are inconsistent in keeping appointments. If they are doing well, this could be a sign that they are ready for counseling sessions to be set for every other week or once a month. Alternatively, the therapist will tell you when the sessions can be spread further apart.

Your counselor, your teen, and you will know that counseling is nearing completion when the goals we encouraged you to develop earlier in this chapter are accomplished. If the counseling relationship was good, then feelings of attachment will need to be processed. The therapist will take a few sessions to solidify what was learned and then set further long-term goals for your teen to implement on his own. Your teen may miss the counseling relationship at first, so don't hesitate to encourage periodic checkups with the therapist. This solidifies the relationship, which can help if the depression symptoms return.

WHAT IF THE THERAPY INTERVENTIONS AREN'T WORKING?

If your teen doesn't seem to be improving after several months, or if you keep getting conflicting treatment from the various mental health professionals working with your teen, then you need to get additional consultation. Unfortunately, sometimes the counselor or psychiatrist could have missed something in diagnosing your teen's situation, or the treatment intervention may not be the most effective for your teen. Sometimes it just takes time for the diagnosis and treatment interventions to come together, so you need to know which it is.

During frustrating times like this, parents often wonder if their teen's lack of improvement is their fault or if they are with the right professionals. The truth is it might be a bit of both. It's difficult to accept the reality of your teen's "special needs." It requires a shift in your mind-set to view your teen as being in crisis and not place expectations on him to "act normal" and snap out of it. Seeing your teen act so differently than he did as a child can be disconcerting. For these and other reasons, it's important to keep open the option of family therapy or even your own individual counseling at times.

A successful treatment of depression depends on the correct diagnosis of symptoms and the process of elimination by trying to find the right antidepressant and interventions. This can take time—sometimes a long time! Remember, each antidepressant will take about six weeks to show effects, and counseling interventions might not show dramatic results until the physiological brain functioning is restored.

GET THE HELP YOUR TEEN NEEDS

As we have tried to show, counseling is an essential part of the treatment of all depressions. In the case of reactive depression, it is the main form of treatment because there is nothing wrong with brain chemistry. In genetically and stress-induced depressions, because disrupted brain chemistry is the primary problem, antidepressant medications may be necessary to speed up recovery. However, even then, ongoing psychotherapy or counseling is essential to include for effective treatment. The best road to recovery includes a comprehensive integrative approach.

So why do so many teens suffering from stress-related disorders not get the help they need? Many times it's because the parents who make treatment decisions for children—even parents who hold strong Christian beliefs—regard this form of treatment (both psychotherapy and medication) to be taboo and even "un-Christian." The truth is your teen's ability to recover and overcome depression is directly with your willingness to seek help. You cannot do it alone. Getting help—whatever forms that comes in—is essential for your child's well-being.

> *I would say to other parents that there's no difference*
> *between your child having diabetes or depression.*
> *It can be a long journey, but when you see the light at*
> *the end, you realize that you have saved your child.*
> — Harold S. Koplewicz, M.D., *More Than Moody*

7

SENSIBLE MANAGEMENT
OF MEDICATION

Then God came back . . . I have not been neurotically
depressed since . . . though to be honest, God also comes to
me each morning and offers me a 20-milligram capsule of
Prozac. . . . I swallow every capsule with gratitude to God.
— Prof. Lewis Smedes, *A Spiritual Memoir: My God and I*

T HE TREATMENT OF DEPRESSION HAS MADE SIGNIFICANT
advances in recent years with the development of new medications. I (Arch) started practicing as a clinical psychologist when antidepressants had not yet reached widespread use and when the side
effects were worse than the depression. Suffering from depression was
like a bit of "hell on earth" for the unfortunate few. Of course, most
serious depressions in those days had a genetic cause. These days, as
we have pointed out several times in this book, the most common
form of depression is less genetic and more stress-based. Stress now
eclipses bad genes as the cause of serious depression.

The good news, however, is that the treatment of our modern-
day stress-induced depression uses the same antidepressants as the
genetic depressions to correct the problem. Having lived in a time

when these treatments were unavailable, I thank God every day that we now have effective treatments available for depression.

Despite the great progress in the development of antidepressants, research on the use of these medications in children and teens is still in the early stages. Most of these medications developed to date have been studied primarily in adults. Still, things are changing, as specific guidelines regarding the use of antidepressants for adolescents are now emerging.

PARENTS MUST STAY INFORMED

In this chapter, we want to help you, as the caregiver of a depressed teen, to understand how these medications should be used and the precautions you need to exercise in giving these medications to your teen. It is not our intention to usurp your doctor's role; you need to trust your doctor. However, this doesn't mean you should not keep yourself informed of current developments and guidelines, if for no other reason than that you can be a safeguard against mistakes. Furthermore, since you will be responsible for actually administering the medication, you should be informed about therapeutic effects, side effects, and the dangers of combining with other drugs or overdosing. We believe that a fully informed parent or caregiver is vitally important to the effective treatment of a teen's depression.

START WITH A MEDICAL EVALUATION

Anyone needing antidepressant medication needs to have a thorough medical evaluation. There are many medical conditions that can cause depression, and these need to be ruled out via an evaluation. You can also help by gathering information about family history of depression for the doctor, and especially about what type of treatment has been effective for other family members.

You may discover a disorder such as low-thyroid function. This condition may not be serious or life-threatening from a medical

point of view, but it may be the cause of some emotional disturbance. Make sure that you stay informed about what tests are
being conducted on your teen, such as a blood workup or thyroid
and liver function tests. Request a copy of all the results for your
own file.

A common question parents ask is whether or not their general
physician can prescribe the appropriate medication for their teen.
Yes, a GP can prescribe these medications; but the younger the teen
or the more serious the depression, the more likely it will be that
your physician will request a consultation or even ongoing treatment by a psychiatrist who specializes in children and teenagers.

CONSIDER COUNSELING

Research shows that when counseling or psychotherapy is combined with medication, you have the best possible outcome — particularly the prevention of future depression episodes. The reason
for this is twofold. First, therapy provides an ongoing method of
accountability to ensure that a teen is taking medication as prescribed and that the teenager is motivated to stay on track. Second,
counseling strengthens a teen's healthy thinking patterns, resolves
emotional turmoil, and provides an opportunity to learn good
stress-management techniques. This is crucial if stress is one of the
major causes of depression in your teen due to damage caused by
the stress hormones.

HOW DO ANTIDEPRESSANTS WORK?

Earlier we described how either genetics or stress can cause endogenous depression, which is a depression caused by something within
the body or brain. This type of depression alters the levels of some
of the chemical messengers in the brain, called neurotransmitters.
The three principal chemical compounds involved are noradrena-
line, dopamine, and serotonin. Nerve cells in the brain constantly
produce, release, and reabsorb these neurotransmitters. Lower levels

are responsible for the transmission of faulty messages to the rest of the brain; hence, they are also to blame for some of the symptoms of depression. Drugs such as SSRIs (selective serotonin reuptake inhibitors) increase the levels of serotonin, while others increase the other neurotransmitters. It is this increased brain activity that improves mood.

The brain is mainly made up of neurons, which are interconnected brain cells. Messages travel along these cells. When a message reaches the end of a neuron, it has to jump a gap (called a synapse) to get to the next one. To do this, the neuron releases tiny amounts of a neurotransmitter into the gap between the nerve cells. Ideally, a nerve impulse starts in the new nerve, and thus the message gets from one nerve to the next. For the original nerve to recover and get the next message, it needs to replace its stocks of the neurotransmitter in the original neuron to make itself ready to send the next message. The "healthy" body thus takes the neurotransmitter back into the originating neuron. This is called "reuptake" and is the brain's form of recycling.

In depression, these neurotransmitters, such as serotonin, are too low, so they cannot be taken back in full to the originating neuron. In other words, without the recycled messengers, the brain cannot produce enough for its use. And that's where antidepressants enter the picture.

ANTIDEPRESSANTS TAKE TIME TO WORK

The delay in seeing results with antidepressant medications can be frustrating for you and your teen. Antidepressants are unique in that, unlike other medications that treat emotional disorders, they cannot be delivered directly to the brain—as, for example, by injection. They have to be taken orally. Although taking an antidepressant by mouth means that it enters the body through the blood stream, a protective mechanism in the brain, called the "blood brain barrier" prevents this type of medication from going directly to the brain. In this sense, antidepressants are not as mind-altering as, for example, a tranquilizer that can enter the brain. In effect, an antidepressant like Prozac is not a serotonin pill that you can take to transfer serotonin into the brain. (Remember, it is a low level of neurotransmitters like serotonin that causes depression.) Rather, Prozac does something quite different. What happens is that it goes into the liver, where a biotransformation occurs. The Prozac is transformed by the body into a substance (still not serotonin) that can enter the brain, where it acts to inhibit the brain's recycling system.

Yes, you read that right. Since creation, the brain has known about recycling and uses it to save having to manufacture whatever neurotransmitter has been used along the nerve's pathway. This recycling action of the brain is called "reuptake," which literally means there is a garbage collection system that captures the used neurotransmitter and returns it to the sending side of gaps in the nerve pathway (remember those synapses?) to be reused. Sometimes this garbage collection system is too aggressive and literally sucks more serotonin out of the synapse than it should; the result is that after several weeks of this depletion the receptors on the receiving side begin to shut down—which, after a while, leads to the experience of depression. Depression results, therefore, in both a deficiency in serotonin (or other neurotransmitters) and in diminished receptors. This deficit is called "down regulation," simply meaning that one doesn't have enough receptors to maintain a normal flow of information along the brain's nerve pathways.

What does the antidepressant do? It encourages the brain to do what only it can do—increase the supply of serotonin to the synapse. It does this by blocking or inhibiting the garbage system from taking too much serotonin and putting it into the recycle bin. In so doing, it causes a backup of serotonin in the synapse. It's like running a bath with the tap open and the plug out of the outlet; the bath will never fill. But if you block the outlet, it will start to fill. This backing up of serotonin tells the nerve to start increasing the number of receptor cells (a situation called "up regulation"). When there are enough of these receptors in place, the system starts functioning normally again and our depression lifts!

MINIMUM DOSE FOR MAXIMUM RESULTS

It is important to understand that these medications are not like painkillers—of which a small dose kills a small amount of pain, and a big dose kills a lot of pain. With antidepressants, you have to get the amount in the body up to a steady state above a certain threshold, and then, only after two to eight weeks, do you see an improvement. This means you cannot take a "little" antidepressant to feel a little better; you have to take a full dose before your concentration can get above this threshold. Taking higher doses than what is needed does not give any further improvement. In fact, it may only make the side effects worse. Because of this, the goal is to find the minimum dose in a given person that provides a concentration in the blood that is above the threshold. It's an on-or-off phenomenon; you either have enough or you don't!

Also, if you stop the medication once it starts working, the depression does not come back right away. It takes as long for the depression to return as it took for the depression to go away. This means that if your teen, once recovered, inadvertently stops the medication for a day or two, and then comes running to you saying, "Look Mom, I'm not taking any medication and I feel fine. Can I stop it now?"—your answer should be a definite no. Explain that the depression will come back in a few weeks because the effects take time to go away. Many have been misled into stopping their medication after they feel better, only to discover that this brings back the depression after a while.

So how long should your teen continue taking antidepressants? It depends on several factors. If there is a strong genetic factor causing the depression, he may have to take the medication for the rest of his life. Generally, psychiatrists encourage young patients to take an antidepressant that is having good effects for one year. At this point, the depression may be reevaluated with a trial without antidepressants to see if the depression returns. If it does, then your teen will have to go back on the antidepressant. Remember that it takes at least six weeks after stopping the medication to see if the depression returns.

COMMON FEARS ABOUT
ANTIDEPRESSANT MEDICATION

There is a pervasive resistance in our culture in general, but particularly in our Christian subculture, to the use of antidepressants. We encounter this resistance in every seminar we teach and patient we treat. We find this to be even truer among teens whose parents fear the effect it might have on their beloved children. Is this resistance justified? Not if a teen's depression is serious or incapacitating. There is too much at risk to willynilly oppose this form of treatment, if it is what is needed. So let us examine some of the major fears that feed this resistance and then dispel the myths behind them:

1. The fear that antidepressants are addictive
Often parents, as well as the teens themselves, equate antidepressants with tranquilizers or mind-altering drugs and believe, therefore, that they are addicting. It's common to hear a parent say, "But I don't want my child to be on drugs this early in his life!"—meaning, of course, that "drugs" are always addictive. The belief that antidepressants might be addictive is a carryover from the pervasive use of tranquilizers a few decades ago; and there is no doubt that tranquilizers can be addictive, especially if not used correctly. Therefore, let us right here and now stress this very important point: *antidepressant medications are not addictive.* They are not like the medications given for Attention Deficit Disorder, nor for those given for anxiety.

Part of the reason antidepressants are not addictive is the way they work. These medications do not go directly to the brain but indirectly. The liver has to first convert them to something else that can pass through to the brain.

2. The fear that teens will have to take the medication the rest of their lives
This is an important and valid concern. For a small percentage of teens, especially if the genetic factor is strong, there is a likelihood that they may have to take an antidepressant for the rest of their life.

But if this is the first time your teen is on an antidepressant, it is premature to even be thinking about the long-term outcome. The focus now should be on getting your teen out of the depression. Usually, treatment will last for six months to one year and will then taper as your doctor checks to see if the depression is still present. Hopefully, counseling will have helped and the depression may have passed. If however, it is still present, or genetic factors are strong, or after a while the depression returns a second time, your psychiatrist may very well recommend ongoing treatment.

To understand this, think of the depression as something equivalent to diabetes. Both diabetes and depression have deficiencies—the former insulin and the latter neurotransmitters. No one would

PARTIAL LIST OF ANTIDEPRESSANTS

Note: all of these are considered suitable for teens, and the "Age Considered" list may be modified for a given teen.

Type	Trade Name	Generic Name	Age Considered
TCA	Sinequan	Doxepin	12 or older
	Tofranil	Imipramine	6 or older
SSRI	Celexa	Citalopram	18 or older
	Luvox	Fluvoxamine	8 or older
	Paxil	Paroxetine	18 or older
	Prozac	Fluoxetine	18 or older
	Zoloft	Sertraline	6 or older
MAOI	Nardil	Phenelzine	Not used for teens
	Parnate	Tranylcypromine	Not used for teens
OTHERS	Effexor	Venlafaxine	18 or older
	Remeron	Mirtazapine	18 or older
	Serzone	Efazadone	18 or older
	Wellbutrin	Bupropion	18 or older

even think about stopping the insulin treatment of a diabetic. So why would you deprive your depressed teen from the same treatment? If the medication is used for a long time, it may be necessary to have liver function tests done regularly, but your doctor will know this and recommend it when necessary.

3. The fear that taking antidepressants will lead to suicide

There has been recent concern in the media on the possible link between teens just starting to take antidepressant medications becoming suicidal. This is an example of misapplied information. Sadly, it caused many uninformed parents to stop their teens from taking the medication, causing other serious consequences. A recent report has provided some hope, however. According to a national study by the U.S. Centers for Disease Control and Prevention (CDC) in February 2005, suicide rates have dropped in association with increased use of selective serotonin reuptake inhibitors (SSRI) and the more recently developed non-SSRIs, two of the most common antidepressants. This reduction is not as evident, however, in rural areas where cheaper TCA-type antidepressants (these are the older medications with many bad side effects) are being used. The risk of suicide in teens can be reduced dramatically with the proper management of the medications.

TYPES OF ANTIDEPRESSANT MEDICATIONS

Using the most effective antidepressant medication in the right dose is especially critical in the treatment of teen depression. It's easy for a teen to become frustrated with uncomfortable side effects and not want to take her medication anymore. But ineffective treatment— such as taking the medication inconsistently—can result in an increased risk for suicide (the adolescent becomes more demoralized and fears that nothing will fix the depression), and the need to then hospitalize the teen becomes necessary. It is far better to use medication correctly right from the start than to try to repair a failed attempt at treating the depression.

Not all antidepressants used in adults are recommended for treating children or adolescents. For instance, the group called TCAs (described later) is not recommended for children, but they may well be effective in older teens. Both the age of your teen as well as her level of maturation has to be taken into consideration. There is general consensus that all of the SSRI antidepressants are effective and acceptable for teens, though there is no clear, unequivocal research data to prove that they work in all teens. The MAOIs are usually used only in adults, as they have strict dietary restrictions that teens may not be able to follow.

Here is a brief summary of the antidepressant medications, listed in the order in which they were discovered:

1. *Tricyclic Antidepressants (TCAs)*. These were the first to be discovered (early 1960s) and include elavil, imipramine, trazadone, doxepin, and nortriptyline. Most work mainly on a brain neurotransmitter called norepinephrine (NE), but some also on serotonin, the other major neurotransmitter implicated in depression. TCAs are all now available in generic form, which means they are cheap. Unfortunately, they have a lot of side effects, including sedation, dry mouth, and urinary retention. They are, therefore, reserved for use as a last resort. (However, some men do better on these than on the newer ones.)

2. *MAO Inhibitors (MAOIs)*. Next in order of discovery, MAOIs include Parnate and Nardil. Many depressions that don't respond to TCAs respond well to these. MAOIs act by slowing down the brain's "garbage collection system," thus increasing the essential neurotransmitters. Their downside is that they have dietary restrictions (aged cheese, beer, caviar, anchovies, smoked meats, and yeast products), though with the level of health consciousness we have today, few people complain about these now.

3. *Selective Serotonin Reuptake Inhibitors (SSRIs)*. These include Prozac, Zoloft, Paxil, Luvox, Effexor, and Celexa. The discovery of Prozac revolutionized our treatment of depression, especially in women because of their unique type of depression, and opened up a new battery of medications called SSRIs because they

work mainly on serotonin. Despite many early attacks on these medications by those opposed to all medications, they are really miracle drugs. I (Arch) call them a gift from God, which they certainly are to those who have "rediscovered" life. SSRIs are now the drug of first choice among depressed teens because they treat most depressions well and have fewer side effects than TCAs.

4. *Other antidepressants.* Several newer medications that work on combinations of neurotransmitters or that have fewer side effects have now emerged, and many more are in development that could revolutionize these revolutionary medications. We are truly on the verge of a major breakthrough! One emerging medication is called an atypical antidepressant (Wellbutrin), and it is used for a particular type of depression. For several of my male patients, this has been the only medication to work for them. Another new drug called Remeron is selective for certain serotonin receptors, and therefore has fewer side effects.

No medication is perfect. Each has a slightly different profile of side effects, which means it may be necessary for you to try several different preparations or even a combination to get the optimal response.

Caution should be used when mixing these agents with weight-reduction pills, agents used in smoking cessation (Zyban-buproprion), tryptophan, St. John's Wort, or other substances marketed in health-food stores.

SIDE EFFECTS

The most important consideration in using all medications—not just antidepressants—is the side effects. Sometimes the side effects are worse than the disorder! All medications can have side effects, and no two individuals will experience the same effects to the same extent. This makes it virtually impossible to generalize (and is the reason for the comically extensive list of side effects mentioned on television ads for new medications). For instance, your teen may have had a bad reaction to one antidepressant, but this does not mean another teen will react the same way. Some medications, for example, have more universal effects. For instance, TCAs cause your mouth to run dry—meaning that those taking it have to drink more water. SSRIs may cause weight gain, especially if they work! You feel better, so you eat more. But they also stimulate the brain to want more food. That simply means being more aware of healthy eating habits and exercising. Many side effects diminish after a few weeks, while others can be managed by taking the necessary actions to diminish them.

The important point is that if a side effect is really serious, talk to your doctor about it right away. Just because your teen feels some side effect doesn't mean he should stop the treatment. The best approach is to manage these effects so as to minimize them. You can do this by lowering the dose for a while to let your teen's body get used to it, and then raising the dose again. I recommend this all the time with patients. We would never get anyone better if we didn't.

What's important is that anyone taking antidepressant medications should not stop them abruptly. This is when many of the bad side effects occur. All changes—whether increasing, decreasing, or stopping a medication—should be done under the care of a knowledgeable mental health professional. A serious reaction could jeopardize any future use of this medication by creating a fear that it will occur again.[1]

QUESTIONS TO ASK

Since medication is such an important part of treatment for serious depression in teens, become as informed as possible about what this means. It is common for patients to simply trust their doctor in ordinary medical situations; but in an emergency, many parents freeze under the stress and can easily become so confused that they make poor decisions. Remember that, except for extreme depressions in which your child may have to be hospitalized, you will be the primary person to supervise your teen's treatment. The more you know, the better will be your handling of the crisis, and the less anxious you will be about the process. Your teen should be included in the discussion about medications, how they should be taken, and the side effects to watch for. But make sure you use language your teen can understand—which means forcing your doctor to explain things to you rather than speaking medicalese!

Here are some important questions you may want to ask your doctor:

1. What is the name of the medication?
2. Is it known by other names? If so, what are they?
3. Are there any known risks in taking this medication?
4. How will this help my child, and how long will it take before we can expect any improvement?
5. If it doesn't work within this time, what will be the next step?
6. What serious side effects commonly occur with this medication?
7. What should we do if these effects occur or if they don't go away or if a problem develops?
8. Are any of the medications addictive? Can they be abused?
9. Are there any laboratory tests that must first be carried out before we start the medication (heart, liver, etc.)?
10. How often should we come to see you for follow-up?
11. What should we do if my teen accidentally or deliberately skips taking the medication?
12. Are there any activities my teen should avoid (alcohol or recreational drug use, driving, stimulants such as caffeine, extreme addicting behavior such as video games, risk taking, etc.)?
13. How long will my teen have to take this medication, and how will we know when the time has come to stop?
14. Should I inform my teen's school nurse of the medication?

15. Is there anything else I need to be aware of?
16. What other options do we have if the depression does not respond to conventional treatment?

WHAT ABOUT INTEGRATIVE AND HERBAL MEDICINES?

Recently, there has been a great surge in the field of integrative medicine. This is evident in the medical and mental health fields that are expanding their scope of practice to further help people prevent illness, recover, and get well. The best of traditional, herbal, and other fields of health care are now considered to meet mental, emotional, and relational needs. As a result in expanding this view of whole-person health, some profoundly biblical and practical living resources are being emphasized in current health trends.

We now have solid scientific evidence of the benefits of living a healthy lifestyle that includes exercise, adequate sleep, good nutrition, healthy connections, and even prayer. They provide recovery from stress, optimism, hope, and meaningful connections. And remarkably, these findings are profound truths based on Judeo-Christian values and principles for living, such as: Let your medicine be your food and your food your medicine. A merry heart is like medicine. Prayer provides peace in your heart and mind. There are even benefits to having pets, listening to music, and smelling certain herbs (aromatherapy). We will explore many of these in the next few chapters.

Likewise, there has been interest to find other alternative "natural" substances that can alleviate depression and anxiety. Health-food stores are growing across the country, providing a plethora of natural remedies to every malady possible. Although some of these are viewed to be equivalent to old-fashioned "snake oil," there is increasing research evidence that some of these natural herbs and neutraceuticals are worth considering.

There is no question that God did create many herbs and plants for our healing benefit. That is not the problem. It is in how we use these in treating children and teens that we want to caution you to. Here are a few important issues to consider.

1. "Natural remedies" aren't always harmless.

"Natural" doesn't mean it can't be dangerous. There are still active ingredients in natural healing substances. These remedies need to be seen as medicines, as they are substances that can have an effect on the body and mind. Even marijuana is natural (as some would justifiably argue).

For example, one of the most commonly known herbs is St. John's Wort. It has been discovered it is dangerous to take this in combination with other medications, as it interacts directly with them. You cannot take it if you are on an antidepressant, as well as a long list of other things. We don't fully know the effects on children or teens of some of these herbs.

A more promising natural remedy is Sam-e; however, it cannot be used on those with bipolar depression, and child and teen dosage has to be clarified. (We are not providing extended information on the range of alternative treatments in this book. If you are interested in knowing more, please refer to the "Natural Complimentary Therapy" chapter in our book *Unveiling Depression in Women*.)[2]

2. Always get professional supervision when taking any substance.

Don't try to treat your teen yourself with over-the-counter natural remedy products. It's key that you not administer anything without your mental health professional's agreement or with a trained physician in integrative medicine overseeing the products and correct dosage.

As you explore options for the best way to care for your teen and get treatment, consider the first rule of medicine: do no harm. Never do anything where there is a risk of causing harm either physically or emotionally. Remember, your teen's life is at stake.

GETTING WELL TAKES MORE THAN A PILL A DAY

We started off the treatment section with the importance of considering counseling help for yourself and your teen. Then, in this chapter, we discussed medication treatment as an important additional treatment consideration. Antidepressants can be a crucial source of relief and brain chemistry restoration aiding to your teen's healing journey.

However, the greater challenge to overcoming depression is in living and staying well. That is the venture for the next few chapters. A pill a day won't take all your teen's troubles away. It won't provide him with physical health or the nutrients necessary for his body to optimally metabolize the medication. Neither will it equip him with the effective skills for managing stress. Your teen needs and wants to be equipped to solve problems, make necessary changes in his life, and find happiness and spiritual meaning. But all these require practical, daily tools.

In the next chapter, we will reveal how you can help your teen build an ongoing recovery and protective plan based on doable lifestyle strategies. As your teen integrates these practical self-care activities, he will continue feeling better when he is depressed, as well as ward off looming depression.

8

GETTING BETTER AND STAYING WELL

Therapeutic effectiveness will increase when other
factors in life are considered such as physical health,
stress levels, rest, and recovery, as well as finding
happiness and meaning spiritually. —"Living on Purpose,"
Psychotherapy Networker (September/October 2003)

E FFECTIVE WELLNESS TOOLS CAN ENHANCE RESTORATION from the ravages of stress and depression on your entire teen's being. You can help your teen build an ongoing recovery and protective plan that incorporates specific lifestyle strategies. These practical self-care activities will help him feel better when he is depressed and can ward off looming depression.

Good therapy is important, and antidepressant medication may be essential. However, popping pills and getting forty-five minutes of counseling a week will not cut it. Stressed or depressed teens need more to shape their lives—and they want more. They want to know how to live. They are looking for practical guidance and steps to apply to their lives outside the therapy room or doctor's office.

The fields of medicine and mental health have recently begun taking an integrative, comprehensive, whole-person approach to preventing and treating maladies such as depression. Solid research is validating the importance of spiritual practices and daily wellness living, proving their effectiveness in treatment outcome and offering empowering strategies that can be applied daily.

This approach is nothing new. In fact, it's straight from the Bible. And the good news is that things are changing across the mental health field. In just the last few years, the focus is no longer solely on the treatment of mental disorders such as depression (good as this is), but instead on finding ways to prevent these disorders, enhancing positive strengths and emotions, and implementing a healthy lifestyle. What is even more exciting is that these strategies are inherent in every aspect of the Judeo-Christian faith, values, and lifestyle.

STRATEGIES FOR LIVING WELL

There's no plainer way to put it: living well enhances effective treatment. By helping your teen apply practical lifestyle changes, you can accelerate healing, recovery, and resilience. Conversely, you can sabotage even the best clinical work and medication by not implementing wise patterns of living.

For example, if your teen is taking an antidepressant but is deficient in vitamin B and omega-3s, her body will not metabolize the medication as effectively. If she is having great counseling forty-five minutes a week but is eating junk food, not getting enough sleep, or filling her mind with negative, fearful stimuli, her counseling may not be as effective.

Granted, all teens may do this from time to time. That's where you come in as a parent. Remember, the goal is complete recovery, which includes being aware of what will minimize symptoms as well as prevent a recurrence or relapse. Lifestyle issues are crucial in getting better and staying well—and you can aid in administering positive changes.

BUILDING A WELLNESS ACTION PLAN

Wellness is about feeling better and staying healthy through basic self-care. For instance, some teens taking antidepressants may experience increased appetite, which can lead to weight gain. However, by eating a balanced diet and exercising regularly, this side effect can be managed quite easily, even if your teen is taking a SSRI-type antidepressant that has this side effect.

Drawing from effective treatment results, we have devised a "wellness-building action plan" that you can use as a guide to provide practical skills and resources for your teen. This can also teach her to take responsibility for a lifelong wellness lifestyle. Following are some of the simple wellness skills your teen can apply to improve her overall health, to feel better, and to keep from getting depressed again.

1. Physical activity

As already mentioned, exercise is good for your overall health, but it is especially helpful for boosting moods. It increases levels of endorphins, the body's own mood-elevating natural antidepressant. Vigorous exercise also helps to burn off stress hormones like adrenaline and cortisol, improves sleep quality, increases the immune system, and generally tones up and energizes the whole body. Here are some key considerations to get the full benefit:

- Exercise at an age-appropriate level for at least sixty minutes, three to four times a week. Six days a week is best.
- Choose an exercise that is enjoyable and that will increase the heart rate for at least twenty minutes continually (e.g., a team or individual sport, running with the dog, biking, going to the gym). Check with your doctor about what would be an appropriate level of physical activity for your teen.
- Exercising with a friend, a trainer, or a family member can help your teen stay motivated.

2. Good nutrition

There is a connection between stress, depression, the brain, and the food your teen puts in his mouth. Nutrients from food are like drugs and medicine. A proper diet can actually help your teen improve tremendously and enhance the effects of medications. Basically, envision his plate as divided into thirds: each meal should be balanced with a source of lean protein, complex carbohydrates (whole grains, fruits, and vegetables), and some healthy fats (monounsaturated).[1]

Maintain a stable metabolic rate for energy and brain fuel. Healthy meals help keep the metabolic rate steady, supplying the body with necessary nutrients and energy that may be depleted during times of stress or depression.

- Focus on helping your teen eat well-balanced, nutritious mini-meals throughout the day, along with taking a vitamin and mineral supplement.
- Start with a good breakfast that includes quality protein.
- In his breakfast, lunch, and snacks, include plenty of fresh fruits and vegetables; whole grains, such as wheat bread; healthy cereal, such as granola, pasta, and brown rice; and lean proteins, such as meat, cheese, eggs, or beans.
- Throughout the day, your teen should drink eight to ten 8oz. glasses of water a day (more when exercising). Avoid sodas, as it takes more water from the body than it puts in. This dehydration is harmful to the brain and metabolism.
- Get creative with meals.

Many parents find that feeding healthy nutrients to teens is the big challenge. Teens naturally tend to crave empty carbohydrates (junk food), especially when stressed or depressed. Many haven't yet acquired a taste for food that is close to its natural form. However,

GETTING THE ESSENTIALS

Provide your teen with high-quality supplements of the following essential nutrients. We've included some examples of food that includes these nutrients

- Vitamin B's, especially: Vitamin B6—bananas, avocados, dark leafy greens, chicken, legumes, fish, whole grains; Vitamin B12—eggs, fish, cheese, yogurt, milk, and meat—chicken, turkey (Vitamin B12 works with folic acid)
- Folic Acid—leafy greens (spinach), legumes, asparagus, broccoli, cabbage, oranges, and whole grains
- Vitamins C and E—brightly colored foods (broccoli, peppers, summer squash, tomatoes, asparagus, avocados, green leafy vegetables and lettuce, strawberries, papayas, raspberries), seeds, nuts, whole grains, and oats
- Omega-3 Fatty Acids—salmon, flaxseed oil
- Calcium—cheddar cheese, greens, yogurt, whole milk, broccoli, cottage cheese, peanuts, romaine lettuce, oranges, carrots, sweet potatoes
- Magnesium—tofu, legumes, seeds, nuts, whole grains (wheat germ and bran), green leafy vegetables, fresh green peas, garlic, molasses
- Zinc—fish, red meat, whole grains, legumes, nuts, seeds

Check with your doctor on particular supplement formulas and appropriate doses for your teen.

to the best of your ability, offer food around the house, in packed lunches, and at dinnertime that will provide lean protein, complex carbohydrates, and vitamins and minerals that are essential to your teen's recovery. He may have a picky appetite, so talk with him about what kind of healthier meals he would prefer.

Try to include meals that will boost depleted nutrients and serotonin levels (even if you have to disguise it). These will have a lasting effect on your teen's brain chemistry, mood, and energy levels. If you need help, there are plenty of books and online sources that provide examples and suggestions for naturally healthy meals.

SAMPLE MEAL OPTIONS

Breakfast
- Oatmeal, whole-grain cereal, toast, fruit, vegetables
- Egg whites, egg substitute, omelet, yogurt, turkey, bacon, sausage, cottage cheese, protein shake

Snacks
- Low-glycemic fruits and vegetables, such as apples, grapes, strawberries, oranges, melons, raw or steamed vegetables
- Yogurt, cottage cheese, string cheese, cream cheese, protein shake or bar, beef jerky
- Whole-grain crackers, peanut butter, nuts

Lunch
- Salads, soups
- Sandwiches: use whole-grain bread, lean meats, natural peanut butter with no-sugar-added fruit jam or spread
- Tomatoes, lettuce (on sandwich), carrot sticks, celery
- Protein shake or bar

Dinner
- Salads, soup
- Chicken, lean beef, lamb, fish (salmon is highest in omega-3)
- Vegetables

(Avoid fatty fried foods, high-starch carbohydrates, and other junk food at dinner. This will help with weight maintenance and a better night's sleep.)

Use supplements to compensate for deficiencies. Nutritional deficiencies can cause feelings of apathy, depression, insomnia, irritability, nervousness, personality changes, and confusion, as well as lowered mental functioning. There are several nutrients that play a role in contributing to or preventing depression, irritability, and mood swings.

- Nutrients to supplement include: calcium, iron, magnesium, selenium, and zinc. Low levels of omega-3 fatty acids and vitamin B6 have also been associated with depression and are important to supplement.

NATURAL SEROTONIN BOOSTERS

Besides the practical suggestions already covered, here are some additional ways to alleviate mild depression or curtail it when you notice early warning signs:

- Get social support: tell someone (family, friends), call a counselor, and visit your support group
- Get involved in sports, clubs, or other areas of interest
- Be physically active, visit the gym, and join team sports
- Focus on the positive, your strengths, hope for the future
- Keep busy and productive with positive, enjoyable activities
- Get involved in something that will build authentic self-esteem
- Journal thoughts and feelings
- Laugh (it's great medicine), watch a funny movie
- Avoid negative people and places
- Pray and think of things to be thankful and grateful for
- Listen to enjoyable, uplifting, or calming music
- Take a mental health day, doing something enjoyable
- Smell pleasant fragrances (herbs and flowers) to stimulate and calm the brain (lavender to relax)

• Antidepressant medication will be even less effective if
there are low levels of B-vitamins and folic acid.
Supplementing for these deficiencies can be essential to
relieving depression and helping the treatment work more
effectively.

(For more details on nutrition and natural complimentary therapy, please refer to our *Unveiling Depression in Women*.)

Limit unhealthy substances. Teens will naturally want to eat
their fair share of junk food. Though it's unrealistic to try to get rid
of all of the junk food your teen is exposed to, keep an eye on how
many Cokes, french fries, slices of pizza, candy, or doughnuts he is
consuming without including other necessary nutrients. These
cause energy depletion, irritability, and mood swings, and they can
even trigger anxiety.

As much as possible, encourage your teen to limit or avoid:

• Refined sugars, sodas, high-sugar fruit juices.
• White flour, white rice (all "white trash" foods).
• Fried, fatty-processed foods like fries, chips, fast-food
  type foods.
• Caffeine (coffee, sodas, chocolate). This substance is
  the culprit for interfering with sleep and causing
  jitteriness and anxiety; it can worsen depression.
• Alcohol, marijuana, and other drugs. Besides being
  unhealthy, these sabotage everything else your teen
  does to stay well.

3. Sleep and rest for recovery

In the chapter on stress, we emphasized how important sleep is for living a healthy life. It is also crucial for recovery while overcoming the
damage done by stress and depression. REM sleep is when fragments
of thoughts and emotions are sorted out, and when important growth
hormones are released. Sleep disturbance can be one of the symptoms
of stress and depression, which interferes with necessary recovery and

---

WAYS TEENS CAN EXPRESS
AND RESOLVE EMOTIONS

- Talk about it to a friend, parent, peer counselor, or a therapist.
- Write about it in a journal or diary. Write songs, poems, letters, or just your thoughts or feelings. Use one of the depression workbooks for teens.
- Do creative, enjoyable activities.
- Do a relaxation exercise.
- Listen to music.
- Watch a good movie.
- Get involved in an enjoyable activity you are good at such as a sport, the arts, a hobby, etc.
- Engage in activities that you like and that will help you relax.

---

development. Encourage and allow your teen times to take a break from everyday activities at regular intervals, in order to give her body time for recovery. This helps to clear the mind and be restored to full health. Encourage her toward restful, low-stress activities, such as:

- Stress-reduction exercises, such as deep breathing, progressive muscle relaxation, guided imagery, and biofeedback
- Chatting on the phone with a friend
- Playing with the family pet
- Listening to music
- Hanging out around the house and reading magazines
- Watching a funny movie or television program
- Doing something she finds fun, like playing games on the computer

Consistent, full nights of sleep will help your teen feel better overall, especially if she is feeling fatigued. Sleep deprivation is a major concern with teens, resulting in reduced concentration and compromised emotional and physical health. Teens usually need about nine hours of sleep a night; occasionally on the weekend they can sleep up to twelve hours to recuperate from a full week of activities or disturbed sleep. More sleep than that will usually make them feel worse.

4. Sunlight or full-spectrum light

For centuries, natural healers relied on heliotherapy (using sunlight for healing) to cure many maladies, including simply cheering up an ailing patient. Apart from the obvious benefits of a sunny day, bright, warm sunlight shining down from heaven has proven to chemically alter moods, lift the blues, and even prevent depression.

Just ten minutes of daily exposure to sunlight will supply your teen with all the vitamin D he needs. This is essential to promote calcium transfer across cell membranes and calcium absorption in the gut, both of which contribute to strong bones and a contented nervous system.

In climates that have long, dark winters or a lot of rainy days, a unique form of depression called Seasonal Affective Disorder can occur. This miserable condition is caused by a suppression of serotonin and an excess of a hormone called melatonin, which is produced in the brain by insufficient sunlight. This hormone triggers winter hibernation in animals, but in humans it is secreted with the onset of darkness and is the hormone that helps us fall asleep.

The problem in these places is that because sunlight is minimal, the production of melatonin doesn't get turned off as it should—creating a sort of hibernation state in the brain that feels like depression. In dark climates with long winters, therefore, this can be prevented by spending as much time outdoors on bright days, or by having at least one room in the house that is overlit with full-spectrum light (light closely resembling sunlight), where the family can spend several hours every day. Your local hardware store can recommend such a light source.

5. Hope and optimism

An important part of building mental and emotional wellness is learning to curtail negative thinking. Thoughts of regret and disappointment are natural reactions while going through difficult times. It's common for depressed teens to mull over outcomes and situations that are not what they wanted or expected. This only fuels the despondency over a loss, tragedy, or breakup. And what results is a pattern of negative thoughts that feed off each other and become entrenched beliefs.

A pessimistic teen will think he is a failure, doomed to always be like this. He will feel trapped and helpless with what he doesn't like about his life or who he has become. Over time, these can become dominant thought patterns in his mind that weave a complex pattern of sadness, helplessness, and anxiety. Every setback confirms the negative and bolsters a self-fulfilling approach to life. And as the mind and body are connected, these thoughts influence physical health, emotions, relationships, and spirituality.

You have most likely already experienced this downward cycle with your teen and can attest to how influential a negative mental state is on every part of life. Over time, pessimistic, distorted thinking causes people to give up and give in when faced with overwhelming, unsolvable problems.

It is this negative thinking that you as a parent can confront head-on. Pessimism isn't just about your teen thinking poorly of himself; it is a deeply entrenched system of beliefs that has to be changed. You can guide your teen on his day-to-day journey by bolstering hopeful, reality-based thinking. (We expand on this further in chapter 10.)

6. Emotional awareness and expression

When teens are stressed or depressed, they tend to be even more moody than usual as they struggle with inner pain, frustration, and confusion. Helping your teen to identify, label, and express her deeper emotions (such as fear, sadness, anger, or disappointment) can help her understand herself better, as well as develop strategies for constructively dealing with her emotions in a healthy way. Various studies have shown that verbally naming an emotion has a

WELLNESS BUILDING CHART

Use this chart as a guide to keep track of your teen's wellness-building activities.

Indicate a 1, 2, or 3 for each statement.
1—Never 2—Sometimes 3—Often

Physical

__ Eats a variety of healthy food in the most natural form, such as fruits, vegetables, and lean protein

__ Eats balanced meals evenly distributed throughout the day—breakfast, lunch, and dinner (or five to six mini-meals)—with each meal including protein and low-glycemic carbohydrates

__ Limits or eliminates harmful substances such as excess fat, caffeine, white flour, refined sugar products, salt, junk food, sodas, alcohol, smoking, and other possible food allergens

__ Avoids unhealthy substances (smoking, drinking, drugs)

__ Takes vitamins, minerals, and other helpful supplements necessary for enhanced health

__ Drinks at least eight to ten glasses of water daily

__ Exercises for at least twenty minutes three to four times a week or as much as physically able

__ Gets adequate rest and sleeps at least nine hours a night (occasionally even more)

__ Rests and relaxes when body and/or inner being needs it

__ Has effective, positive ways to periodically reduce stress and anxiety in life

__ Gets regular medical checkups to determine physical health needs

__ Takes medication regularly as prescribed

Spiritual

__ Has an open heart toward God and spiritual things

__ Spends time daily reflecting through devotional, Bible reading, prayer, and journaling

__ Is developing a stronger relationship with God

__ Listens to worship and praise music

__ Attends worship services

__ Is connected with a youth group

__ Has friends who share the same faith and encourage each other toward spiritual growth

Mental/Emotional

__ Cares for self by doing special, nurturing things, especially as rewards.

__ Identifies, expresses, and resolves emotions through talking, journaling, etc.

__ Exposed to healthy media and music

__ Looks for the positive aspect of a situation

__ Is able to stop and replace self-directed negative thoughts and words with reality-based, optimistic ones

__ Is building a positive, authentic self-image by doing well in life and relationships

__ Is growing in personal strengths

__ Takes a break from regular routine to do fun activities, and/or try something new

__ Makes good use of leisure time and is seldom bored

__ Has family and friends who are loving and accepting

Social

__ Has the support of friends and family to stay depression-free

__ Spends time with people who are positive, energizing, and overall good influences

(continued)

__ Actively seeks out enjoyable people
__ Avoids people who cause negative feelings about self
__ Has good boundaries; is able to avoid harmful situations and say no
__ Dresses and grooms in a way that is generally pleasing
__ Is involved in enjoyable activities
__ Does thoughtful gestures for others
__ Is building healthy friendships and peer connections
__ Is not being negatively influenced or pressured to compromise
__ Avoids "partiers" and the party scene

Staying Well and Depression-Free
__ Partners with the professional help needed for treatment and healing
__ Learns about depression, possible causes, and most effective treatment
__ Is aware of implementing areas of improvement on a daily basis.
__ Is becoming aware of vulnerability to depression and possible triggers for future episodes (see the list from stress and depression chapters)
__ Is aware of early warning signs for depression (see list in depression chapter)
__ Has an action plan for eliminating depression—what to do, choices to make to alleviate early stages of stress and depression
__ Has a plan for when symptoms gets worse

quieting effect on the nervous system, which can help teens recover faster from emotional stress.

When something is bothering your teen, she can't always identify her feelings. At the same time, she has no idea what to do with these feelings—how to communicate them, how to handle them, or how to resolve them. These deep feelings are usually vented through behaviors like irritability, anger, and negative talk, which become the main focus of interaction and distract parents from the primary underlying emotions.

You can help your teen to identify emotions by building an "emotional vocabulary." Challenge your teen to try to accurately verbalize and label her emotions. Be patient with her responses. A nonjudgmental, listening attitude will go far in allowing your teen to express what's really bothering her deep inside. At the same time, your attitude toward emotions, especially negative ones like sadness or anger, can shape how she learns to handle her own feelings. So be mindful of how you process your own emotions. (In chapter 11, we provide guidance on how, as a parent you can emotionally coach your teen to healthy emotional resolve.)

7. Community

Studies show that students with the highest levels of happiness and fewest signs of depression have the strongest ties to friends and family, and are committed to spending time with them.

Relationships matter. They are part of the main reason for which God created us. Because of that, strengthening close attachments and community is a key strategy for improving the life of your teen. We are all hard-wired for intimate relationships. Starting with parents and expanding to a broader community, your teen needs healthy connections to support him through difficult times. When we are part of a community, such as the church, extended family, or a neighborhood, the commitment to one another over time creates an environment for modeling and passing on part of what it means to live well.

PREVENTION AND RESTORATION

Here are some basic prevention and restoration strategies you should put into place for your teen.

1. Decrease the risk factors and increase the protective factors.
The following have been proven through research to increase protection against risk for depression:

Be aware of risk factors and change what you can. Depression can result during times of increased family conflict, depression in a parent, trauma or death, financial crises, and other negative influences. Some of these you can do nothing about; a loss is a loss and must be grieved. Other factors in a family's life can be avoided or controlled. How are family dynamics and your parenting impacting your teen's depression?

Build a positive, encouraging parent-teen relationship and connection with the family. This can be a significant protective factor for improving your teen's health and behaviors.[2] This will not prevent your teen from facing various troubles and challenges in the real world. However, it will serve as a buffer against added stress and provide a concerned safe place to make it through.

Show interest in your teen's life and use positive discipline methods. Parents who show interest and use positive discipline methods provide boundaries ("Please be home no later than 10 p.m."), monitoring ("Please call me when you leave the theater after the late-night show so I know you're on your way home"), and supervision ("Will there be parents at home for the party? I'd like to speak with them.").

Of course you want to be reasonable. Though your teen may think of this "tough love" as unbearable, who knows what he's being spared from? Eventually, he will appreciate the value of your prevention when he realizes what potentially could have happened.

Teach healthy social, family, and personal values. By strengthening character traits such as honesty, trust, loyalty, cooperation, self-restraint, civility, compassion, personal responsibility, and respect for others, you equip your teen to overcome adversity and make progress in his development to adulthood.

2. Know the warning signs of depression.
Stress and fatigue can trigger more serious problems such as depression. Learn to recognize the early warning signs and triggers

for depression so they can be avoided and progress can be monitored. Treat any residual symptoms the same way you would a broken bone that is vulnerable to reinjury. Whether these are difficulties with sleeping or appetite problems, keep in mind the future implications of current issues. Because of the lifelong implications associated with depression, prevention of recurrence—both for depression itself and for surrounding symptoms—should be a high priority.

What early warning signs do you need to be on the lookout for, signs that either your teen's depression is returning or that she is not recovering well? Mostly, these indicate that stress is overloading your teen and taking its toll on her body and mind. Here are the important signs to watch out for:

Physical signs
- Increasing fatigue; tends to vegetate (sits around doing nothing all day); frequently complains of being tired; has no energy or interest in physical activity
- Complains of aches and pains (headaches, backaches, etc.); has low tolerance for pain (e.g., when going to dentist)
- Complains of stomach problems, persistent nausea, frequent diarrhea or constipation, or irritable bowel syndrome (i.e. bowel pain, gas, bloating, and irregular bowel movements)
- Vague complaints of itching or burning in different parts of the body (called parasthesias) including chest, mouth, arms, soles of feet; shooting pains in arms or legs

Emotional signs
- Frequently appears tense, fidgety, restless, and can't relax
- Worries excessively or ruminates over past events; can't let things go

- Feels panicky or has panic attacks; hyperventilates or feels as if she can't get enough air; avoids certain public or crowded places like church or movies; won't leave the house or go into crowded places
- Cannot enjoy anything; nothing gives; and claims to hurt when she does feel something
- Worries about dying or wishes that she was dead or could die

Behavioral signs
- Gets angry easily; has a very short fuse and cannot stop the anger when it starts
- Frequently irritable; has a low tolerance for any delays or things not happening quickly enough
- Breaks or damages things; cruel to animals or other children; cuts or defaces pictures or is generally destructive
- Engaged in illegal activities; in trouble with the police or developing tendency toward criminal or dishonest behavior
- Frequently absent from school (with or without permission); finds excuses not to go to school; avoids school friends or extracurricular activities
- Cheats, lies, and steals from family members; conceals activities of which you would not approve

Spiritual signs (don't overlook these, as they could be important)
- Has lost all interest in God, church, youth group, etc.
- Refuses to go to church or Sunday school; prefers to stay home alone
- Blasphemes or blames God for the bad things in her life
- Feels excessively guilty about real or imagined failures; believes she has committed the "unpardonable sin"; thinks God is out to punish her

3. Watch out for recurring depression.

Once a teen has experienced an episode of clinical depression, there is a fifty percent chance of it recurring again at least once. For many, it often repeats itself several times in their lifetime, especially if they don't take steps to reduce their stress levels. The younger a teen is when the depression first hits, the greater the likelihood that it will recur.

To complicate things, once a teen gets depressed, several other problems can arise. Although treatment for depression is extremely effective, these lingering problems often end up becoming the most difficult part of staying well. Because of depression symptoms, a teen may have problems in school, causing an educational setback, which can itself be a source of stress. He may also develop problems with eating disorders, substance abuse, cutting, or withdrawal from friends. These secondary consequences will also need to be considered when looking for ways to prevent a relapse.

A long-term tendency toward recurring psychological problems should be taken seriously. Parents must make every effort to help their teen get better and build a wellness lifestyle that reduces the likelihood of recurring problems. By doing this, you increase your teen's resilience, foster better relationships, improve his school and job performance, and enhance his overall quality of life and physical health. As a result, he will be more likely to enjoy a happy adult life, free of recurring depressions.

9

BOUNCE-BACK ADAPTABILITY

We also have joy with our troubles, because we know
that these troubles produce patience [perseverance].
And patience [perseverance] produces character,
and character produces hope. And this hope will
never disappoint us, because God has poured out
His love to fill our hearts. — Romans 5:3–5

I want to suggest that the best buffers we have
against substance abuse, depression and violence
in our children have to do with a person's individual
strengths . . . [finding] their area of giftedness and
determining ways to build them. — Dr. Martin Seligman

PARENTING TEENS THESE DAYS SEEMS TO BE MUCH MORE challenging than in times before. What used to be considered a troubled or hurting teen thirty years ago is not the same as today. Teens deal with more stress and depression today than in any generation before them. The numbers of teens who use drugs, smoke, or are sexually active, depressed, or anxious are alarming. But what these numbers really reflect is that teens are unequipped to cope with the diversity and enormity of stress they are facing.

What teens desperately need is to learn how to solve their problems, negotiate relationships, and persevere through adversity. Teens want to do more than just survive, adapt, and cope with hardships. They want to be empowered to change the world around them and grow stronger through struggles. But this means they will need more than just a basic education to live productive, meaningful, and happy lives, free from the cloud of depression.

RESILIENT PARENTING

You can develop specific parenting skills for guiding your teen toward greater resiliency. Here are ways to encourage her in each arena of life:

Emotions—Provide caring love and support. Help your teen feel and express emotions, teaching her how to manage difficult emotions

Thinking—Build a healthy mindset of hope and optimism for success in your teen. Help her put things into perspective. Teach her to avoid negative self-talk traps by evaluating beliefs, and to dispute negative thinking through accurate reality-talk.

Spirit—Model to your teen how a relationship with God can change daily existence, especially when knowing He has a plan and purpose for the future. Talk about how He uses hard times in our lives to build character. Show her scriptures that show how He comforts us, answers our prayers, heals our broken hearts, transforms us, and restores us.

Relationships—Support and connection with family and meaningful friends are essential to making it through hard times. Provide opportunities for meaningful participation.

Personal Character and Behavior—Set clear, consistent boundaries. Teach practical life skills for doing well and being resilient. Build on character strengths, Christian virtues, and personal qualities. Urge your teen to take personality and character strength tests for fun and for self-discovery.

And this is where parents play an essential role. Many parents today grew up with a remedial approach to raising children: use good discipline to correct wrong behavior, and eventually an exemplary teen will emerge. Many a parent will attest (as will the Bible and even current scientific research) that this in not a foolproof, guaranteed formula; it's an incomplete approach to parenting. Sure, we are to "train a child in the way he should go" using discipline (Prov. 22:6 NIV). However, parenting that is only about correcting weaknesses and pointing out flaws and errors does not equip children with essential life skills, nor does it give them opportunities to identify their divinely infused strengths and virtues. Children need and want to learn how to use their strengths as much as possible to overcome and flourish through the stresses and troubles that come their way.

In this chapter, we will explore some of the effective ways you can equip your teen to experience courage, perseverance, character, and a resilient life through:

- meaningful connections
- spiritual resilience
- hopeful perspective
- goals, passion, and purpose
- confidence and competence
- character growth opportunities
- a safe place at home
- good self-care
- caring and contributing

While at the movies the other night, we watched an animated film before the main feature about a little sheep being helped by a jackrabbit. Each sheering season, the sheep would become sad and insecure when his wool was shaved off. He was embarrassed by his puny, pink, smooth body. But with the jackrabbit's inspirational optimism, the sheep adjusted to his changes, learned how to feel proud, and felt unashamed of who he was—wool or no wool.

He was once again cheerful as he joined his friend in doing the "bounce-back" dance.

This cute vignette echoes the positive message of resilience and buoyancy that has surged in a post-9/11 world among children, teens, and parents. It encourages ways to actively manage stress, avoid negative outcomes, and persevere in even the worst of life's adversities.

Although an emerging psychosocial research interest, the concept of human resilience is as old as creation. The Bible gives us many examples of those who had to persevere with patience, run the race with endurance, and overcome despair. Throughout this chapter, we will draw from both the best of resilience research and Judeo-Christian faith.

RESILIENT LIVING

Some teens do well in certain stressful conditions yet struggle through others. No one is consistently "resilient" in every situation. Teens respond uniquely to stress in a given circumstance and at different times in their development. There are many interrelated factors that contribute to empowering resilience in them.

Think about what skills your teen draws upon to problem-solve, maintain a healthy perspective, and manage everyday stress. How do teens overcome genetic predispositions, temperament traits, and obstacles from their childhood that put them at greater risk for trouble? What makes some recover from trauma and setbacks, allowing them to move forward with an intentional path of change and growth? And when it comes to your teen, what can serve as a protective buffer to help him move ahead, overcome, and even flourish through stress-filled, turbulent times?

Resilience is what makes the difference. Psychosocial specialists use this term to describe a person's capacity to respond and grow from major stressful challenges. The Bible refers to it as fortitude, endurance, and courage. We will use these terms interchangeably. From a Judeo-Christian perspective, they all refer to the ability to persevere through adversity and move courageously through hard times by drawing on intrinsic qualities and God's power and presence. As a result of these difficulties, the Lord makes us stronger and builds character. He redeems the situation for our good, impacting the present and offering a hopeful outlook for the future. Spiritual resilience is when human and divine support sources collaborate in the midst of a stressful situation. And the result is a positive outcome.

A "resilient-living" perspective can equip your teen to overcome challenges and threats, suffering and sorrow, confusion and loss. It's the undergirding that helps a person make it to the finish with a positive outcome. It doesn't enable him to avoid and get rid of all the hardships. But it does allow his strengths, resources, and skills to be used to protect him. And as a result, he can learn and grow from both good and bad events.

Whenever something bad happens, your teen can be empowered to not give up or just survive, but instead experience God's power in turning a negative situation into one of growth and redemption. Resilient living can enable him to keep in touch with his larger goals while grappling with immediate ones.

LEARNING RESILIENT LIVING

What we do now know is that the factors that build resilience can be learned. Some can even offset the genetic "givens." These can be incorporated into daily strategies and guiding principles to help make life less difficult and painful for your teen, while also enhancing his ability to live well in the midst of hardship. Resilient living is more than just coping with a situation, only to return to status quo. It often involves avoiding certain situations or changing friends, habits, or surroundings. True resilient living requires having a sense of control that empowers a person to break the mold by finding a new way through, making significant changes, and eventually being set free.

The exciting part for you as a parent is that you can join your teen on his journey toward building resilience by increasing your own resilient parenting skills. Together, you and your teen can successfully find new opportunities for growth and building strengths as you struggle through challenges and flourish in the face of adversity.

The journey of resilient living is unique. Personal experience, relationships, and divine support will each have profound impact. Although the following biblical principles and resources apply generally to struggling teens, remember that each teen has a unique set of genetic, personality, and circumstantial needs. What resources, principles, or methods you use to build resilience in your teen will depend on the complexity of situations in his life and what he is going through internally.

Here are some of the major ways you and your teen can discover resilient living.

1. Meaningful connections

Our teens are in the most trouble when they are not connected with parents, family, school, workplace, leisure, or positive peers. The way to prevent disconnection is to build our teens' assets, to invest in their strengths at least as much as, if not more than, we correct their weaknesses. Lots of self-correction takes place when teens feel appreciation, contribution, competence and confidence, and positive belonging.

— Elias, Tobias, and Friedlander, *Raising Emotionally Intelligent Teenagers*

We have expanded on this theme in chapters 2 and 8, so here we will summarize the key elements:

- Build a secure attachment with your teen.
- Teens need to talk and get together with friends.
- Build and draw from a strong family support network.
- Connect your teen with outside support and health professionals.

2. Spiritual Resilience

Spiritual resilience is the capacity to get through hard times. It involves using spiritual resources to resist despair and defeat, and instead construct something positive in light of God's perspective and purpose for life. As a parent shared with us recently, it is "taking your pain and letting God transform it into power."

It's proven that having a personal faith in God and embracing Christian virtues provides meaning, motivation, encouragement, hope, and caring friendship. A 2003 national study involving 3,300 teens found that teens who attend church services, read the Bible, and pray feel less sad or depressed, less alone, less misunderstood and guilty, and more cared for than their nonreligious peers.[1]

Other research has also shown that spiritual enrichment and expression is deeply comforting and transforming. Personal spiritual experience has been shown to positively impact mental health by increasing appropriate social behavior, freedom from worry and guilt, personal competence, self-control, open-mindedness, and flexibility.[2]

As a parent, you can model building a relationship with God through spiritual disciplines of family devotions, Scripture reading, and prayer. Practically apply biblical principles as you are overcoming hardship and embracing God's promises and His constant love. Gain encouragement—for you and your teen—through His Word and through the love and gifts of other believers. Use teen-appropriate resources to strengthen your teen, and encourage her input.

Remember, however, to be flexible and not have unrealistic expectations in this area. Your teen may not show any interest in spiritual things at the moment. If that is the case, do what you can and then pray, pray, pray.

3. Hopeful perspective

It is difficult for troubled teens to automatically respond with an optimistic perspective, much less maintain that attitude. They usually see a problem as a "bummer," not as an opportunity for growth. Here are some ways you as a parent can intentionally be a hope giver.

Remember that stressful times are temporary. This journey can be overwhelming for everyone involved if you don't keep coming back to the perspective that things do change in time and bad times end. This too shall pass. It's not the end of the world. God will see you through. You, your teen, and your family can all learn and grow. If your family's mind-set is one of high hope, promise, and opportunity for growth, your teen will feel more empowered to help himself. You can then become a partner in his struggle to prevail, rather than be just a supervisor.

Gain perspective. Your teen might doubt that he has what it takes to get through this. If so, help him remember a time when he faced up to his fears or got through a difficult time. Refer to how you or someone else was able to get through hard times. Help him learn to combat negative self-talk and relax the stress response, whether that's thinking of a particular song in times of stress or simply taking a deep breath to calm down.

Going through hardship can consume time, energy, conversation, and the focus of life. Encourage your teen to think about the important things that have stayed the same, even while he is in turmoil and the outside world is changing. When you do talk about hard times and problems, make sure you talk about strengths, hopes, and good times as well.

Try to find something redeeming. Nurture a hopeful outlook, one that is optimistic and thankful, one that finds some redeeming consequence in the bad situation. This is more than just looking on the bright side; it is looking for something that gives hope. Even the worst of experiences can teach you something valuable about yourself. Encourage this viewpoint in your teen.

After a teen girl broke up with her boyfriend, she felt it was the end of her life. Yet as she grieved the loss over time, she also discovered that she was grateful for what she learned in the relationship and how it had prepared her to look forward to being in another meaningful relationship.

Your teen will be better equipped for future challenges if she learns not to catastrophize or overreact, but to find something about the disaster that she can hold onto that is objective and optimistic.

Avoid seeing the situation as insurmountable. Although problems and forced change can be scary for everyone, help your teen realize that this is a necessary and normal part of life. Those who

AUTHENTIC SELF-ESTEEM

A teen's healthy sense of worth and value will come as a result of him doing well in his world and thus feeling good about himself. The key to building a healthy authentic self-esteem in teens is not to just say nice things, regardless of how true they are. True self-esteem in teens must reflect the reality of how well they are really doing.

To build your teen's fragile self-esteem, teach him the skills for doing well in life. Improved study skills will result in getting good grades. Making good friends and mending broken relationships will provide meaningful connections. Identifying and pursuing interests and talents will bring meaning and fulfillment. And as a result of these things, he will feel proud of his accomplishments, and develop a satisfying, healthy realistic view of himself.

And that will feel good!

can adapt to change are more resilient in seeing setbacks and problems as temporary and solvable.

Change involves both loss and gain at the same time. New opportunities and goals are always waiting to be discovered, but only at the expense of releasing what has passed. Talk with your teen about how the stress of change is impacting her life and how there is always a hope for the future, even though she can't see it now. Here is a sample of how you might approach the topic in person or through a note:

"Honey, I know this is so painful and difficult, but it's going to be okay. I am so sorry you are hurting right now. But you're (we're) going to make it through. Nothing is impossible with God. We are going to find help to get us through this, and we'll become even stronger as a result. It might not seem like this is possible right now, but we'll just take it one day at a time and deal with one thing at a time. I love you, and I'll always be here for you."

When Winston Churchill, the great leader of World War II, was young, his father, who was a British lord, disliked him and sent him off to boarding school. Often Churchill couldn't go home and had to remain all alone in the boarding school. He would go to bed and sob himself to sleep because everything looked so hopeless. Years later, as prime minister, his nation was fighting a terrible war. When the invasion of the Nazis seemed imminent and things looked bleak for England, he gave a famous speech that rallied the whole country to fight back. The famous line from that speech was: "We will never, never, never, never, never, never, never... give up!" He learned to never give up out of his own pain growing up!

Remember that a merry heart is good medicine. A good sense of humor can contribute much in building resilience. Laugh at yourself and with others. In retrospect, laugh at how you reacted or at the funny side of situations you were in. Even in the most difficult of situations, there is always a humorous side to be found. Humor has become a natural essential in my (Catherine's) counseling practice and with family and friends. We even laughed at my sister's husband's funeral when the priest's wig started to slip off as he was doing the graveside eulogy. I have laughed at myself while telling a friend of my meltdowns and overreactions. I laugh regularly with my daughters reminiscing over the humorous side of dramatic moments. We imitate each other in the way we react to things, mimicking our facial expressions and gestures. Laughter and humor help keep things in perspective, and they make the heart glad and hopeful.

4. Goals, passion, and purpose

One of the strongest factors that can increase teen resiliency is when parents help teens develop their dreams, goals, and purpose in life. Dreaming big is a great incentive. In *The Dream Giver* Bruce Wilkinson shares how each person has been created for a life of purpose and significance.[3] It is his "dream giver" message that is giving hope to thousands of teens stricken by poverty, hunger, and AIDS

ESSENTIAL VIRTUES AND STRENGTHS
FOR RESILIENT LIVING

In the course of your observations and conversations with your teen, look for and point out some of the following life skills. Ask questions about how he has used these qualities in the past. How can he apply these to current life problems, crises, or stressors?

___ Relationships—ability to be a friend, form positive relationships

___ Sense of humor—able to see humorous side, laughs a lot

___ Inner direction—centered and grounded in his sense of self

___ Perceptiveness—insightful, understanding of people and situations

___ Independence—self-sufficient, able to distance from unhealthy people and situations

___ Optimism—positive view of the future, hopeful

___ Flexibility—can adjust to change, copes positively

___ Love of learning—a reader; likes new and different things, people, and situations

___ Self-motivation—takes initiative and gets positive inspiration from within

___ Competence—is good at something and gets joy from it

___ Self-worth—possesses authentic self-esteem and confidence, has sense of dignity

___ Spirituality—has personal faith and hope

___ Perseverance—hangs in there, gets up and keeps going

___ Creativity—gets fulfillment in a creative outlet, expresses feelings and thoughts

Other strengths to build on include: boundaries, honesty, responsibility, respect, obedience, insight, constructive use of time, work ethic.

in Africa. And the same principles will inspire your teen to journey from feeling like a loser to having the potential for his life to count. He truly can do something great for God.

During extremely hard times, just getting out of bed and going to school may be an accomplishment for your teen. Hard times can leave teens feeling out of control. Having a focus and being able to take decisive action—even if it is small—can put a little bounce in your teen's step and boost his self-esteem. When he makes an effort, notice and applaud him for it. Let him enjoy being proud of his little and big achievements along the way.

5. Confidence and competence

Help your teen keep a balanced and positive view of herself by developing her confidence in her natural and divinely infused abilities. Affirm qualities you see in her life that can help her as she struggles with the effects of her hardship. Tell her what she is good at. Help her hone a special talent, something to be better at than anyone else.

There have been many studies conducted on what characteristics influence successful growth and help teens get through to adulthood without major problems. Conclusions have resulted in a cluster of traits known as the five C's: competence, confidence, connection, character, caring—and recently a sixth C was added, contribution.[4]

A parent shared with us a time when her teen was depressed and experiencing a negative perspective on her life and abilities. The mom was actually struggling to see the positive herself, but in her desire to parent intentionally and build positive resilience, she went into her teen's room and noted one positive accomplishment she had observed. "I know you've been having a hard time lately, and you aren't feeling really good or positive about your life. But you did a great job cleaning up your room today, and I know that must have been a big effort for you. That's a great quality, to be able to persevere and get something done even though you don't want to, and it takes effort."

The next day, to the mom's surprise, the teen girl seemed perkier.

In passing, she said, "Mom, thanks for saying the positive thing about me yesterday. I was feeling so down and couldn't think of anything good about myself. After you said that positive thing, it helped me see one good quality in myself, and I've been holding onto those words."

This is a perfect example of how when teens notice the positive outcome of their efforts and competence, it reinforces their strengths and confidence. They no longer see themselves as losers or damaged goods. The emotional pain no longer dominates their awareness. By taking pride in your teen's courage and determination—no matter how small a step—and letting her know about it, you infuse authentic self-esteem in her.

6. Character growth opportunities

It is a fundamental biblical principle that we learn and grow through the tough and difficult times of life—yes, even through depression. It is in these hard times that God does His finest work in us, and we learn about ourselves and have opportunities to grow and mature. Your teen's current trials and tribulations will stretch her, revealing who she is and how she is able to handle these trials.

That's why it is so important that you help your teen look within, to brainstorm on who she is and the ways she can handle situations. Teens like taking self-discovery quizzes. So take personality tests as a family, and share the results you discover about yourselves.

This is a great coaching opportunity for your teen to learn about the stages of development and why she gets angered easily (the part of her brain needed to control anger is not yet fully developed) and depressed (her brain chemistry is temporarily in upheaval). Share with her your own strategies that helped you to be resilient in your life. Explore her personality traits and natural strengths, and point out where she can grow stronger. What strengths does she wish she could develop through this bad experience? How can she compliment her natural weak spots with her strong points? Empower her to have the courage to change and explore a new direction if necessary.

AUTHORITATIVE PARENTING

There are several effective parenting styles mentioned in this book that you can learn about in more detail. One of them is "authoritative parenting," which has proven to be more effective than the permissive and authoritarian styles of parenting.

Representing one extreme of parenting methodology, permissive parenting is taking a hands-off approach to raising children. Many see this as neglectful and ultimately damaging. Authoritarian parenting, on the other hand, is a controlling style that usually focuses on rigid rules and harsh punishment. Parents using this method often maintain a cold, distant relationship with their children. Dealing with stressed, anxious, or depressed teens in this way is unwise. It can easily provoke them to anger and rebellion while worsening their problems. Rules without relationship lead to rebellion.

In contrast, numerous studies have validated that authoritative parenting provides a balance of being warm and involved, while also being firm by establishing boundaries, limits, and expectations. Parenting in this style provides a balance of relationship nurturing, connection, and guiding boundaries, all of which have been proven essential to optimal health and growth. Parents using this method realize that rules matter, but so do close relationships. This style most closely reflects the grace and shepherding heart of God.

Among teens, authoritative parenting instills and increases the characteristics that promote resilience. These teens do better scholastically and socially. They cope better with stress and approach problems with a sense of curiosity and purpose. They develop a healthier theology of God and a more realistic view of His love and nature.

7. A safe place at home

Teens have enough to deal with in their world of stress, disappointment, and decision making. They need home to be a constant in their lives. Although they are starting to want to be with their friends more and pull away from their families, they still need the comfort and stability of a place to go back to.

Allow your teen to create a "hassle-free zone" by making her room a haven free from stress and anxieties. She may do this by the way she decorates, the amount of time she spends there, and the kinds of activities she engages in there.

After a disaster or major stress such as loss, it's important to try to get back into a routine, even if that means finding a new one. A safe, consistent place of refuge at home and in daily routines gives your teen stress relief, comfort, and consistency. Little rituals like taking a relaxing bath at night, playing with the family pet, skateboarding after school, talking with a friend at night on the phone, or exercising regularly are all familiar, meaningful routines that can be a source of comfort. The rhythm and routine of life creates a secure place in times of turbulence.

8. Good self-care

We emphasized the importance of self-care, healthy lifestyle habits, and strategies for living well in chapters 3 and 8. Here are a few additional considerations.

Learn to manage strong feelings and impulses. Stress or tragedy can evoke the deepest of conflicting and painful emotions. Teens can have a hard time figuring out what to do with all these extreme feelings. An important resilience skill is to be able to identify and feel deep emotions, while also integrating those into life without feeling a loss of control. This is called emotional regulation and impulse control. The best way for your teen to learn this is through your modeling it.

Start by encouraging your family to talk about their feelings and identify them accurately. If your teen is in counseling, he will be getting help on how to do this and could possibly come home and challenge you to be honest about your feelings as well. Don't dismiss or resist this. Go along with it, as you might learn to improve your own emotional regulation. Other methods of capturing emotions, such as journaling or artistic expression, are also helpful and likely to be used by your teen's counselor.

Allow your teen to take a break. As you gain understanding and grace toward your teen and she begins to show progress, be careful you don't push her too hard and add more stress. Periodically call a time-out and let everyone take a break. This might be a weekend away, a short vacation, or going to the beach or mountains for a day out. It could also be a day at home staying in pajamas, or an occasional "mental health day," when your teen is allowed to stay home from school to rest and recuperate.

The added challenges of therapy and trying hard to achieve a good recovery can easily add new stress that, on top of everything else, can exacerbate the problem. Things will eventually settle down, but in the meantime, encourage your teen to take it easy, take a break from the sad or scary stories of real life in the media, and take good care of herself.

9. Caring and contributing

We truly do help ourselves by helping others. When a teen feels helpless, he can be empowered by helping others—even animals. This is another way of curbing loneliness or not being the only person with a problem.

I (Catherine) have a friend, Beth, who was undergoing some heavy-duty chemotherapy a while ago. One day she received a home-cooked dinner from a mom at her daughter's school who was herself going through a really hard time.

"I feel so bad that you did this for me when you're going through so much yourself," Beth said. "Oh, please don't," the school mom insisted. "This morning I was feeling so terrible and sorry for myself. Then I thought of you in your wheelchair, barely able to swallow. So I decided to bless you, and now I feel doubly blessed myself."

When you bless someone else, you actually receive a blessing for yourself. Nothing gets your mind off your own problems like helping someone else in need. Don't overwhelm or burden your teen; but when appropriate, encourage him to try doing something nice at school, helping around the house, being kind to a sibling, or aiding a friend with homework. Mission trips are also a great way for your teen to go on an adventure and discover passion for life. There, he can get beyond his day-to-day self-centered perspective of living and make an impact in others' lives, while also feeling valued.

THE RESILIENT LIVING JOURNEY

In this chapter, we've tried to provide you with practical ways for building your teen's resiliency. We've stressed that developing resilience is a personal journey for each teen. The resilience concept allows you to honor the efforts your teen is making to help herself, whether or not those efforts lead to breakthrough results. It is an approach that fosters the respect and affirmation teens need in order to persist and that you need to support them. Explore and discover what is meaningful to guide your teen. Not all these approaches are going to hit the spot and work for her. Remember also that these strategies should not be substituted for professional medical and healthcare.

Although your teen can increase her resilience skills, she may still feel stressed or anxious at times. She might have some happy times that follow with some down times. That's to be expected, and it's okay. Simply keep in mind that what she learns and discovers during the challenging times will continue to be useful for her future everyday life.

10

TEACHING HEALTHY WAYS OF THINKING

Think about the things that are good and worthy of praise. Think about the things that are true and honorable and right and pure and beautiful and respected.
— Philippians 4:8

Do not change yourselves to be like the people of this world, but be changed within by a new way of thinking. Then you will be able to decide what God wants for you; you will know what is good and pleasing to Him and what is perfect. — Romans 12:2

ONE OF THE MOST EFFECTIVE, PROVEN INTERVENTIONS IN treating teen depression has to do with transforming the way a teen thinks. Teenagers are engaged in a battle of the mind that involves distorted, hopeless, pessimistic, and ruminating thoughts. This battle must be confronted in order to live well.

Thankfully, this isn't an overwhelming fight. Teens' unhealthy thoughts can chip away at every moment of every day! Changing entrenched negative, distorted thinking habits into accurate optimism can be hard work, but over time, they will reap the benefits.

Thought, emotion, and behavior are all linked. By addressing your teenager's thinking (cognition), you can change his emotions and behaviors (behavioral). A teen is literally what he thinks, his character being a complete sum of all his thoughts. The mind is like a garden that must be cultivated or allowed to run wild. We need to plant intentional, useful seeds of good and right thoughts and weed out wrong, useless, and impure thoughts. This process of guarding and tending our minds shapes our character, circumstances, and ultimately our destiny. The inner state of your teen's thoughts, emotional attitudes, and perceptions will directly impact character, choice, action, and other aspects of his outer life.

In this chapter, we will offer biblical and cognitive behavioral principles that you can use to prevent distorted thought patterns from emerging in your teenager. Essentially, these are ways to identify thoughts that produce negative, painful, or inhibiting feelings, as well as maladaptive behavior or reactions. Negative self-talk conditions low self-worth. Although there is no instant cure for the complexity of depression, these healthy thinking skills are a powerful intervention that can bring relief and enhance treatment outcome by dealing with both negative, inaccurate thinking and the resulting emotions and behaviors.

WINNING THE BATTLE OF THE MIND

Teens (even nondepressed ones) are notorious for negative self-talk. Instead of dwelling on either reality or hopeful outcomes, they choose to ruminate over pessimistic, self-deprecating thoughts. One study estimated that as much as 77 percent of self-talk during an average person's day is negative and berating in nature. We can only imagine how much more this would be for a depressed teen.

This negative self-talk usually includes statements such as, "I can't do this, I give up." "I feel so confused and uncertain about life. I'm an idiot." "I feel so unfulfilled and disconnected; there must be something wrong with me." But God has a response to every one of these thoughts. He wants your teen to know His reality and His promises, and He wants him to turn his mind toward those. When your teen is despairing, the Lord assures both you and him that you can get through with His help. And when your teen is confused, uncertain, and disconnected, He offers His care, guidance, value, and comfort.

NEGATIVE SELF-TALK VERSUS REALITY TALK

A fourteen-year-old girl comes home from school, throws herself on her bed, and starts sobbing in front of her mother. "Mom, nobody likes me in my school. They all hate me. I want to go to another school. I hate my life! There is nothing positive about my life."

What's irrational and inaccurate about this? For starters, the words *nobody*, *all*, and *nothing* couldn't possibly be true. Even the word *hate* is probably an exaggeration. If she had said, "Melissa doesn't like me anymore," or even, "Melissa and Mary are upset with me at the moment," they would have been rational and probably accurate statements. You would have no basis for challenging them. And a possible response would be, "Sweetie, I'm so sorry to hear this. It must feel terrible to have your best friends turn on you like this. I'm sure it seems like your entire life is affected. Now, why don't you tell me about what happened, and we'll see if there is a way for you to change how they feel about you. So where do you want to start?"

Healthy thinking is able to go directly to problem solving. Irrational, inaccurate thinking, or cognitive distortions, on the other hand, can't move you directly to problem solving because the real problem hasn't yet been identified. In a situation like this, you would have to help your daughter backtrack her thinking, unravel her emotions, and use more rational, honest phrases that can identify the real problem: "Honey, I can see you are very upset." (Always affirm the legitimacy of what is being felt at the moment, even if the feelings are unjustified.) "But let's backtrack. Tell me what happened and who is upset with you, and we'll try to figure out a way to resolve the problem. I'm quite sure everyone couldn't possibly hate you. Now, who are you talking about, what happened, and what did that person say?"

Gently steer your teen to making a more rational statement (so as to reinforce the value of doing this) and determine what has really occurred.

THE DIRTY DOZEN DISTORTIONS

The above example encompasses several clearly identified cognitive distortions: overgeneralizing, filtering, catastrophizing, and even mind reading. These and other irrational, downward-spiraling thoughts have to be stopped. They can create significant changes in attitudes, emotions, and behavior, and need to be replaced with reality-based thinking. There are at least twelve cognitive distortions that have been identified as common to many of us. We'll call them the "Dirty Dozen Distortions."

1. *All-or-nothing thinking.* You see things in black-and-white categories. If your performance falls short of perfect, you see yourself as a total failure. Example: your first attempt at getting a date for a school dance fails, so you vow to never try dating.

2. *Overgeneralization.* You see a single negative event as a never-ending pattern of defeat, or you reach a conclusion based on just one bit of information. Example: when your friend forgets to call, instead of accepting the fact that she simply forgot, you jump to the conclusion that she doesn't like you anymore.

3. *Mental filter.* You pick out a single negative detail of a situation without considering the whole and then dwell on it exclusively. Your vision of all reality becomes darkened, like the drop of ink that discolors the entire beaker of water. Example: you miss a shot at basketball and say, "I'm just a lousy player!" No, you are not—you simply missed this shot.

4. *Disqualifying the positive.* You reject positive experiences by insisting they don't count for some reason or other, whereas you never challenge a negative experience. In this way you can maintain a negative belief that is contradicted by your everyday experiences. Example: "Sure, I got the ball in the hoop that time, but it was just a fluke. That time also! That too!"

5. *Jumping to conclusions.* You make a negative interpretation even though there are no definite facts that convincingly support your conclusion. Example: "He totally ignored me at the party; he kept looking at Jennifer. I don't think he wants to date me anymore."

6. *Mind reading.* You randomly conclude that someone is reacting negatively to you, and you don't bother to check this out. Example: "The teacher didn't ask me to answer the question. I think he thinks I'm dumb and stupid!"

7. *Fortunetelling.* You anticipate that things will turn out badly, and you feel convinced that your prediction is an already-established fact. Example: "Every time I dream that dream, something bad happens to me. I can feel it follow me all day waiting for it to happen. Maybe it means I shouldn't leave the house."

8. *Catastrophizing (maximizing or minimizing):* You exaggerate (or diminish) the importance of things, such as your mistake or someone else's achievement; or you inappropriately shrink things until they appear tiny (your own desirable qualities or others' imperfections). This means you always expect the worst to happen. Example: "I just know that this strong wind is going to become a tornado and we are all going to die."

9. *Emotional reasoning.* Believing what you feel must be true, just because you "feel" it. You assume that your negative emotions necessarily reflect the way things really are. Example: "I feel that God doesn't like me, therefore it must be true."

10. *"Should" statements.* You try to motivate yourself with "shoulds" and "shouldn'ts," as if you have to be whipped and punished before you can be expected to do anything. "Musts" and "oughts" are also offenders. The emotional consequences are guilt. Example: "I should go and return Mary's CD right now because I can feel her talking behind my back about borrowing it." "Every Christian must enjoy old-time gospel music or else they are not really Christian."

11. *Labeling and mislabeling.* This is an extreme form of overgeneralization. Instead of describing your error, you attach a negative label to yourself. (Example: "I'm a loser because I'm getting an F in math.") When someone else's behavior rubs you the wrong way,

you attach a negative label to him. (Example: "He's a liar; I'm never going to talk to him again.") Mislabeling involves describing an event with language so emotionally loaded that it cannot be questioned.

12. *Blaming.* A common irrational belief is that "everything that happens must have a blame." Example: if the traffic on the freeway is jammed, then someone has caused an accident. When you drop and break your glasses, your first reaction is, "If you hadn't have distracted me at that moment, I wouldn't have dropped my glasses."

ACCENTUATE ACCURATE THINKING

W. Clement Stone once wrote, "There is very little difference in people. But that little difference makes a big difference. The little difference is attitude. The big difference is whether it is positive or negative."[1]

It also matters whether it is accurate and realistic. A positive, optimistic attitude protects against illness and depression. In his book *The Optimistic Child,* Dr. Martin Seligman presents an antidote to the epidemic of depression. He calls it "psychological immunization" and bases the remedy on a reality-based optimism. The healthy mind-set that Seligman discusses does not avoid natural, negative feelings of sadness or anger. These are part of life and often compel us to understand or change what is upsetting us. However, a reality-based optimist thinks something like this: "Where there is opportunity to be grasped and there is hope, things get better. When there is no hope, things do not. What can I do to help the cause of providing opportunity and hope?"[2] The implication is that every parent can be a hope giver to her teen.

Accurate optimism and reality-based self-talk are tools that encourage your teen to reflect on her beliefs, which then equip her to take an active role in persevering and overcoming problems. The Bible provides a similar solution in various proverbs: "A happy heart is like good medicine, but a broken spirit drains your strength" (Prov. 17:22). "Pleasant words are like a honeycomb, making people happy and healthy" (Prov. 16:24).

ATTITUDE ADJUSTMENT

From observing human experience throughout time, it's not what happens to us that has the greatest impact on us, but rather our perception, attitude, and response. Holocaust survivor Viktor Frankl knew firsthand of this profound principle. In his book, *Man's Search for Meaning,* he wrote, "Everything can be taken from a man but one thing: the last of human freedoms—to choose one's attitude in any given set of circumstances."

In the light of such overwhelming evidence, the importance of parenting children toward positive, optimistic, accurate thinking is compelling. The problem is that distorted perceptions can get there first! Day after day, week after week, your teen is being influenced in how he thinks. If that influence is inaccurate and negative—complaining parents, unhappy home environment, critical teachers, peer rejection, or low-self esteem—then the brain adopts it as the "normal" way of thinking.

Yet it is not as difficult to change negative thinking as you might imagine. It merely takes an effective plan and an objective approach. Every time your teenager says something optimistic, positive, and accurate about anything, notice it, reflect it back to him, and praise him. "I really liked the way you responded to that bad news about not making the team. You're right; you can just try a little harder next time."

Responses and actions that are praised have a better chance of being repeated than behavior that is condemned. What you feed will grow. Remember, teens find it most helpful when we point out their strengths and what they are doing right, rather than how they are failing and what they are doing wrong. Although both perspectives can be accurate, emphasizing a hopeful perspective is more productive in helping them improve, cope, and flourish.

CHALLENGING NEGATIVITY

Parents can play a key role in helping their teen overcome the destructive self-talk that contributes to and is part of depression. By utilizing the "Dirty Dozen Distortions" and challenging your teen's negative assessment of herself or a situation, you can help her decipher between optimistic reality and dysfunction. Here are three ways to do this.

1. Increase your teen's awareness of inaccurate, pessimistic thinking.

Help her see the connection between negative thoughts, the emotions they create, and the behaviors that follow. Without being critical, reflect back to your teen what you are discerning. "Just because you're having difficulty getting ready for the school dance doesn't mean that the rest of your evening is ruined."

2. Challenge the accuracy of the negative or pessimistic statement.

Aid your teen in recognizing and monitoring negative thoughts or distortions of reality. Examine the evidence for and against such distorted thinking or perceptions of reality. What does the evidence indicate? "I heard you say you were stupid when you noticed you got a C in math. You got As and Bs in all your other subjects, and the C was mostly because you didn't get your assignments in on time."

3. Encourage your teen to substitute a more accurate way of thinking, believing, and responding.

You can do this even if she doesn't want to believe it yet. Just saying it can help the brain and heart accept it. Following the example above, you could suggest your teen substitute her thoughts with the following: "I know I am disappointed in my grades. I also know I can do better. But these grades don't define who I am. I have two choices: I can find ways to improve next time, like get my homework in on time, or I can just accept that this is my best and be content with it!" Then identify and help change the inappropriate assumptions that predisposed your teen to distort the experience in the first place.

Here are some other examples of alternatives to inaccurate negative attitudes your teen may think or say.

DISTORTED SELF-TALK	ACCURATE REALITY-TALK
No one loves me.	God loves me. My parents love me.
I am a failure.	One failure doesn't make me a complete failure.
I feel like I want to die.	I can't always trust what I feel.
There is no hope for the future.	I'll feel better in the morning.
Good people never make mistakes.	You learn more from mistakes than successes.
I don't know what to do.	I can get advice from others and God.

TRANSFORMATION THROUGH AFFIRMATION

In his book *Saving the Millennial Generation*, Dawson McAllister tells of a pastor friend who characterizes his ministry as "transformation through affirmation."[3] He says that people live for encouragement and die without it. Parents must pour constant affirmation and love on their teens, even when they don't feel like it or their teens don't deserve it. Along these lines, you may have to work on your own tendency to see only the negatives in your teen. Challenge yourself to view him in a positive light more frequently by aligning yourself with God's perspective of him, which will come through prayer.

Ultimately, God is the one who counsels us in all wisdom and leads us to freedom from the past. He gives us hope, heals our broken hearts, and teaches us how to overcome those things that hold us down. He truly transforms us all—including your teen.

The most effective way to begin accentuating the positive in your teen is through reflecting and focusing on regular truths, or affirmations. Affirm the affirmatives. Encourage him to be more aware and affirming of what God is doing in his life. Allow Christ to affirm him through you, and help him to feel a greater love and tenderness than he experiences in this world. (As a parent, this should always be the case!)

THE MAGNIFICENT SEVEN
AFFIRMATIONS FOR YOUR TEEN

Following are seven Christ-based, optimistic truths and affirmations that you can reflect and teach your teenager to believe. Write him a personal letter in which you express these. It will leave a lasting impression that he can always turn back to for renewed hope.

These affirmations help to express an optimistic view of God while emphasizing His deepest love and concern for your teen. We call them the "Magnificent Seven Affirmations." You can add to these any that you feel would more specifically reflect who your teen is in Christ, His love, and His promises. Accentuating these in your teen's life from day to day provides the skills and food for thought that develop a healthy mind, attitude, emotions, and actions.

1. *I am a child of God. I am loved and accepted.* As I receive God and believe in Christ, He gives me the right to become a child of God (John 1:12). God loves me more than I can imagine, and I can never go outside the reach of His great love (Rom. 8:38–39). Hating myself doesn't make God love me more; it just makes it harder for me to see His love (Ps. 103:10–12).

2. *I am forgiven.* No matter what my sin, God will forgive me if I repent and return to Him (1 John 1:9). If I seem to fail because circumstances are against me, God will always give me another opportunity (Ps. 37:24). I am free from condemnation (Rom. 8:1).

3. *I am safe and secure.* There is nothing I can do that will cause God to turn His back on me or abandon me (Heb. 13:5). When I am in trouble, God will rescue me from darkness and bring me into the light and a secure place (Ps. 27:5). When I go to God for protection, I can trust He will be a safe place for me (Ps. 91:1–2).

4. *I can do and face anything with Christ's help.* God never wants me to give up—never, never, never, never ever (Joshua 1:5, 7–9). Whatever I attempt to do, if it is God's will for me, He will give me the strength and wisdom I need to do it (Phil. 4:13).

5. *I have hope for my life and the future.* I am confident that the

good work that God has begun in me will be completed (Phil. 1:6). God has a plan for my life, to give me a hope and a future (Jer. 29:11).

6. *I can have the mind of Christ and the Spirit of God in me.* I can be transformed, grow, and change by renewing my mind with God's Word and His Kingdom ideals (Rom. 12:2). I can become like Christ and be filled with God's love (1 John 4:13). I can be led completely by the Holy Spirit (Gal. 5:18).

7. *I was created for a purpose. I am significant.* The Lord takes pleasure in me (Ps. 149:4). God created me with specific gifts and talents to contribute to His kingdom and do good (Eph. 2:10). Out of the comfort that God shows me in times of trouble; I am able to bless others (2 Cor. 1:4).

Part III

PARENTS PARTNERING
WITH TEENS

11

SAFE-PLACE PARENTING: PARTNERING SO TEENS WILL TALK, LISTEN, AND CHANGE

> *Grace-based parents spend their time entrusting*
> *themselves to Christ. They live to know God more.*
> *Their children are the daily recipients of the grace these*
> *parents are enjoying from the Lord . . . . They are*
> *especially graceful when their children are hardest to love.*
> —Dr. Tim Kimmel, *Grace-Based Parenting*

EFFECTIVE PARENTING HAS PROVEN TO BE ONE OF THE most powerful ways to reduce adolescent problem behaviors. Teens need their parents' support in their lives, especially while they're going through a difficult time. As a parent, you play a vital role in the recovery and prevention of your teen's depression. Not only can you notice behaviors and symptoms of depression in your teen, but you also have the opportunity to contribute to his progress on a daily basis. You have the crucial responsibility of implementing and overseeing the essential involvement of professional treatment interventions and medications.[1]

When the forty-five minutes of counseling are over, you are the one providing 24-7 care. At home, in the evenings, on weekends . . . at any time, you're the one who must deal with a crisis situation when

203

it comes up. As you have learned from previous chapters, you are the essential foundation for preparing your teen for adulthood, helping him get better, build resilience, prevent relapse, and stay well.

PARENTING STYLES FOR HURTING TEENS

The way a parent approaches and interacts with a hurting teen makes a huge impact on his growth and recovery. Given this truth, most parents want to know the best approaches and styles of parenting. In this chapter, you will discover some of those parenting methods, though this may require a paradigm shift in how you approach being a parent. It may even require you to become more intentional instead of reactive. But it will be well worth it!

Let's begin by highlighting a few helpful parenting approaches that are essential to nurturing your hurting teen.

- You first need an effective plan and goals to properly care for your teen. If you don't have a strategy in place, begin forming one by recognizing your teen's healing needs, where she is developmentally, and her strengths and vulnerabilities.
- You will also need a guide and model for how to relate to your teen during this crucial time. This begins by understanding the heart of God as He models His care for you. The way you experience God's relationship and care toward you will determine how you parent your teen.
- As you parent purposefully and from the heart of God, remember that this is an assignment from God. How you care for your hurting teen is your way of obeying, pleasing, and worshiping Him.
- Finally, a helpful perspective in caring for your hurting teen is to assume the parenting role of life coach and heart shepherd. You are partnering with your teen on her journey to wholeness and adulthood,

helping her develop life skills that she will use for the rest of her life.

PURPOSEFUL PARENTING

Being purposeful in your parenting means daily having a sense of what you're up against, where you're going, and how you plan to get there. Other parents of hurting teens will attest that trying to just wing it or simply doing what comes naturally doesn't work. By being reactive instead of proactive, you allow your teen to take the lead—with potentially disastrous consequences. Here are a few primary goals to keep in mind as you seek to maximize the effectiveness of your parenting.

1. Learn as much as you can about your teen and his struggle.

Become an informed parent who knows about the impact stress and depression is having on your teen. Become an expert of sorts in what challenges your teen. Observe carefully what he is experiencing, and try to put yourself in his shoes to understand his strengths and struggles. Identify the symptoms and triggers for stress and depression in your teen so you can help monitor his progress in getting well.

2. Develop an action plan.

As you learn about what your teen is experiencing and her particular needs, explore a plan for the best course of action and set your priorities. Have purposeful goals for getting there. You may want to include professional input from a therapist or psychiatrist for this task. Work in partnership with these professionals on a treatment plan for your teen, asking for parenting help and tips along the way.

Copy the charts and checklists throughout this book, and use them daily if necessary. Being able to refer to a set of written guidelines will help you from feeling powerless and stressed. Don't stress about being on top of things all the time; you just have to have a sense of direction and a way to take positive action to move toward positive results.

3. Know your role.

It helps as a parent to have the same sense of mission and purpose as you do in other important jobs and assignments. Here are some biblically based parenting models that you can consider including as you write your own expanded parenting job description and mission statement for a hurting teen.

- **Home-based pastoral work.** Listening, observing, teaching, and mentoring teen growth and development.
- **Soul care.** Providing nurture, guidance, and restoration for a hurting and developing teen.
- **Shepherding the heart.** Directing the purposes and heart issues in which God is bringing about lasting change.
- **Servant leading.** Serving God by serving the needs of a hurting teen. Seeing the interruption of turmoil in his life as a divine appointment for ministry and transformation.

4. Grow as a parent and as a person.

To begin with, accept that you are not going to be fully prepared for the challenges of parenting a hurting teen. As a bumper sticker I recently saw says, "Pray for me—I'm parenting a teen." This process will stretch you beyond imagination, forcing you to learn and grow along with your child. Take a parenting class. Get family and parenting counseling. Talk with parents who have gone through raising teens, especially if they have had similar challenges.

This process is not just about accumulating how-to and what-to-do answers for parenting; it's about a deeper expanding of you as a person. Your character, personality, parenting styles, strengths, weaknesses, and past will all be highlighted as you aim to be a positive influence with what God is doing in your teen's life. You will be challenged to become purposeful in your spiritual growth, journeying through your own adversity and crucible as a parent of a hurting teen. Parents who have been through this valley all recall the opportunity they had to grow in their Christian character as they were challenged in the areas of love, patience, kindness, forgiveness, and perseverance.

In his book *Sacred Parenting*, Gary L. Thomas shares that the process of parenting is one of the most spiritually formative journeys a man and women can ever undertake. Thomas says parenting has taught him how to sacrifice, to handle guilt, to listen and pray, to laugh, to grieve, and to live courageously. Parenting can touch us all this way as we face our inadequacies, ultimate needs, and complete reliance on God.

PARENTING FROM THE HEART OF GOD

Our children see a reflection of the heart of God in us as we love, lead, and guide them into a healthy, Christlike life. As parents, our primary model is God the Father and Shepherd. So how does the Lord "parent" us as His children? How does He treat us? How does He ask us to treat others? What would Jesus do in these difficult life situations? What would Jesus say? The answers to these questions provide a foundational model and guide for how we are to parent our teens. The Lord teaches us to love one another as He loves us. He is the model of a wonderful counselor. He sympathizes with our weaknesses and gives mercy and grace to us in our time of need. Based on His perfect example, here are a few suggestions for learning how to parent from the heart of God.

1. Parent out of grace.

Most effective parenting styles embrace fundamental elements of how God loves, approaches, and raises us all as His children. But the styles that mirror God's example the most combine boundaries with care and nurture. Merely enforcing rigid rules and checklists and punishing with fear to ensure good behavior will only lead to emotional injuries and rebellion. Most parents of teens already know this from experience.

Instead, parenting your teen the way God parents you—with love and grace—can set an example for her that models God's secure love and purpose that enables us all to flourish—especially during hard times. This approach communicates:

- God has a purpose and a plan for your life, and He loves you passionately, no matter what.
- You are going to struggle through hard times in life, but don't be afraid; God is with you.
- You will make mistakes and wrong choices, but God will forgive you and restore you.

Living and parenting from God's grace will help you become more grateful and confident, knowing God loves you. The result is growing in humility, love, and compassion toward those hurting and in need. And obviously, this is key to parenting a stressed or depressed teen. As you approach parenting from a grace perspective, you create a safer environment of trust for your teen. This will be much more appealing for him and will make for a healthy, healing environment.[2]

2. Relate to your teen as another believer.

There are many passages throughout the Bible that reveal how the Lord treats us and how He asks us to treat each other. For example, in Ephesians 4:1, we are urged to live the life that God has called us to live. In verse 2, we are urged to always be humble, gentle, and patient, accepting each other in love.

This passage also says we are to make every effort to live in love and peace. That's because it is going to be difficult. There will be times when as a parent, your stressed or depressed teen is going to appear very unlovable as he rejects your love (just as we do to God sometimes). It will take an effort to ask God to give you His love and perspective in order for you to reflect that to your teen. But she desperately needs to know how wide, long, high, and deep the love of Christ is for her. That, in turn, will convince her of your own love.

It is the love of God that draws us all to Him. And your teen needs to know she is loved and accepted by you for who she really is.

If your strong emotions and reactions often get in the way, think about treating your teen as you would another believer. Imagine her as someone who has yet to know God's love and freedom, and whom God has asked you to take into your home and mentor. Often we can get a little too comfortable with those closest to us, not making the effort to do and give our best. Think about how your teen's counselor would treat her. What would her youth pastor say to comfort her? What would Jesus want you to do?

As we serve God, we are to make the most of our opportunities to do what is good for everyone, especially for the family of believers. This great opportunity to serve God has been presented to you in the ordinary, daily ministry to your teen.

3. Parent heart-to-heart.

Our walk with God is all about Him changing us from the inside out and transforming us to become like Him (2 Cor. 3:18). God looks at the heart, and so we should also look at the hearts of our children. He desires for you to guard and cultivate your heart, because it is the wellspring of life. Everything else in life overflows from the heart of a person, and the more Christlike the heart, the more Christlike your life.

In the same way, parenting your hurting teen is all about the heart. Your role is to do everything out of the heart of God; only then can your teen achieve the needed transformation of his inner being. You are a partner with God, given the task to nurture and nourish your child in order that he might fulfill his destiny and please God. As you parent, reach, cultivate, and nourish the heart of your teen, handle it as God would, and align it with the heart of God.

A parent I (Catherine) was counseling recently shared the following: "Early on in parenting I realized that the greatest challenge was going to be me. I realized that I would have to be aware of and accountable for my reactions that so transparently reveal who I really am and who I am becoming. Parenting is all about what God is doing in me and how I am going to grow with my children. I have to deal with my expectations and disappointments, and that terrifies me! I am going to have to parent from my heart—day by day—being flexible to my children's changing needs and adjusting my approach and strategies."

Most parents like formulas, lists, rules, and programs for doing things. You can read all the seven-step methods and how-to books on parenting, but when it comes time to really be a parent, you quickly realize that each child is unique. Likewise, there are no foolproof formulas or pat answers for all the complexities of parenting a hurting teen. You will have to parent from your heart as well as your head. Be flexible each day with each changing need, adjusting your approach and strategies to meet each unique problem. Remember, the value of who you are as a parent and what you do is in who your teen is becoming. Your relationship counts more than anything else, so go for the heart.

4. Use your spiritual gifts in the home.
Christians are to use the gifts entrusted to them by the Lord for the strengthening and encouragement of fellow believers. The primary way we have opportunity to use these spiritual gifts and natural abilities are with those closest in our lives—in the home. The Lord teaches us to have enthusiastic love for one another, to open our hearts and homes and minister to others without complaining. He asks us to be kind, forgiving, tenderhearted, and loving. We are also told to comfort the fainthearted, uphold the weak, and be patient, as the following scriptures emphasize: Ephesians 4:1–3; 4:32; 5:2; 1 Peter 4:9–10; Colossians 3:12–13; 1 Thessalonians 5:11–14.

The Lord wants us to encourage and help those closest to us through times of adversity. Your primary assignment as a parent is to nurture and disciple the teen God has given you. This is your assignment and priority. Don't look down on the day-to-day, mundane tasks of parenting in order to accomplish the extraordinary in your teen. In reality, God's finest work is done when parents simply focus on raising healthy, godly children. To this end, God has given you spiritual gifts to help you encourage your teen. May the following prayer help turn your perspective and heart toward your Father God as your role model.

Jesus, more than anything I want to get to know You more intimately as I go through the challenges facing me as a parent. I want to become more like You, growing in character and in surrender to Your Holy Spirit living in me. Lord, I want to follow Your example as a parent. I need Your wisdom and guidance, because in my humanness I fall short, Lord. I want to be faithful to You in this glorious assignment. I need to know what You would have me do. Empower me today so I will use every situation as an opportunity to think, speak, and act in a way that reflects Your love, grace, and mercy. Amen.

PARENTING AS TO THE LORD

A parent recently shared the following story of an epiphany of sorts she had one day in the kitchen with her daughter. They had been going through a particularly difficult time, and one evening before dinner the daughter approached her mom with an apology: "I'm so sorry for all the trouble I have caused you and Dad. I really don't want to hurt you or be an inconvenience to you the way I have been. I'm really sorry."

Sensing her child's shame and helpless regret, this parent became profoundly aware of a clarity rising to the surface of her fragmented weariness. In the next few moments, a strong, purposeful focus engulfed her. "I forgive you," she replied. "Sure it's been difficult, but we'll get through this. Don't take unnecessary guilt on yourself. My part as your parent is an assignment from the Lord, to partner with Him as best I can. Your part is to learn, grow, and seek what He has for you."

In all we do, we must serve Christ with all our heart, not to impress others or get our "fair share" in return, but simply because we love Him and want to please Him.

IT'S NOT ABOUT YOU; IT'S ABOUT HIM

In Colossians 3, Paul talks about what the Christian home looks like. After instructing wives, husbands, fathers, and bondservants on how they should treat each other, he says this: "And whatever you do, do it heartily, as to the Lord and not to men, knowing that from the Lord you will receive the reward of the inheritance; for you serve the Lord Christ" (3:23–24 NKJV). Rick Warren's best-selling *The Purpose Driven Life* reminds us what life is all about. He doesn't present anything new or profound in this book. And yet the fundamental truth he drives home is so often forgotten. Let's apply this important principle to parenting.

1. It's not about you.

You were created to serve God—and this applies to your being a parent as it does to anything else! Christlike servants (parents) think about the needs of others and let God use them for His purposes. You will walk alongside your teen through his journey, not merely for your own joy and fulfillment, but because you purely desire to see him become everything the Lord has made him to be. Forget that he is an "extension" of you or that he brings you joy and happiness just by being himself. Give up trying to redeem the childhood you never had through him. Don't try to impress others or work out your own problems through your teen. It's not about you; it's about living for God's purpose.

2. It's not about your teen.

Your life and fulfillment don't revolve around your teen. You don't even own her. You are a steward of the assignment to parent her. Sure, you want the best for her, to see her get well and live a happy life. But if you're parenting just for her, you won't get the appreciation, immediate feedback, and results you had hoped for. Until you realize this assignment is for a purpose beyond your teen, you will be unhappy and disappointed.

3. It's about Him.

Remember, the Lord sees what is done in secret. He catches each tear that falls. He is with you when you are going out of your way to sacrifice yourself. He appreciates the effort to extend yourself and lay your life down for your teen's needs, and He promises a reward. Your labor is not in vain but can be offered up as a sweet aroma of worship to the Lord.

LIFE COACHING AND CONSULTING

Now that you have the purpose and heart focus of parenting in perspective, let's talk more about practical parenting styles. Your parenting style will change as your child ventures through each phase of adolescence. Most parents, however, are unprepared for the challenging assignment of reevaluating their parenting stage and style.

As a child moves through the teen years, parents often become frustrated and angry because their parenting methods aren't working as they did before. The teen is no longer responding to the style of parental authority in which you spoke and she simply obeyed. Parents also express feeling frightened, helpless, and angry about the shift in this parenting journey with teens who are struggling emotionally. We encourage you to grow with your teen. Adjust your relationship with her—and your role as a parent—according to her development and needs.

When children are young, parents cater to their needs while also managing and controlling them. Then, as kids become teens, parents move from primarily protecting them from the dangers of life to preparing them to live their lives. The parenting focus shifts from controlling them to influencing them, assuming the roles of life coach and consultant.

Teens who are stressed or depressed will naturally make these shifts also, but it will be a more complicated journey. As a parent, you may have to function in many roles, often going back and forth between managing, consulting, and coaching. Your hurting teen may need extra protection and supervision at times. She may need you to make some decisions with her. She may struggle with intense, conflicting emotions that she expresses through confusing, negative behaviors, simply because she's unable to regulate them. This can be easily misinterpreted and misunderstood if you aren't looking beyond her words and actions.

One of the primary ways parents of hurting teens can have a profound impact is by learning to shift to a healthier and happier parenting style such as "emotion coaching." This is another way of mentoring, discipling, or teaching. This approach enables you to empathize with your teen's emotions. You are better able to label her feelings, help her regulate those emotions and solve problems, set limits on her behavior, and guide her through difficult periods.

FOUR BASIC PARENTING STYLES

John Gottman, a well-respected researcher in the field of relationships, identifies four basic parenting styles in his research on families and the emotional climate in the home.[3] These fit well with the Judeo-Christian approach toward handling hurting teen emotions.

1. *The dismissing parent.* Treats the teen's feelings as trivial and unimportant. Disengages from or ignores the child's feelings. ("Just get over it." "I can't deal with your feelings, so I'll just avoid or dismiss them." "I'm uncomfortable with those feelings, so you'll just have to do what I do.")

2. *The disapproving parent.* Dismisses feelings, judges and criticizes the teen's emotional expression, and tries to demean and suppress her ("You shouldn't feel that way." "Your emotions are wrong, and you should just suppress them.")

3. *The laissez-faire parent.* Freely accepts all emotions, but offers few boundaries and little guidance on what to do. ("Anything goes." "You can run amuck until I've had it, and then I'll lose control.")

These first three approaches deal with emotions in an

unhealthy manner. Unfortunately, they also tend to produce the following negative results in hurting teens:

- Have a hard time trusting their own judgment
- Grow up feeling that something is wrong with them
- Have trouble regulating their own emotions and solving their own problems
- Often lack the ability to calm down when angry, sad, or upset
- Aren't able to use negative emotions and challenges as learning opportunities

4. *The emotion-coaching parent.* Values all the teen's emotions as an opportunity for intimacy and growth. She is aware of her own emotions and can tolerate teen's emotions. These parents empathize and guide their teens.

In contrast to the first three, this parenting style best nurtures your hurting teen's emotional development. It begins with empathy, which is at the heart of caring parenting. By empathizing with your teen's feelings, your teen can learn how to identify, trust, and deal with her emotions in positive ways. It takes some commitment and practice on your part to nurture her emotions, but the result will be noticeable in your teen. Here are some tips as you begin this new approach to parenting.

- Be patient with your teen.
- Be honest with your own emotions.
- Avoid excessive criticism and humiliating, negative comments.
- Avoid calling your teen negative names, specifically ones that label her ("selfish," "jerk," etc.).
- Notice your teen's successes and boost her confidence and self-esteem.
- Empower your teen to experience her emotions, understand them, and regulate them.

BECOMING AN EMOTION COACH

You can learn more about emotion coaching through the resources mentioned in the back of the book. For now, here are the five basic steps the emotion coach follows.

1. Be aware of your teen's emotions.

Make a concerted effort to identify and be sensitive to your teen's feelings. When you show your teen that you care about her, she is more likely to welcome your support during times of anger, sadness, and frustration; and she'll jump at the chance to share with you during times of happiness and laughter.

There are two types of feelings to be aware of: primary and secondary emotions. The deep-down, gut feelings that your teen experiences are primary feelings. These can include deep hurt or rejection. They're often disguised, unclear, and expressed by secondary emotions like anger, aggression, and sadness. When you see these surface reactions, ask yourself, what is underneath these more obvious feelings and behaviors?

With depressed teens, the primary feelings often reflect unmet emotional needs; the secondary are the obvious ones. For example, if your teen is acting unusually selfish, boisterous, or loud, you may interpret her extreme actions as a cry for attention. Beneath the surface of her cry for attention, however, may be feelings of self-doubt, insecurity, or even loneliness.

So how do you become more aware of this in your teen? Start by being aware of and understanding your own emotional makeup. How do you handle your primary and secondary emotions, especially the negative ones like sadness or anger? How do you handle different feelings and emotions at the same time? Gottman's research found that parents who are in touch with their own emotions are better able to relate to those of their teens. When appropriate, share your own emotions. Remember, your teen is learning about emotions by watching you handle yours.

Notice what is causing your teen to be stressed, anxious, or depressed—or, on the other hand, happy and fulfilled. Accept her feelings. Value them and explore them. Try seeing the world through her eyes when she's struggling, and explore ways she can regulate her emotions and problem-solve.

2. Recognize emotional times as opportunities to teach and build intimacy.

Times of intense, conflicting emotional upheaval or outbursts are opportunities to connect and teach your teen life skills and problem solving. In his book *Age of Opportunity*, Paul David Tripp reminds us that "those dark days are meant by God to be times of growth and repentance. These are times when God is exposing the hearts of our sons and daughters for the purpose of rescuing them from the domain of darkness and transporting them to the kingdom of His dear Son . . . We need to see these tough times as huge God-given redemptive opportunities."[4]

This attitude of making the most of the opportunity allows you to enter into your teen's life and become a safe place for him to turn to in times of need. Let your teen know that you accept him, no matter what feelings he has. Assure him that he is not alone, that you are with him to understand and share his feelings. Help him think of solutions to the situation, and allow him to suggest his own ideas. This is how your teen can stay connected and learn.

3. Listen empathetically and validate your teen's feelings.

Listen to your teen's words and actions, using your head and your heart. Let her know you are paying attention and taking her seriously. Your teen needs comfort, understanding, and validation of her feelings. As you listen with empathy and comfort her, she will learn more about how to soothe herself during times of trouble.

Once your teen is done expressing herself, help her get a grip on those feelings using simple statements like, "It hurts when a friend turns on you, doesn't it?" "Fridays seem to be overwhelming and exhausting." "It's a bummer when things don't work out as planned, isn't it?" Reflect back to your teen what you sense her feeling, staying attuned to her emotions without belittling how she's expressed them. A wise strategy is to let your first statement be one of understanding rather than advice. This often defuses any potential defensiveness and turns her problems into opportunities to teach.

4. Help your teen verbally label emotions.

This isn't as easy as it sounds because hurting teens often feel multiple emotions at the same time. Explore the full range of possible emotions with your teen, helping him identify them and validating each one. Develop a rich, accurate vocabulary for emotions, and allow your teen to "name" what he is feeling.

Various studies have shown that verbally naming an emotion has a quieting effect on the nervous system, which can in turn help teens recover faster from emotional stress. This has to do with the brain's structure and how emotions are processed. By verbalizing an emotion, the language area in the left side of the brain is engaged, which also impacts logic and other higher-level types of thinking. Activating the connections between the logic areas and emotional processing areas of the brain may help your teen think about his emotion in a different way, thus leading to a calming effect.

5. Set limits while helping your teen problem-solve.

Never punish your teen for her feelings. The emotions in and of themselves are not the problem; it's how she acts on those feelings and the way she behaves that become the issues. Discipline your teen for what she does, not for what she feels.

You can set limits and boundaries on what are acceptable and unacceptable ways of expressing feelings. Angry feelings are understandable, but destroying other people's property in frustration is not. Stress and frustrations are part of life, but smoking, drinking, or taking drugs is not the most constructive way to deal with it. Ask your teen upfront, "What would be an alternative way to express your feelings and resolve these problems?"

You won't be able to intervene on every "emotional drama," but when possible, slow it down and try to help her explore acceptable solutions. Much of the learning happens in retrospect, rethinking through possible solutions and outcomes to her problems. Talk through what your teen would like to accomplish as you help brainstorm for appropriate solutions, while always valuing her emotions.

THE BASICS FOR LOVING YOUR TEEN

Provide a loving and happy home. Take care of yourself, then your marriage, then your teen. Keep your marriage bond strong and secure. Value your relationship with your teen. Go for the heart. Become a safe place. Love her unconditionally. Model the heart of God as a parent. Give her focused attention. Be there. Enter into her world. Listen to her words, feelings, and her heart. Take your time, use self-control, and respond thoughtfully. Love her with hugs and affection. Grow with her. Say you're sorry. Ask forgiveness often. Forgive always. Take a good look at yourself, and parent intentionally. Pray for her. Become a mentor, a life coach, and a consultant to her. Prepare her for adulthood. Be alert to early warning signs of struggles and trouble. Get help before these become serious. Learn about these problems and how you can be most helpful. Embrace support and prayer. Know God, so you may become a hope giver, applying the life of Christ in everyday life. Live out faith, hope, and love.

12

THE PROPER CARE AND NURTURE FOR HURTING TEENS

*A parent who has his hope in the gospel will pursue his
teenagers and will not stop until they leave home . . . .
With hearts full of gospel hope, we will question and
probe, listen and consider, plead and encourage, admon-
ish and warn, and instruct and pray. We will wake every
day with a sense of mission, knowing that God has
given us a high calling. We are walls of protection
that God has lovingly placed around our teenagers.*

— Paul David Tripp, *Age of Opportunity*

YESTERDAY, THE EXOTIC AFRICAN TORTOISE I (CATHERINE) was taking care of for my sister suddenly died. Besides being a symbol of Africa, he was a charming character with great sentimental value to the family. My friend, Staci, picked him out at a reptile fair, and when my sister, Sharon, adopted him, he could fit in the palm of a hand. Yesterday he was almost too heavy for me to pick up. Although he was only 10 years old, his life expectancy was much longer. We had all enjoyed him and anticipated our grandchildren enjoying him as well. I am still reeling from the loss.

I woke up this morning with a typical day-after reaction, mulling over questions in my head. *What did I do wrong? What did I miss? Had I not properly fed him? What signs and symptoms did I not recognize? What could I have done to care for him better and prevent this?*

And then it struck me that these musings are similar to what parents have to face when finally discovering that the hurt, loss, and problems associated with their teen occurred on their watch. As a parent of a hurting teen, you want to know: What's going on with my teen? Is it normal, or is it serious? What does my teen need? What are the practical ways to intervene and help?

HANDLE WITH SPECIAL CARE

I have been told that it's tricky to know when an African tortoise is not doing well. Tortoises need special care and feeding to survive well in captivity. I knew some of these basics, but obviously not enough to know what was wrong and nurse him to health. I missed something.

In the same way, it's tricky for parents to know whether their hurting teen is experiencing something normal or serious. Depressed teens undoubtedly require some "specialty" of understanding. It is important to learn about stress, depression, and other related problems your teen is experiencing. Earlier in this book, we discussed how you can become aware of the signs and symptoms, and how to go for professional help. We have also explored how you can compliment treatment with effective practical strategies to get well, stay well, build resilience, and prevent recurring episodes of depression.

In this section, we continue to share proven fundamental and essential strategies that will better equip you as a parent in helping your teen overcome stress and depression through your care and nurture.

THE HEALING HEART OF THE HOME

We've talked about the need every teen has for a secure, safe place to go to when hurting or struggling in life. This certainly doesn't change when your child enters the teen years; in fact, it becomes even more needed. Such a relationship and home environment offers her hope for the future and a place where she can flourish in who she is becoming. The bottom line is that you are your teen's most valuable supporter.

BUILDING A SAFE PLACE

Here are the essentials for building a safe-place connection with your teen.

1. Give unconditional love and concern.

When a teen is hurting, he needs triple the amount of love, kindness, and support that he needs when everything is going fine. Go out of your way to be kind and considerate. Bite your tongue when you feel the urge to criticize or, worse still, say, "I told you so!" Spend quality time with your teen. Let him know you are there for him whenever he needs you. Tell him that you love him, and be sure to communicate that with your actions as well.

On the other hand, as one teen suggests, "Don't smother them with overconcern or by micromanaging their lives." Don't panic if at first your teen shuts you out or seems to reject your care. Make small gestures of love toward him and just trust that love wins out in the end—it always does!

2. Offer and create trust.

Relationship is what's most valuable, so go for your teen's heart in establishing trust. Be kind and considerate to his struggles and developmental journey. After all, how can your teen share deep, painful feelings with you if he can't trust you? If you've already broken trust, have hope; it can be restored over time, though usually not as quickly as we'd like.

Be genuine in your interest to learn about your teen's everyday life and how to better partner with him in overcoming daily challenges. Assure him that you will do everything in your power to earn and maintain trust. One way to do that is by being honest and trans-

---

WHAT ARE THE BENEFITS OF A SAFE PLACE?

· Creates a kind, warm, solid relationship between parents who show respect for their children and teens who appreciate their parents.
· Provides unconditional love, regardless of mistakes and wrong choices.
· Teens aren't scorned, judged critically, or dismissed as delinquents with silly feelings.
· Sets firm, caring boundaries for a teen's activities.
· Has a profound effect on teens overcoming the challenges of stress and depression, as well as deterring other possible maladaptive behavior.

---

parent in every area of your life. In case you haven't already discovered, teens don't trust hypocrites! They need to see you practice what you preach. When you make mistakes (notice it's not if), be quick to apologize because this also earns trust.

When your teen can sense that you love him unconditionally, that you have his best interests at heart, and that he matters more than anything else in your life, he will believe and trust you wholeheartedly.

3. Be emotionally available.
Don't underestimate the power of consistently being present in your teen's life. Being present means being available unconditionally, through the good and bad times. It means making your teen a priority and giving her your full attention when you are with her. Even when your teen pulls away, being launched into adulthood, she still cares what you think. She still needs your love and guidance, just in a different way. Don't overreact and take it personally. Stay involved as you slowly let go.

Let your teen know that the communication lines are open, that she can talk about whatever is on her mind, even if she comes home late at night. Commit to being available for your hurting teen. Show her that you're willing to put aside what you are doing to spend time with her. For some parents, this means cutting back on work hours or even taking time off work. Others have had to cut back on social time, hobbies, and recreational activities. Whatever it takes, you need to be there to extend a listening ear, infuse hope, and triple the love and support.

4. Be responsive.

Becoming a safe place for your hurting teen also means being emotionally responsive. Listen objectively and be genuinely involved in your teen's struggles. Be honest about some of the struggles you face yourself as an adult. Although you may have different views, try to take into consideration your teen's perspective. Don't judge harshly or become critical, as this will only make it seem as if you were walking on eggshells around her. When you enter into a conflict with your teen (and this is inevitable), try to be constructive in mending and resolving the conflicts. Be kind and considerate of what she's going through—and then respond to her pain rather than brushing it aside. Ask her how you can be most helpful, and follow through.

LEARNING PARENTAL SELF-CONTROL

It is extremely important that you as a parent exhibit emotional and behavioral self-control. If you cannot control your emotions, don't expect your teen to either. Parents who have been challenged by rough teen years say that being patient and learning emotional self-control—especially with negative emotions like anger, resentment, and guilt—is one of the most important skills they had to master.

Nothing productive ever comes out of reacting from your negative emotions. You only push your teen away when you are angry, to the point where he doesn't feel safe and will begin building walls in the relationship. Emotional overreaction will hurt your relationship with your teenager in several ways.

- Excessive and uncontrolled anger will make it difficult for your teenager to come to you when he wants to talk or get emotional support. You will not be a safe place for him.

- Your emotional overreaction tends to cause your adolescent to trust you less—a very natural response to anyone who lacks self-control. He won't respect you if you're acting like a delinquent teen yourself (especially if you swear or act like most teens do).

- If you are not a safe place your teen will tend to be pushed toward the only other safe place he knows: the influence and comfort of his peers, who won't overreact and will accept him for who he is. This is not necessarily a good thing, as it's possible that your teen's peers are the source of the bad behavior.

THE WAY OF THE SPIRIT

An old African proverb describes a struggle that goes on inside all of us as follows: There are two dogs living inside each of us, who are competing for dominance: human nature and the spirit. The one you feed the most is the one that wins. In Scripture, Paul presents us with the same idea: the "flesh" (our sinful human nature) is struggling against the "spirit" (God indwelling us) to see who will dominate (Gal. 5:17). Paul tells us that the spirit and the flesh are opposed to each other and describes how we are constantly making the choice as to whether we will live the way of the spirit, which is empowered by God's Holy Spirit, or the way of the flesh, our natural human nature. The two cause inner conflict, and only with the strength of God's love and Holy Spirit can we be victorious in making the right choice—that is, to live in the spirit and not the flesh.

When you choose to feed your spirit, it becomes stronger, enabling you to respond and act in ways that reflect the fruits of the Spirit, which are love, joy, peace, patience, kindness, goodness, faithfulness, gentleness, and self-control (Gal. 5:22). But when you don't feed your spirit or choose the higher way, you do what comes naturally. That's when you tend to react in negative ways that Paul describes in verses 19–21—with anger, hatred, selfishness, discord, and resentment. Obviously, these are the things that cause you and your family turmoil.

My mom (Catherine) teaches a simple, biblically based way to remember how to direct yourself to respond and act in a positive way rather than to react in the flesh. Think about how you can apply these to caring for your hurting teen as you become a safe place and a hope giver.

Put up your hand, and starting with your pinky finger, recite each one of these affirmations for each finger:

- Do good to your teen (pinky)
- Bless your teen (ring finger)
- Pray for your teen (middle finger)
- Love your teen (index finger)
- Forgive your teen (thumb)

1. Provide a secure attachment

As we mentioned earlier, emotional bonds among family members are essential to healthy psychological development and functioning. Through attachment bonds, we all develop internal beliefs and attitudes about ourselves, relationships, and ways of interacting based on our early care giving experiences.

John Bowlby, a development psychologist and leading founder of the attachment theory, has greatly contributed to our understanding of interpersonal relationships. After directly observing many children over the years, he suggests four ways of nurturing, bonding, and relating in relationships. The emotional connection between people is known as an "attachment bond" and starts with the parent and child. We are born into the sheltering relationship of our parents and other caregivers, and this is where we are nurtured to grow and learn ways of relating to others.

Your responses to your teen and the way you communicate with her tell her how lovable she is, how lovable she is to others, and how safe the world is. Early interactions between a parent and a child literally create neural pathways for how, as an adult, your child will deal with emotions, express needs, regulate stress, be resilient, and soothe herself. These interactions (along with expectations, beliefs, and values regarding relationships) are internalized and impact how other close relationships become a source of comfort and security or pain and distress. They will even be brought into your child's marriage relationship and the way she parents.

To develop a healthy attachment style, a child must bond with a caregiver who offers consistent nurturance, soothes negative emotions, and tolerates the child's full range of emotions toward herself and others. Conversely, she is at risk for forming an unhealthy internal relating style (which will have long-term impact on other relationships) if her caregiver fails to respond to her emotional distress in a consistent, empathic, and supportive way. This could result in a child developing an "insecure" attachment relationship, which causes her to feel that others cannot be relied upon for help in regulating negative emotions. As a result, she will fail to develop the ability to deal with and regulate negative emotional states and is at risk for depression.

There is a complex interaction between the parent-teen attachment and depression. Teens who report greater attachments to parents report less depression and more positive perceptions of family expressiveness and connection than teens with less secure attachments. Those with an insecure attachment style exhibit many of the signs of depression, including low self-esteem and difficulty with emotional regulation. Remember, your teen will need to connect somewhere—with you and with friends. If she doesn't have a good relationship with you, she is more likely to make poor choices in friends or romantic interests.

2. Stay connected
Research shows that loving parents and connected families (both of origin and extended) are the strongest determinant for reduced levels of emotional distress, drug and alcohol abuse, suicide, and violence among teens.[1]

Staying connected earns trust and the right to influence. Here are a few strategies for building a positive, connected relationship with your teen.

- Spend time with your teen and show your love in direct, not just indirect, ways. Play games, go to a movie with him, go shopping at the mall, or go out to dinner.
- Create a safe place for him to feel shame-free and secure to talk and connect. Edit your "award-winning" lectures to brief summaries.
- Make the most of unexpected opportunities that lead to deep sharing: at bedtime, when he comes home late at night and shares a snack, when he's home sick, when you're shopping together, during a meal, while watching TV.
- Don't get immobilized simply for making mistakes and not being the perfect parent. Learn, forgive yourself, say you're sorry, repair the damage . . . and never give up.
- Show affection, just pick the timing. Even if your teen rolls his eyes and flinches, he still needs physical affection and connection.
- Make the most of the holidays. Make a big deal out of special events such as the prom, homecoming, birthdays, anniversaries, and graduations. Keep and make new traditions. Go on family vacations. Take lots of pictures.
- Laugh a lot, and see the humor in the everyday things around you. Laughter is good medicine. It is also "the shortest distance between two people" and can be a great way of connecting with your teen (as well as helping you manage stress and keep things in perspective).
- Remember, the power of parenthood and caregiving is stronger than biology or peer culture in making your teen's world safer, more joyful, and more meaningful.

Connect with the regressed child and the emerging adult. In the early to mid teens, the developmental process will seem to advance rapidly toward adulthood at times and then regress to childhood at other times. Your teen can act like she's 18 one day, then, before you know it, stage a fit like a 2-year-old. Parents need to connect with both the emerging adult and the regressing child in their teen. Yes, it is confusing, but that's how teens are. This is true of all teens, not only stressed or depressed teens.

Stressed, anxious, or depressed teens might vacillate between these two extremes more frequently and with more intensity. Some will regress more often, wanting the comfort and ease of childhood. You might be disappointed (fathers usually are), thinking your teen should "grow up and act her age." Be assured that this is typical. So be flexible and sensitive to meet your teen where she is, responding in ways that are comforting and necessary for her security.

Some teen regressive behaviors include starting to suck their thumbs again; watching cartoons; or turning to their transitional objects such as old toys, stuffed animals, and "blankies." There is nothing wrong with these regressive behaviors, as long as they are temporary. Let them act silly with younger siblings or do appropriate childish things like ordering a happy meal and enjoying the free toy. This oscillation of emotional and behavioral maturity is a normal part of development. However, if at any time it seems a little over the edge or gets serious, consult a professional counselor.

Connecting may be difficult, so be willing to adjust. It gets old trying to hug a porcupine or talk to a mute teen. Some hurting teens just aren't interested in being connected the way their parents want them to be. For these parents, this can be painful, lonely, and even feel abusive.

It can help to know your teen's unique love language—that is, the way your teen expresses his love. Teens differ here. In fact, if you have more than one teen in your household, you can probably attest to how different they can be. Some might hug you after getting over their hurt, while others want to tease you. Each has a unique way of demonstrating love and affection.

In the same way, learn your teen's frustration language. When teens are stressed out, they can be irritable and often reject any effort to approach them. What we think is helpful can be downright irritating to them. Parents can take this rejection very personally, but don't. Personality styles, physical space, and other differences play into this as well. Remember, you are the adult. Act like it!

When you try to be there for your teen in a way that is imposing, that doesn't match his needs or love language, he will often feel misunderstood and even rejected. While it seems you are doing all the right things for your teen, be aware of the much deeper issues surfacing. Growing up is not a straightforward, trouble-free process. It can be frightening for both teen and adult. It takes a lot of emotional discipline on a parent's part not to get caught up with feelings of rejection or not being appreciated.

3. Listen when your teen talks.

In *Life Together*, a book about how we are to live in community, Dietrich Bonhoeffer says that "the first service that one owes to others . . . consists in listening to them." He goes on to suggest that if we stop listening to one another, we will soon not be listening to God either.

If listening to one another is important to begin with, then listening to our children—especially teens in distress—must be even more important. Your hurting teen needs a listening ear and an open heart. Be available and make time to interact with her. She needs your focused attention. Though it may be hard, avoid criticizing or passing judgment once she opens up and starts talking with you about her feelings. The key is for you to just listen.

Here are some ways you can fine-tune your listening skills.

- **Listen to and understand your teen's heart.**
  - Focus on listening, and keep your mouth shut unless you have thought through and filtered what you want to say.
  - Don't lecture or offer unsolicited advice or ultimatums as your immediate response.

- Use good communication tools such as open-ended questions to continually engage your teen in the discussion.
- Don't try to talk her out of her feelings.
- Observe her behavior and actions. These are just as important forms of communication as her words.
- Go for the heart. Reach for the "real" teen inside, and connect with where she lives.

- **Listen to and understand your teen's interests.**
  - Talk and listen during her "down periods" of everyday life—when she's hanging out in her room, getting ready for bed, or coming home from being out at night.
  - Include her in making decisions. Ask for her opinion so she feels valued and important.
  - Spend more time with her doing what she's interested in. Get involved in her activities.
  - Listen to her music and ask what she likes about it.
  - Take her to movies and concerts, and talk about them afterward.
  - Know her friends and listen to them as well.

- **Make it safe for your teen to open up.**
  - Create an emotional "holding environment"—a shame-free zone for talking and emotionally connecting.
  - Show your teen that disagreements and painful feelings can be safely expressed and resolved.
  - Allow her to share feelings of confusion, sadness, loneliness, shame, and other strong emotions. Once she opens up and starts sharing, it makes way for real communication and decreases the intensity of holding these feelings inside, which can contribute to depression.

A WORD OF ADVICE TO FATHERS

As teens go through ups and downs, so do their dads. The National Center for Fathering shows that fathering satisfaction reaches its lowest level during the teen years. However, fathers still have a crucial role in teen development. Fathers provide hope and purpose. The challenge for them is finding the balance between being supportive and caring, while still monitoring behavior and enforcing family rules.[2]

While we were speaking at a family conference in Pietermaritzburg, South Africa, my (Catherine) teen daughter shared her insights with the fathers:

Children crave acceptance and attention. A lack of this will leave them hungry and weak. They see their father's role the same as God's. Focus on what you want your child to focus on. Feed your attention to the good in her. Have a real honest relationship with her (like a friend) and not just a "father." Be willing to show your weakness as well. You will not be seen as a failure, but a model for how we all need to act. If you do not, your child will also want to hide her areas of weakness. This will create low self-esteem and will interfere with her knowing herself honestly. She will be guarded and become strong-willed to protect herself, rather than strong in character.

- **Be understanding and empathetic.**
  - Don't overreact and vent your anger or other negative emotions toward your teen. If you do, say you are sorry and mend things when they go wrong.
  - Don't judge her, shame her, or reject her. None of these things are helpful. Although you may not understand, agree with, or approve of her thoughts

or actions, she still needs your unconditional love and support, no matter what she has done wrong.

- Although her perspective might be distorted and catastrophic, don't brush it off with "That's ridiculous," or, "You shouldn't feel that way." Instead, tell her you're sorry she feels that way, and you can imagine how hard it must be. ("I admit I don't understand the pain or feelings you're experiencing, but I will love you and support you through this time.")

- **Be honest and sincere about yourself and in the way you relate.**
  - Share how you made mistakes and how the Lord is working in your life.
  - Admit that you are growing on this journey together, and that you're committed to learning, growing, and changing.

4. Be a hope giver

Show me some hope! It's the heart cry of every hurting teen. Parents, therefore, must be hope givers. The reason your teen craves hope is that she feels helpless, which always leads to hopelessness when life situations get scary and there seems to be no way out. With all the negative stuff going on in your teen's life, who can she turn to for hope? What can she hope in? Deep down inside, she may be saying to herself, "Is there really any hope for me, or am I a lost cause?"

Our culture offers a pseudo-hope that is temporary. Mostly it is wishful thinking, unrealistic dreaming, and empty distractions. True hope and purpose is founded on knowing God and understanding that these temporary struggles will soon pass. There is a hope and a future because God keeps His promises and will never leave us or forsake us. He has also promised to use the hard times to make us stronger.

This isn't just optimism for optimism's sake. It's the truth, and it's the message and attitude we need to convey to our teens. Effective parent leaders live in the balance of reality and possibility. Expect the best in and for your teen—and help her to adopt the same hope. Being a hope giver means you don't catastrophize the hard times. It means you can take strength in knowing that you will come through these challenging times with God's help. When your teen sees you walk out this attitude and faith, she will feel more prepared to face the tough times. By refusing to take the setbacks so hard, she will build her confidence in her own progress.

Ways to build hope in our teens include:

- Smile more at your teen.
- Let him hear you speak of and see you experience the hope you have in God and in His promises.
- Be a positive reflection of who your teen is becoming. Help him figure out goals.
- Talk about the future with optimism. Encourage his dreams to discover purpose beyond typical teen self-absorption. Provide opportunities for him to explore the world and find a calling.
- Praise him daily for his progress, or for anything you can see that is positive. Don't wait until he has it all together. He will progress forward, and he will have setbacks—that's part of growing up and getting well. Focus on his progress, even if it's small.
- Look for character traits you can praise (honesty, responsibility, trustworthiness, thoughtfulness, patience, courage, diligence, genuineness, etc.).
- Turn the most difficult situations into learning opportunities. Every challenge is a chance to learn and grow.

5. Establish boundaries and discipline

Research shows that positive discipline, monitoring, and supervising boundaries are also important factors in preventing and facilitating stress recovery and depression in teens. Get to know your teen's friends and the activities she is involved in. "If you love your children, you will correct them" (Prov. 13:24). This models the way God parents us because the Lord corrects those He loves (Rev. 3:19), just as parents correct the child they delight in (Prov. 3:12). He loves us too much to leave us the way we are.

Pick your battles or you'll be battling all the time. Decide what the most important issues are to stay on top of and where the boundary lines need to be drawn for your teen. Choose what matters and what's not worth making a big deal about. A recent nationwide survey of parents conducted by the Barna Group offered some surprising insight. When parents were asked if they were more likely to battle their children over every issue that emerged in order to establish control or limit those battles to particular issues they deemed significant, three out of every four parents took the "pick your fight" approach.

If you say no to everything, your teen will feel oppressed and frustrated. If you say yes to everything, you become a pushover and lose all disciplinary control. So there must be a balance and willingness to reasonably compromise. You may be tempted to take Mark Twain's suggestion and lock your teen in a barrel, feeding him through a hole until he's eighteen. But unless you want to go to jail, here are some general—and far more realistic—guidelines to follow:

- *Be firm on the issues that have lasting moral significance and long-term negative consequences.* For instance, drugs and drinking are out. God's clear-cut instructions must be obeyed. Delay your teen from making major decisions while depressed, such as running off to get married or dropping out of school with no other plans.
- *Be more lenient on matters that do not have lasting moral implications.* No matter how much you may detest the idea, body piercing (within reason), hairstyle (and color), or clothing fashions (within the bounds of

modesty) can have minimal moral consequences, so a compromise may be permissible for some families.

- Be flexible in matters where circumstances vary. Enforcing a bedtime might be important during exam times but no big deal at other times. While rest and sleep recovery is essential for a stressed and depressed teen, be open to allowing him late nights every now and then. Your teen will appreciate your flexibility.

What issues are important for you to monitor and set boundaries for your teen? Which ones can you be lenient on, and which ones are nonnegogtiable? Here is a list you can review from time to time, asking yourself, "Do I put my foot down, do I reconsider, or do I let it go?" Remember, as your teen matures and becomes well, you might become more flexible, and the answer may depend on other circumstances at the time:

__ Basic self-care (eating, sleeping, exercise)
__ Curfew limits
__ Body piercing
__ Tattoos
__ Keeping a clean room
__ Choice of friends
__ Swearing and talking back
__ Secular music and movies
__ Lying to parents
__ Hairstyles and styles of clothes
__ Chores around the house
__ Doing homework and grades at school
__ Drinking
__ Smoking
__ Using drugs and other illegal substances
__ Being sexually active
__ Being on birth control
__ Being involved in a serious dating relationship

__ Choice of where your teen goes, what he does, who he goes with
__ Having to know where he is at all times—a phone number, address, etc.
__ Allowance, how much money he receives and how it is spent
__ Use of the car or having his own car
__ Going to church with you or to a church of his choice
__ Not being forced to go to church if he doesn't want to
Others:

_____

_____

_____

_____

_____

Discipline styles for hurting teens. Because depression symptoms can cause teens to easily feel negative about themselves, harsh discipline can be harmful to a depressed teen because it compounds these feelings. While troubled teens can be frustrating and even infuriating to parents, they must be handled with care. Take into account the demoralization that your hurting teen already feels, and move your strategy toward being more considerate of these feelings.

Here are the two most successful forms of discipline and how they apply to stressed and depressed teens.

1. *Discipline through natural consequences.* This is an important way for all kids to learn important life lessons. Basically, it follows the biblical principle that we reap what we sow. Every action has a consequence. Teens can't learn this from a book. Every teen has to discover on his own that he can make good and bad things happen as a result of his choices and behaviors, and that he is in control of his life and actions. This is a hard lesson for parents to allow their teens to learn, but it builds maturity and authentic self-esteem.

There is a balance, however. Let your teen learn on his own—to a point—while also monitoring whether he is at risk for danger. Depressed teens tend to not think ahead of the consequences of their actions. Your child may act impulsively, be oblivious, or think he is exempt from natural laws; and the only way he will learn to control it is to "reap what he sows." Obviously, you should intervene in worst-case scenarios. But, as difficult as it is to stand by and watch, your teen will never begin to feel the impact his choices have until he feels the brunt of a bad one.

Actually, the rest of the tortoise story fits here. Not long after my (Catherine) sister's tortoise died, she spoke with her gardener who knows a lot about tortoises and knew ours for years. He speculated that the tortoise might have eaten something poisonous in my garden while wandering around. He ate something he didn't know was harmful for him, and neither did I. The point is we can't always be there to jump in the middle of every situation and save our teens from making bad decisions. We can't always prevent them from running into dangerous situations, or from slamming headfirst into the natural inevitable challenges of life. Some of their choices will result in hard lessons learned; others will have more lasting ramifications.

It's the bad decisions that will have far-reaching, painful consequences that you want to prevent. These are the ones in which you should intervene. Going to jail for breaking the law is a serious consequence, but better avoided, as is getting pregnant, becoming addicted to drugs, or getting expelled from school. You can bring your child home from the hospital, but you can't bring them home if they have to go to jail. If you are aware of any behavior that could lead to serious consequences, take action so that these consequences can be avoided.

2. *Discipline through logical consequences.* The idea here is to try to teach, usually through logic, ways your teen can learn the connection between his choices and his actions and behaviors. This is not punishment. It is discipline in as much as your teen is learning that when he chooses to go outside of the rules, boundaries, family contract or law, there are also consequences.

For example, by choosing to violate a curfew, your teen also chooses to lose his freedom to drive the car. Or if he won't put his helmet on while skating (even though you have nagged him repeatedly), then he forfeits skating for a prearranged time period. Good discipline spells out the consequences ahead of time and then enforces the rules without question. No anger, just plain action.

The challenge in using this form of discipline with a depressed teen is that he doesn't, or can't, think about the consequences you have set up. He simply doesn't care. He lives for the moment, for the pleasure or escape it can offer. His internal motivation for keeping boundaries is extremely low.

Parents are often baffled at how irresponsible a teen can seem. After five skateboarding-no-helmet violations, you'd think the boy would get it! After the first one he should have gotten the message. But he didn't care; he just kept skating without a helmet. Only when he has to get a part-time job to pay for the tickets he receives will he realize what he has done. And only his regret will motivate him even then. Yet perhaps this is what it will take for your teen to start putting his helmet on when he skates.

6. Don't give up—pray!
In parenting your hurting teen, you may have reached a point where you want to just give up, close your heart permanently, and shut out your teen. Parents often say that this is the time when they feel they have to reach outside of themselves, when they cry louder and longer. But it's also the period when they realize that prayer is essential for help and hope.

Whether God ushers in the miracle of healing or the miracle of bringing peace to your mind, He hears our prayers and the cries of our heart. If you are feeling overwhelmed and desperate about your family situation, remember, just when you think all is lost, there is always hope.

NEVER GIVE UP HOPE

Never give up hope for your teenager, no matter how hopeless things appear. Never give up hope for your family. Never give up hope for the future. Without this future, there is nothing in which to hope!

In this life, we won't win all the battles, and we will experience loss and pain. You might be at your end, desperately praying for God to reach your teen, wondering if she will ever come through this turbulence. In case you think all is lost and want to give up, seek God in prayer first, because there might still be a little life left yet for God to do a miracle.

I (Catherine) once read about the "miracle dog." She got that name because the veterinarian couldn't believe what this dog had gone through. Dosha was hit by a car and then shot in the head by a police officer to put her out of her misery. Presumed dead, she was put in a freezer at an animal control center. Two hours later, when the vet opened the door to the freezer, Dosha was standing upright in the plastic orange body bag. At the time I read this story, it was reported that she was in fine spirits, doing amazingly well considering what she had been through.

Dosha's story struck me as an incredible picture of how parents can feel during the turbulent journey with their hurting teen. Your situation can leave you feeling beat up, shot to death, and put away as "stone cold." Yet the Lord so profoundly reminded me that He is capable of doing miracles in many situations and people's lives. Even when you think it is all over, there is still a spark of life yet.

We want to encourage you to be hopeful. Be persistent in fasting, praying, reading the Word, and worshiping. Jesus had victory at the cross, and He will have victory on the final day. For now, your part is to turn to Him in prayer to battle on your behalf during painful and fierce struggles. And as you trust and have faith in God, the Holy Spirit is preparing a kingdom victory. Anticipate God to breathe life and do miracles in you and in your teen's life.

13

HOW TO PRAY
FOR YOUR TEEN

Praying always with all prayer [conversation
with God, hope] and supplication [pleas and requests]
in the Spirit, being watchful to this end with all
perseverance [determination, resolve, insistence] . . .
—Ephesians 6:18 (NKJV; meanings added)

It is during suffering that we learn to pray our most
authentic, heartfelt, honest-to-God prayers. When we're
in pain, we don't have the energy for superficial prayers.
—Rick Warren, *The Purpose Driven Life*

GOD HAS A REDEEMING PURPOSE BEHIND THE PROBLEMS
your teen is going through and the struggles you are having parenting him. Though He doesn't enjoy watching you agonize through the process, He still uses it to develop character in you, so you can become more like His Son, Jesus. At the same time, your difficulties present a prime opportunity for you to draw closer to the Lord. When your heart is broken, and you feel desperate and all alone, that is when you can turn to God for your hope and comfort. There is no better way to do this than through prayer.

Prayer is basically spending time with God and being in conversation with Him. It's sharing what is on your heart, listening, and receiving His response. Prayer is simply being with God—

inviting and being aware of His presence in your life, and turning your awareness and thoughts towards Him.

BE IN CONSTANT CONVERSATION WITH GOD

This relationship of prayer can be shared and expressed in so many ways. You can utter short, one-sentence silent prayers throughout the day. *Lord Jesus, have grace and mercy on me. Help me, God, to know what to say and do. Lord, may Your perfect heavenly ways be done in my teen's life. Protect and heal my teen, Lord. Fill me with Your love and Holy Spirit; I need Your presence in my life.* You can also communicate thoughtfully and specifically by using Scripture as your guide to formulate prayerful conversation with God. Or you can simply talk, as if you were talking to a neighbor. No one knows you as well as God, so there's nothing you can't share with Him.

However you converse with God, there is power in prayer. The Lord desires that you pray not because He needs to have you ask for things, but so you can partner with Him as He moves around your circumstances. Prayer can change things in you as well as in your teen's life. In his book *With Open Hands*, Henri Nouwen states, "Those who live prayerfully are constantly ready to receive the breath of God, and to let their lives be renewed and expanded."[1]

We want to encourage you to make prayer a priority, to draw close to God so He can draw close to you. Take all your cares to Him, surrendering your heart, your teen, and the circumstances in your lives. He wants to show you grace and mercy in your time of need. He desires to bring healing and wholeness to your body, mind, and hurting broken heart—and, of course, to every part of your teen.

Yet never forget that prayer is not just you talking to God. He desires to talk to you just as much. Listen so you can hear His heart and receive His life that renews and transforms. Feel his love for you. Hear His soft whispers of comfort. When you are tired and burdened, He will give you true rest.

Remembering the importance of prayer throughout the process

of your hurting teen's healing, we offer the following reflections on prayer. Consider this as a supplement to your own prayer conversations with God. We offer meaningful words that you can pray for yourself and your teenager not because this is exactly what you should be praying, but because we know at times we all need direction to formulate specific, purposeful prayers. Interwoven in these prayers, we suggest you just sit quietly, by yourself, allowing God to draw close, comfort, and encourage you.

DON'T WORRY; PRAY

Let's begin by taking a look at several reasons why prayer is important.

1. Pray for your teen and your own peace of mind.

Your teen needs you to pray for her. If you don't pray for her, who will? Without being covered by prayer, it's easy for your teen to feel abandoned. When you pray for her, do it as if you are interceding for her life—because that's exactly what you are doing. "Get up, cry out in the night, even as the night begins. Pour out your heart like

---

A PRAYER FOR PARENTING A HURTING TEEN

Lord, help me communicate love, understanding, grace, hope, and life to my teen. Empower my efforts at parenting with the power of Your presence. Teach me to relate calmly and confidently. Lead me as I correct in a spirit of acceptance, forgiveness, and hope. Build the connection between my teen and I, so I can enjoy his presence and so he will feel safe to talk about things that other teens hide or ignore. And as our relationship deepens, may he progressively become well, maturing and taking on the character of Christ.

In Jesus' name, amen.

water in prayer to the Lord. Lift up your hands in prayer to Him for the life of your children" (Lam. 2:19).

We show great care and nurture for our hurting teens when we give them what they need by surrendering them to the Lord and upholding them in prayer. Medical science has even proven the remarkable effectiveness of praying for others who are ill and struggling. They recover, get well, and make it through their ailing much more rapidly, and with much greater progress. By covering your teen in prayer, you further her healing.

"Anyone who is having troubles should pray" (James 5:13). "Do not worry about anything, but pray and ask God for everything you need, always giving thanks. And God's peace . . . will keep your hearts and minds in Christ Jesus" (Phil. 4:6–7).

Prayer and peace of mind are closely connected. When we share our concerns with God, then our hearts and minds will be calmed and assured by the peace of God. We can receive great help and support from friends, counselors, and books, but nothing will give us the powerful peace and inner strength like being with God.

2. Don't battle alone—get prayer support.

While you are going through a difficult season of parenting a hurting teen, it's crucial to get support by asking others to pray for you. Surround yourself with those who will help strengthen and sustain you. Ask for prayer at church or through prayer chains. Share your struggles with friends and family, receiving comfort and encouragement.

A dear friend of mine, Dr. Beth Fletcher Brokaw, is battling cancer. She has written several short essays on her tumultuous journey that are profoundly encouraging to anyone going through a difficult time. Here is an excerpt from one of those essays:

> Whether we are encountering cancer, ex-spouses, hurting children, crusty parents, cranky neighbors, crazy bosses, or spiritual powers beyond our visibility, we need to connect with each other. We need some comradeship along life's journey. . . . I

read recently that the American troops have one supply soldier for every "fighting" soldier. Yes, I think the workable ratio should be at least one-to-one—or much greater. That's the reality of battle. The number of support and supplies needed are extremely high when sustaining someone in the midst of a raging battle. . . . In truth, I have had a cavalry of supporters around me—friends and family. . . . In life, we are always both the ones in need and able to help others. I have a card some-one gave me with the caption: "We give comfort and receive comfort sometimes at the same time."

Utilize a variety of resources that can build you up, equip you, and encourage you. Read books or link up with Internet ministries and resources. Attend worship services, classes, and gatherings with other believers. No matter how much you think you can be a lone ranger in this process, the truth is that you need the support of others.

PRAYERS FOR HURTING TEENS

You will want to cover your teen with prayer for everything and anything that comes to your mind, for every aspect of his life. To help guide you, here are some major things for which you can pray.

1. Pray for wisdom and direction on what to do.

Parents of hurting teens frequently struggle with knowing how to deal with difficult situations that come up. My daughter has bad-influence friends in her life. What should I say? Should I be stern and put my foot down? My son habitually lies and deceives me. How should I handle this? My son isn't doing well in school. He isn't happy and doesn't want to go. What do I do?

Unfortunately, there is no step-by-step manual to follow when parenting hurting teens. There are some basic guidelines and principles, but every child's needs are customized to them. And with every situation that comes up, there are on-the-spot decisions and responses to be made. This aspect of parenting is stressful,

A PARENT'S PRAYER FOR WISDOM AND DIRECTION

O Lord, help me to know what is the right thing to do. How should I respond? I am winging it as each challenging situation comes up and catches me off guard. I don't always know what the best thing is to do. There are just no absolutes for each situation, so I need the guidance of Your Holy Spirit and your revelation to me. Please show me the way. Give me wisdom, insight, and the right words to say to my teen. May I be led by your empowering love and the gifts of Your Spirit. I know that You love her so much more than I do, and Your desire for her is to have a hope and a future. May Your will be done in her life, and may I be effective to accomplish what You need me to do in her life in this situation. Have grace and mercy on us in our time of need, and lead us in the way we should go.

In Jesus' name, amen.

especially when you don't have the answers or don't know the best thing to do.

There is good news: the Holy Spirit was sent to be your guide in all things. You can ask for wisdom, guidance, and direction. Invite the Holy Spirit to lead your every step. At the same time, talk to the counselor, your pastor, or other parents who have gone through similar challenges, and ask them how God guided them. Many times hearing others' stories helps us recognize God's direction in our own lives.

2. Pray for your teen's healing and development.
As you pray over your teen's development, use the chart in chapter 2, committing to the Lord areas that you discern they need to mature and become stronger in. Also pray for your teen's healing journey by using the Wellness Building Chart in chapter 8 as a guideline, interceding for areas where they need to change and be strengthened.

PRAYING PSALM 23 FOR YOU,
YOUR FAMILY, AND YOUR TEEN

The Lord is my shepherd.
You are our protector, God. You watch over me and my loved ones and take care of us. We are under Your care, therefore I have absolute and peaceful confidence in You, Lord. You love us so much that you even gave Your life for us.

I shall not want.
Everything that we really need, You, Lord, will provide and take care of. With that assurance, I give all my cares and needs regarding my life and my teen to You, not worrying about anything. Instead, I will be thankful and have assurance with a peaceful heart and mind.

He makes me lie down in green pastures.
When I look to You, God, as my resource, You provide the best environment for spiritual food and resources for my restoration and recovery.

He leads me besides still waters.
You give me peace, Lord, as I trust You, taking everything to You in prayer. You calm my mind and heart. You also quench my thirst for deep spiritual intimacy, fulfillment, and meaning—as You do for my teen and loved ones.

He restores my soul.
Lord, thank You for daily renewing and restoring my inward being, my anxious, weary soul. You give me hope. You repair and heal the places in me, my teen, and loved ones that are hurt, damaged and not well. Lord, restore and renew me deep in my heart where only You can see—as well as my teen and loved ones. (Pray for specifics.)

He leads me in paths of righteousness for His name's sake.

Lord, You guide me and give me wisdom to know what is good and right, what is Your will and plan for my life as well as my teen and loved ones.

Yea, though I walk through the valley of the shadow of death.

Lord, I know there are going to be difficult, dangerous, and challenging times in this life—that I'm going to have to go through, and so are my loved ones. And it is going to be scary and dark. The shadow will dampen our joy and we will feel low and far from the mountain top experiences. But Your divine presence will always be with us. I pray that I and my loved ones are able to recognize how You are with us and be comforted, encouraged, and hopeful.

I will fear no evil.

I know evil is real, and all around us. That the enemy wants to see me and my family be destroyed. But I will have courage and not be overwhelmed because You are greater than any evil. The battle is Yours, and You will be victorious.

For You are with me.

As we go through these trials, Lord, I know we are not alone. Your presence will always be with us, God. Even when we feel distant, and not aware of Your presence—You are still there—wanting to care for us, to lead and guide us. Minister to us through many caring people. Fight for us so we can be victorious and overcome.

Your rod and Your staff, they comfort me.

Lord, You have promised that You will protect, defend, and guide us. You have compassion on us, deep empathy for us, and console us through all the challenges in life. It is so comforting to know that as I release my teen and family to You,

You will be their protector and guide, reassuring and consoling them along their journey.

You prepare a table before me in the presence of my enemies.
And when we come through trials, Lord, You will lovingly provide abundantly for us. You encourage us, Lord, with your kindness, generosity, grace, and mercy. Your presence in our life is evident.

You anoint my head with oil.
You, Lord, will show favor to us as Your children, and treat us with warmth, kindness, and generosity. You will cover and wash all the wounded places in our life with Your healing oil. Lord, I pray particularly for healing in myself, my teen and my family in these ways. (Pray for specifics.)

My cup runs over.
My life is so full of blessings and things I can be thankful to You for, Lord. You nourish us with what we need. And the grace and mercy that you have shown to me and my loved ones is the blessing that I can share with others to be an encouragement.

Surely goodness and mercy shall follow me all the days of my life.
I can be confident, Lord, that your unfailing, steadfast, covenant loving-kindness is always going to be part of my life, my teen's, and my family's lives. You will complete the good work You have begun.

And I will dwell in the house of the Lord forever.
My desire is like David's, Lord, to stay in a close personal relationship with You, living continually in Your presence, feeling safe and secure, experiencing Your rest. Through all the hard times and abundant blessings of life, I can be confident that You have an eternal home waiting for me with You, my Shepherd, for eternity. I pray that my teen and loved ones will all be together forever in Your presence worshipping You.

PRAYING THE LORD'S PRAYER
FOR YOU, YOUR FAMILY, AND YOUR TEEN

Our Father in heaven, hallowed be Your name.
Praise and Thanksgiving—Our need for a parent and God's presence
I come humbly into your presence, Lord. Thank You that I can come with confidence and faith that I have a relationship with You, that I am Your child because of the blood of Jesus. I need Your presence, power, and provision in my life and in my teen's. You are Holy God and worthy of my absolute devotion. Work Your holiness, purity, love, mercy, and grace in me—and in my loved ones. I worship and praise You in all aspects of my life. I come to You with an attitude of gratitude, a heart full of thankfulness for . . . .

Your Kingdom come. Your will be done on earth as it is in heaven.
Intercession—God's priorities for our life
Father God, may Your perfect heavenly ways happen in our broken world and lives. I choose to invite and declare Your kingdom living priorities in myself and in my loved ones, friends, community, church, and nation. I welcome the over-ruling power of Your presence into the situations in my life and my teen's life to transform seemingly impossible circum-stances. (Pray for special needs.) I give You my fears, worries, troubles, struggles. I will be still and wait on You.

Give us this day our daily bread.
Personal Petitions—Direction for the day and God's provision
I fully commit myself and the day before You, Lord. Reveal Your perfect plan for this day in all I do and as I parent my teen. I will follow and obey Your direction. I come dependent upon You, Lord, needing insight and wisdom for each situa-tion. Please fill me with Your Holy Spirit. May I do all things

today in the power of Your love. I know that You provide and meet my basic needs. And so, Father, I ask for . . . . (pray for specific requests).

And forgive us our sins, as we forgive those who sin against us.
Repentance and Forgiveness—Receiving freedom through God's forgiveness and forgiving others
Lord, help me to walk in love and forgiveness toward my teen and others. Search my heart, Lord, and help me be honest and keep my life clean. I forgive (insert name) for the wrong they did to me and to my loved ones. I release all resentment and my right to get revenge. Forgive me for the wrongs I have done. (Confess sins.) Thank You for Your forgiveness and freedom.

And lead us not into temptation, but deliver us from evil.
Protection for Our Life—Power over evil, victorious life over barriers
Preserve my family with Your mighty power that we won't fall into sin or be overcome by adversity. And in all we do, direct us to the fulfilling of Your purpose. Help my loved ones and me to learn to obediently walk in Your ways. Strengthen our weaknesses. God, lead us to victory in moral tests. I surrender my will and my desires, and I pray that they do as well. Lord, I pray a hedge of protection about myself and loved ones. I put on the armor of God so I can stand against the enemy.

Yours is the kingdom and the power and the glory forever, amen.
Divine Partnership—Hope and security for the future
The battle is Yours, Lord. I trust You and have faith in You that You are able. You are all-powerful, and You will help us get through these turbulent times. I rest in complete submission to You, Lord. I put my hope in You for today, for the future, and forever.

LISTENING PRAYER

Lord, I am still before You, listening for Your voice. I wait on You, receiving Your presence and Your Holy Spirit to minister to me.

(Write down what you sense God is speaking and confirming to your heart.)

_____

_____

_____

_____

_____

_____

_____

---

3. Pray using the Word of God.

The Lord instructs us to pray always, about everything. In other words, we are to be in constant conversation with God, including Him in every aspect of our lives. There are many examples in the Bible of how to intercede in prayer during troubled times and do battle for our loved ones. God instructs us to pray "in the name of Jesus" because He has all authority over the enemy. We are to declare the blood of Jesus over our teen as we pray, which signifies protection from evil.

The Bible also teaches us to fast as we pray in zeal for breakthrough. Often our prayers may be more about a heart's cry than words, and when we don't have the words to express our feelings, the Holy Spirit intercedes for us (Rom. 8:26). By bringing our heartfelt requests to God, we can be thankful and give praise for His promises and assured victory.

PRAYING BLESSINGS OVER YOUR TEEN

The Priestly Blessing (Numbers 6:24–26)

The Lord bless you and keep you.
May the Lord increase your prosperity and keep you from harm.
The Lord make His face to shine upon you, and be gracious to you.
As you worship God, may the Lord take pleasure in you and be compassionate, merciful, and kind to you as you heal, mature, and grow.
The Lord lift up His countenance upon you
and give you peace.
May you sense God's presence in your life, being confident and having peace of heart and mind that He will provide all that is necessary for your well-being.

Other Prayer Ideas:
Paul's Prayer—Philippians 1:9–11
Prayer for Love—Ephesians 3:16–19
See the "Additional Resources" list in the back of this book for additional guidance to help you pray for your teen.

Whether we have words, tears, or simply a heart full of thanks, one of the most effective prayer strategies is to pray the Word of God. When struggling through difficult times and overcoming the enemy, Jesus overcame by praying scriptures. Ask the Lord to bring to your mind specific verses that apply to your situation. Over the years, the Lord has led me (Catherine) to develop expanded prayers from some of the most well-known and loved Bible-based prayers, blessings, and promises. These have been instrumental in my times of interceding and pouring out my heart in spiritual conversation

MAGNIFICENT SEVEN PROMISES OF GOD

God's Word gives us great and powerful promises of His love, provision, and direction for your life and that of your teen. These Magnificent Seven Promises of God will help you and your teen focus your mind and self-talks on God's truth and His loving faithfulness for you. By keeping God's perspective on life through His promises, you can be encouraged and comforted to persevere in hope through the pressures you are facing.

Promise #1: Protection and Provision
God will watch over my loved ones and me when we go through temptations and hard times. I will not be afraid because God will defend and guide us, keeping us safe. He will provide all that we need and take care of us. He is always with us, watching over us, and will never abandon us, no matter what we are going through (Ps. 91:1; 23:1).

Promise #2: Healing and Restoration
The Lord restores my anxious, weary mind and heart, giving me hope. The Lord is close to the brokenhearted. He treats us with empathy and kindness, counseling us and healing those places that are hurt, damaged, and unwell (Ps. 23:3; 34:18).

Promise #3: Guidance and Direction
I will trust in the Lord and not my own understanding because He has a plan and knows what is best for us. He will give us direction and guidance for the future (Ps. 23:1; Prov. 3:5).

Promise # 4: Comfort and Peace
God comforts us when we have trouble, and out of His comfort for us, we can comfort others. When I take everything to God in prayer with thankfulness, I will have His peace in my heart and mind (2 Cor. 1:4; Phil. 4:6).

Promise #5: Hope and Purpose
God has plans to give us a future and hope. I am confident that God will complete the growth in me (and my family) that He has begun. God will use hard times to build patience, endurance, and character, which will bless others. All things will work out for the good because I love Him and I am His (Jer. 29:11; Phil. 1:6; Rom. 8:28).

Promise #6: Strength and Endurance
My help comes from the Lord. I will wait, hope, and trust in Him to renew my strength. I can do everything God allows in my life because He will give me the strength. The joy of the Lord is my strength. I won't lose hope and give up doing good, but will live the life of faith (Is. 40:3; Phil. 4:13; Gal.6:9).

Promise # 7: Grace and Mercy
The Lord is always good, loving, and kind. He will show us compassion, sympathy, kindness, and understanding in our time of need. His grace and mercy are available all the time and are everlasting (Ps.103:17; Heb. 4:16).

with God. I share them as an example for you to personalize your own prayers of the Bible as you seek God daily for spiritual breakthrough, growth, healing, protection, and intimacy—both for yourself and your family.

CHALLENGES IN PRAYER

A parent recently shared with me (Catherine) about her struggle with praying and blessing her teen, and at the same time dealing with strong negative emotions: "I'll be desperately crying out to the Lord for my son: 'Oh God, please deliver him. Break through the strongholds in his life. Draw him to You and soften his hardened heart. Do a deep work in his life to untangle the webs of deception and confusion that keep him bound in a downward spiral.'

"Only a few minutes later, I'll recall an incident that causes me to get in touch with strong negative feelings. As the thoughts begin, I'll become overwhelmed with anxiety, fear, and anger: 'What a jerk. I can't believe he talked to me that way and is talking such trash to his friends. I'm so done with him. I don't care if he doesn't want to graduate from high school. If he wants to mess up his life, it's his choice. I'm not letting him take advantage of me anymore. He's really gone over the line this time, and he's in for a big battle if he comes home with any of that stinking attitude with me.'"

This woman's dilemma is common among parents of hurting teens. James 3:10 says that we bless and curse with the same mouth. While your love for your teen is undeniable, at times it is hard to fight back the raw emotions that come from the various times he has inevitably hurt you. And during prayer, this can be an obvious obstacle. When we hang on to resentment and harbor bitterness toward our teen (even when we don't realize it), we open the door for spiritual attack.

If you struggle with this, it's time to release your anger, fear, disappointment—any negative emotion—regarding your teen to God. Don't let the enemy sneak in at the most unexpected times. Shut those open doors by forgiving your teen, releasing him entirely to the Lord, and thanking your heavenly Father for what He is doing in his life.

FROM CURSING TO PRAYER AND THANKS

We can assure you that counseling rooms and prayer closets are not always filled with the giving of thanks. These are safe places where we can pour out our hearts and express our deepest places of anger, disappointment, and frustrations, as well as our longings. It's not uncommon for me to hear both parents and teens confess to secretly cursing or using inappropriate gestures toward each other. After all, no one can get under our skin like our family members! And in the heat of struggling with a stressed or depressed teen, tensions and frustrations can rise.

As a parent, however, your responsibility is to lead your teen toward healing. Name-calling and cursing aren't a helpful part of that process. Instead of cursing your teen, speak blessing over her. When you make a mistake and come to your senses, apologize. Acknowledge that what you did was wrong and not your heart's desire toward her. You will make mistakes, but being honest and repenting is the best way to mend the harm.

It is one thing to stop cursing your teen; it's another to give thanks for her. This part of prayer can be a challenge for parents of hurting teens. One parent shared with me that he was overwhelmed with such strong emotions of anger, frustration, and despair, he had to sit down and consciously think of things for which he could be thankful. It took him awhile, because in the complexity of his human nature, he had a hard time thinking of positive things about his teen, or even what he was thankful for. It was easier to name-call, be defensive, and feel sorry for himself.

You may find yourself facing similar emotions. Making a list of what you're grateful for can still be helpful. Write down anything that comes to mind, whether you feel grateful for it or not. Then intentionally focus your mind on these things, and allow the other raging emotions to subside. Eventually, this will have a positive effect like it did for this father, who began to feel more tender-hearted, peaceful, and happy. Take a few minutes right now and make this list, keeping in mind that you may not feel connected to those things you write down. Still, you will be happier, more peaceful, and more hopeful after doing it.

If you are struggling to even begin the list, stop and offer up a prayer similar to this:

> Lord, I want to consciously remember Your goodness and faithfulness. Change my heart, and allow my mind to be renewed with reminders of Your blessings. Right now, Father, I am thankful for . . . (list as many things as you can think of).

A PRAYER OF FAITH IN TROUBLED TIMES

LORD, I trust in You.
Listen to me and save me quickly.
Be my rock of protection, a strong city to save me.
I give You my life. Save me, Lord, God of truth.
I trust only in the Lord.
I will be glad and rejoice in Your love,
Because You saw my suffering; You knew my troubles.
You have set me in a safe place.
Lord, have mercy, because I am in misery.
My eyes are weak from so much crying, and my whole being
    is tired from grief.
My troubles are using up my strength.
I am like a piece of a broken pot.
Lord, I trust You. I have said, "You are my God."
My life is in Your hands.
Show your kindness to me. Save me because of Your love.
How great is Your goodness.
Praise the Lord. His love to me was wonderful in times before.
In my distress, I said, "God cannot see me!"
But You heard my prayer when I cried out to You for help.
Love the Lord, all you who belong to him.
The Lord protects those who truly believe.
All you who put your hope in the Lord, be strong and brave.

Excerpts adapted from Psalm 31

A CLOSING PRAYER

Father,
I commit myself and my teen to You.
I realize that to be the parent my teen needs
is beyond my human control and abilities.

Make me the parent You want me to be,
and teach me how to pray for my teen.

You alone know the needs of her heart and what is best,
so I commit her into Your care and protection.

God, I ask You to give my teen wisdom and revelation
so she will know You better.

I pray also that she will have greater understanding in her
heart to know the hope to which You have called us,
and that she will comprehend how rich and glorious
are the blessings You have promised us.

I pray that she will realize how great is
Your power for those who believe.

Lord, I ask that You give my teen and me the power to have
inner strength through Your Spirit,
so that Christ will live in our hearts by faith, that our lives
will be strong in love, and that both will be built upon love.

I pray that my teen and I will have the power to understand
the greatness of Christ's love, to know that love intimately.

I pray that it will grow more and more in our lives so we can
see the difference between good and bad and choose the good.

Father, I pray that we will be pure for the coming
of Christ and do many good things with Your help,
all to bring glory and praise to You.

(Adapted from Ephesians 1:17–19; 3:16–19; Philippians 1:9–11)

14

HOPE FOR PARENTS OF HURTING TEENS

So don't worry, because I am with you.
Don't be afraid, because I am your God. I will make
you strong and will help you; I will support you
with my right hand that saves you. —Isaiah 41:10

Many of us are so tempted to focus on purifying our chil-
dren that we neglect our own spiritual growth. . . . We
must see parenting as the process through which God
purifies us—the parents—even as He shapes our children.
— Gary L. Thomas, *Sacred Parenting*

I N A CONVERSATION THE OTHER DAY, A FRIEND OF MINE MEN-
tioned that she had heard I (Catherine) was writing a book for parents on hurting teens.

"What's the title?" she inquired.

"*Stressed or Depressed,*" I responded.

"That's a great title! Because that's just how parents feel while
going through the hard times parenting teens."

I laughed and explained the main themes of the book. What a
humorous take on the title. Sure this book is about parenting teens
who are struggling with stress or depression, but the impact on parents can be just as stressful and depressing.

Whatever your particular story, it is also undoubtedly filled with times of sadness, anger, guilt, and fear. You have questions and concerns, and losses and challenges to overcome. In fact, perhaps the only thing more difficult than being a teenager is parenting one. If the teen years are considered a journey from childhood to adulthood, then parenting a stressed or depressed teen is a courageous expedition. The more serious the problem, the harder the journey and the greater the consequences—and, might I add, the deeper your despair. As you read this book, we pray that you may be comforted and find hope and direction in your journey as a hurting parent of a hurting teen.

BELIEVE IT OR NOT, GOD IS WORKING

Your greatest challenge in parenting will be your own growth. You have to be aware and accountable for your reactions, who you really are, and who you are becoming. There is no set manual for growing children. This is about how God works in you as a parent and how you mature and become Christlike alongside your teen. Close relationships in life are the crucible for our character development.

Hard times simply add fuel to the fire of this process—and other parents of hurting teens will attest to this. God has a purpose for you even in the trials you are facing. He has plans for you, and He desires for you to grow as a parent and as a believer through these difficulties. It's when we see His perspective that troubled times become opportunities for building character and hope, and to share His hope and comfort with others. "And we are happy because of the hope we have of sharing God's glory. We also have joy with our troubles, because we know that these troubles produce patience. And patience produces character, and character produces hope. And this hope will never disappoint us, because God has poured out His love to fill our hearts" (Rom. 5:2–5).

God has not left you alone to suffer. He promises to be your protection and your strength, to help you in your times of trouble. You do not have to be afraid.

JOY IN TRIALS, DESPITE THE TRIALS

Just because you are God-fearing doesn't mean that your teens or you are excluded from difficult times or illness. You obviously have discovered that by now or you wouldn't be reading this book. However, the Lord has specific instructions on what believers are to do when we do go through times of adversity. During times of trouble, He says we are to have joy.

What?!? Don't worry, that's a common reaction for most people. It's one thing to endure trials; but to endure them with joy? Yet here is our hope: God says that as believers, we can have the confidence that He is always working for our good (Rom. 8:28). That's not just when everything is going great. As hard as it may be to believe, the truth is that right now, in the midst of your (and your teen's) trials, God is at work. When you realize that your troubles test your faith and give you patience, you can find joy. And if you get stuck and need wisdom on what to do, ask God. James 1:2–5 says that He will give generously to you.

It's important to note that this joy is not simply an emotional reaction, but an intentional, intelligent outlook from God's perspective. Jesus defined this in John 16 when He spoke to His disciples about their imminent sadness that would come when He suffered and died. But He was also quick to point out that their sadness would become joy because they would see Him again. Jesus also explained that as believers, we can ask for anything in His name so we can receive and that our joy will be the fullest possible.

God allows difficulty and hard times as an opportunity for us to get closer to Him and for our moral and spiritual growth. We don't rejoice in the actual challenging situation itself but in the possible results that the Lord will work through it. It's not as if you will pray, "Oh Lord, I'm so glad my teen is hurting and messed up right now." But you can pray, "Lord, I trust that You will use this difficult season as an opportunity to teach us, build character in us, and bring us into a deeper, more dependent relationship with You. And Lord, we also look to You for wisdom on how to get through each day, as there are situations we just don't know how to respond to or what to do. We need Your spiritual understanding to know Your purposes behind each difficult circumstance. But even when we don't, we will choose to worship You."

BELIEVING THE NOT YET SEEN

Trials are also for another purpose: to test our faith. As James 1:3 says, this produces patience, which, if you remember from the previous chapter, is one of the qualities that contributes to effectively raising teens.

When our whole person and character goes through hardship, the hope of receiving what God has promised can grow stronger. But the greatest challenge to this is unbelief. Some people have an easier time with having optimistic faith. For parents of a hurting teen, it can be difficult to believing that God is in control and that He will bring you and your teen through the turmoil in His way and in His time.

When parents are bombarded with the ongoing strain of caring for a stressed or depressed teen, their spirit is weary and their energy drained. The loss, negative emotions, and frustrating challenges can dominate parents' daily experience, making it difficult for them to focus on the positive hope, the light at the end of the tunnel—especially if they have no glimpse of it. Circumstances can often get worse before they get better, and it can be a challenge to believe that it won't always be that way.

But this is the essence of faith: believing in something that is not yet seen (Heb. 11:1). You may have no vision for things getting better, yet faith takes you beyond the boundary of what is into what can be. In hard times, you have a chance to be stretched to hope in God for future blessings and help. You can rejoice in God because you know He is with you, leading, guiding, and healing you. Your patience isn't just a passive resignation to the circumstances, but an optimistic faith that endures with courage. For some parents, this season has been relatively brief—a few months or a few years.

Others have endured years of patiently waiting, believing and trusting the Lord to bring healing and victory in their child's life. Either way, your hope can always be in the truth that, as you take one day at a time, God is still at work.

MIRROR TIME

Parents want to be the best they can with few regrets. You might not have had the kind of childhood you hope to give your children. Maybe you're determined not to make the mistakes your parents did while raising you. It's comforting to know that you don't have to have had the greatest parents in order to learn to be a good parent yourself. You can make sense of your flawed teen years and integrate your past into new learning experiences for the present. Being aware of the mistakes made during your childhood can prevent you from overreacting and taking unresolved childhood issues into your relationship attachment with your teen.

If you still struggle with issues from your past and often find yourself treating your teen the way your parents treated you, it might be helpful to journal your thoughts and discuss them with friends or a counselor. How are the struggles in your teen's life impacting you and your teen's relationship now? What does she trigger in you from your own teen experience? As you see her go through these challenges, how does it remind you of your teen years?

DEALING WITH DIFFICULT REACTIONS AND EMOTIONS

1. Fear, worry, and anxiety
Worry is a special form of fear that becomes a heavy load on the spirit. It is what humans do when the fear reaction is processed in the brain and reaches the cerebral cortex, where people then complicate the matter by expanding the fear into the imagination and fueling it with emotion. This then triggers the brain's neurotransmitters to send further messages to the body and the brain, heightening the stress response and embedding our brain with anxiety.

It's easy for caring, loving parents to become concerned and worried whenever their teen struggles. There is a lot to be concerned about, that's for sure. However, worry never solves anything and only leads to anxiety and depression.

So why do we worry, when we could pray? We worry because it's hard to trust God. We are afraid that things won't work out or go the way we want if we are not in control and on top of things. The less we feel in control, the more anxious and worried we become.

Become a prayer warrior, not a worrier. God teaches us in the Bible that we are not to worry needlessly about anything. Instead,

---

A WALK DOWN MEMORY LANE

A deeper understanding of yourself can help you be a better parent to your teen. Ask yourself the following questions, and don't just answer them quickly—think about them!

- What was it like for you growing up as a teenager?
- Do you remember having any challenges like your teen is having?
- How did your parents react to you when you experienced something similar to what your teen is now facing? How did they handle your feelings and emotions?
- How can you respond in a more helpful, healthy way (e.g., parenting style, emotional response)?
- How did you emotionally handle getting through hard times when you were a teen?
- Are there unresolved issues from your teen years that you can now finally resolve?
- What can you do to take responsibility for what your teen is evoking in you, so it doesn't diminish your effectiveness as a parent?

we are to remain calm, pray, and ask God for everything we need, remembering to also give thanks. This is the key to having peace in your heart and mind. Prayer and thankfulness will guard you against worry and anxiety.

That's easier said than done, isn't it? As parents, our hearts often automatically go to being troubled and fearful for our hurting teens. Stressful, disappointing circumstances can overwhelm us, leaving us feeling isolated and out of control. These are all natural automatic fear responses in the brain. However, to have peace and not suffer from the misery that worry causes, we have to intentionally calm the physiological fear response.

In *Praying God's Word*, Beth Moore shares how she turned the biblical prescription for peace (found in Philippians 4:6–7) into a no-fail prescription for anxiety.[1] Her result looked like this: "Do not be calm about anything, but in everything, by dwelling on it constantly and feeling picked on by God, with thoughts like 'and this is the thanks I get,' present your aggravations to everyone you know but Him. And the acid in your stomach, which transcends all milk products, will cause you an ulcer, and the doctor bills will cause you a heart attack, and you will lose your mind."

Sounds funny when you read it this way, but we all do this— which is why God had to tell us so many times not to worry or be afraid. Often when we are worrying or anxious it is more difficult to pray. However, if we spent more time praying, we'd have a lot less to worry about and would experience greater peace. When our troubles (including those concerning our hurting teen) cause worry and anxiety, we often do everything but pray. We get weighed down by struggles and emotions but usually look for tangible answers through people and events. Granted, God can use church meetings, Bible studies, and counselors to minister to us; but when we pray, something powerful happens deep in our lives as we interact with our heavenly Father. Through intimate time with Him, our spirits are changed to mirror His character—which leads to a sustaining peace that can overcome any fear we have.

A trusting heart cures a worried mind. What is the cure for our needless worrying? Plain and simple, it's trust. The Lord connects with us intimately to get to know Him better; and the more we know Him, the more we are able to trust Him. Then the more we trust him, the more we are able to surrender and release our teens and troubles to Him, sensing His peace.

You may be facing some genuinely big problems with your teen that give you certain cause for stress, worry, and anxiety. While all your problems won't be instantly "zapped," through prayer you can come to know His peace. Just before Jesus died, He said, "I leave you peace . . . so don't let your hearts be troubled or afraid" (John 14:27). He promises to give you supernatural peace that will empower you to deal with difficult situations. You may not feel instant relief of the struggle or escape of the situation, but you can press in to receive His promise to calm your troubled heart and mind.

Keep your mind focused on God. Proverbs 12:25 states that worry is a heavy load on the spirit, and this anxiety in the heart leads to depression. But a kind and good word makes it glad and cheers you up. God also teaches us that we will experience His peace when we focus our thoughts on what we are grateful for. Think about things that are good, hopeful, and positive. Meditate on God's Word and promises, and take everything to Him in prayer. Worry is when you dwell on a problem, going over and over it in your mind. It's also known as ruminating (which women are especially good at). Research reveals that this causes more stress, while increasing vulnerability to anxiety and depression.

Meditation is a similar process in the mind, but instead of focusing on the problem, you think about God, His Word, what you are grateful for, and His blessings, hope, and promises—going over and over those things in your mind. It is an intentional focusing of the mind toward hopeful thinking, which results in uplifting emotions and fulfilling results.

If overcoming worry is that easy, then why is it so difficult to do? Because our brains quickly respond in fear, which perpetuates the worry cycle. To prevent that, we have to intentionally intervene in the fear response, calming ourselves down, redirecting our minds and emotions toward thoughts of hope, trust, love, and faith. We have to focus through prayer, as in the following example:

> *Lord, I am so burdened with the issues surrounding my teen, and they are causing me to worry and be anxious. My mind swirls with fearful thoughts. It seems they have stolen my joy and peace. Nothing seems to have helped me, and I often lack the motivation or focus to pray. Forgive me for my prayerlessness. I bring all my worries and anxieties to You now in prayer. I also come with an attitude of thankfulness. I pray that You guard my heart and mind with Your peace as I turn my thoughts and heart toward You and Your hope. Thank You for loving me and comforting me during these difficult times, and for being so patient with me as I learn to surrender and trust You so I can have Your peace. In Jesus' name, amen.*

2. Anger, resentment, and bitterness

You will go through a natural process of grieving after the initial shock of discovering your teen is struggling, and you may become severely disappointed. Allow yourself to feel this, and go through the necessary grieving process. As uncomfortable as it may feel, it is necessary for you to grieve all your losses, find resolve, and to move on.

Setbacks can often be just as difficult to deal with as your teen's struggle. One day everything seems fine, with your teen making progress, and the next day it can feel like you're back at square one when he makes a bad choice, the medication becomes a problem, or he encounters another stressor that sets him back. Although this is to be expected in the process of getting well, you may still struggle with it, especially if your teen has been battling this for a while and you are feeling weary. Just when your hopes and trust are being built up, you may see them dashed to even deeper places of disappointment and heartbreak. This can lead to anger, resentment, and bitterness.

You may ruminate and rehearse lectures, clarify claims to your teen's discredit, expose his despicable character flaws, or vindicate the injustice done to you. You may lambaste him, humiliate him into submission, and spew the most vile, foul language descriptive of such debased emotions. The anger and resentment may grip you by the throat. But all of this cuts you off from the flow of any redeeming infusion of grace and mercy. It will steal, rob, and destroy the chance for God to bring restoration, forgiveness, reconciliation, and breakthrough. And your heart will build walls, become guarded and hardened, and shut out love and compassion that doesn't seem to be deserved.

As a parent, you will get disappointed with your teen for not getting it right—for not listening and obeying everything you say, for making stupid mistakes. But those times force both you and your teen to grow up and come face-to-face with her strengths and weaknesses, her sin, and her need for a Savior. Her tendency to err is a natural part of her need to individuate and try things out for herself. You can't control that by manipulating her every choice and consequence; only the Lord has complete control. And that is when you as a parent must remember that this is about the Lord and you, whether you'll trust His will or attempt to control things on your own.

In *Grace-Based Parenting,* Dr. Tim Kimmel reminds us of God's path of grace toward us during these challenging times. "You may feel extremely inadequate and fragile in key areas of your life, but God comes alongside you in those very areas of weakness and carries you through with His grace. You may be frustrated, hurt, and even angry with God, but His grace allows you to candidly, confidently, and boldly approach His 'throne of grace.' His grace is there for you when you fail, when you fall, and when you make huge mistakes. This kind of grace makes all the difference in the world when it's coming from God, through you, to your children."[2]

3. Disappointment, discouragement, regret, and despair
Parents with hurting teens share that dealing with disappointment is a major ongoing battle. Often you have to let go of expectations, hopes, and dreams and adjust to the reality of what your teen is

experiencing. You may do fine for a while, but then you wake up one morning and feel the heaviness of what you both have to deal with. The healing and developmental journey is a continual process that always includes moving forward and periodic setbacks, which can be discouraging.

You may even get disappointed and discouraged that you aren't able to apply some of what you are learning in this book. We have emphasized the importance of building a safe, connected relationship with your teen, yet he might not want to have anything to do with you or the family. Your family might be going through the turmoil of a divorce, or you're a single parent doing everything you can to survive but unable to fulfill every need. Although church involvement is important, your teen might not want to have anything to do with church. Exercise is an important way to recover from stress and naturally elevate your teen's mood, but he might hate to sweat and has no interest in any physical activity. Don't worry. This is a natural part of what many parents experience as they try to do their best to parent their teens.

Just do the best you can. What most have found helpful is to start with what you can do and build on the things that are realistic and already in place. In other words, do what you can each day, being intentional, applying what you can, and tackling what seems most doable. Though it may be frustrating at times, rest in the fact that you're doing all you can do. Eventually, it all adds up. And it will make a difference, although you might not see any tangible immediate results.

The Barna Group conducted a nationwide survey of parents and asked how they determined whether they had been successful in raising their children. By more than a two-to-one margin (62 percent to 28 percent), they assessed their success by having done the best they could, regardless of the outcomes. Fewer than three out of ten parents say that the results of their efforts define their success at parenting.

No matter what ups and downs you and your teen go through on a daily basis, focus on making the most of every opportunity, one day at a time, just doing the best you can.

REGRETTING WHAT YOU DID OR DID NOT DO

Never let the sense of guilt over failure limit or hinder your new actions. As long as your teen is alive, you have a chance to make a change and a difference each new day. I (Catherine) have heard parents say things such as, "I should have been more alert to the warning signs. If only I could have done something to stop that situation from impacting my teen's life so negatively. Why didn't the school catch the problems and suggest getting help?"

In an earlier chapter, I (Catherine) shared the sad sudden loss of our family African tortoise that was so devastating to me. I felt such guilt and regret over wishing I had known what to do. I wanted another chance to try again. All those nagging regrets were beginning to result in helplessness and despair. Like anyone else, I wanted to be a good caregiver, and I didn't want the tortoise to get hurt or suffer on my watch.

The sense of irreparable damage or of lost time and opportunity is part of life that we cannot change. In the classic devotional *My Utmost for His Highest*, Oswald Chambers reminds us of the time the disciples went to sleep on Jesus when they should have stayed awake and been alert. When they realized what they had done, their first reaction was probably along the lines of, "It's all over now. What's the use of trying anymore?" It's not different with us as we struggle over the losses our teen experiences. We want to give up. But when we sink into despair, Oswald Chambers suggests that Jesus Christ comes to us saying, "Sleep on now. That opportunity is lost forever. You cannot alter it, but arise and go to the next thing."

Let the past go, and leave it with Christ. Instead of mulling over your regrets, go out into the future with Him. When you feel you can't lift yourself out of the guilt of an unforgivable thing, Jesus comes with a spiritual antidote for your despair, saying, "Arise and do the next thing."

So what is the Lord showing you? What are you to leave behind with Him? And what is the next thing He is wants you to focus on

LETTING GO OF RESENTMENT

The only person hurt by holding grudges and unforgiveness is you. Unforgiveness is like stubborn stains on the fabric of your heart and memories. It will eat away at your life. The only power to stop the unending flow of pain is forgiveness, which means giving up your right to get back at someone who wronged you. You don't minimize the wrong or undo the consequences. But when you forgive others, it heals your own heart. Think about the following questions.

· How has your teen wronged you and hurt you?
· What wrong and hurt has been done to them?
· What anger do you need to let go of and start forgiving?

For more on forgiveness, refer to *Forgive and Forget* by Lewis B. Smedes.[3]

or take action on? Live each day with renewed refreshing and opportunity in Him.

THE ULTIMATE DESPAIR

The phone rings for a parent. It's someone obligated to make a mandatory report, informing him that his sixteen-year-old daughter has just confessed that she was raped five months ago and that the problems she has been having are all due to her attempt to keep it a secret and deal with it on her own.

The girl's heartbroken parents weep prayers of desperation and anguish that evil has such power to wound the innocent child God has entrusted to them. They cry out with deep pain, not understanding why God didn't stop such evil from reaching their most precious of jewels. They feel utterly disappointed and helpless. Every morning for weeks they awake disoriented, in disbelief and shock of the life they now have to live. *Why didn't she say something and allow us to help her?* The father cries like a baby, grieving that he wasn't able to be there to protect her and that she has suffered so much pain alone.

When we try to pray but feel abandoned by God and instead become disappointed with Him, we encounter true despair. It's a deep fear that all our fears will come true, that we are alone in our desperation, and that we are helpless and hopeless. Such despair grips those parents who have prayed for their daughter's protection, yet she still becomes a victim of violence. Those who have prayed for their son to meet new, godly friends at youth group, yet he gets caught up with the rowdy crowd. Parents who have faithfully interceded for their son to be freed from his drug addiction, yet it still takes almost a dozen years.

You may have given your life to raising your child in a stable Christian home, but still she somehow drifted away and made choices that have led to troubling consequences, and now you feel like a failure. Like God and His system failed. Like your prayers and the cries of your heart were never heard. You can feel rejected—others speak of answered prayers, but what about the ones for your teen?

We read stories of those whose prayers were answered, and the end of the story for their teen is happy. But there are the other heartbreaking stories in which the teen ends up in jail for life, or pregnant, or a drug addict. Some teens reject the faith, marrying nonbelievers. Others even end their life. If your story has nothing but tragedy so far, it's easy to let despair dominate your life and shape your actions and ways of relating. Where can you go? Where is the hope?

THERE IS HOPE

When you are made desperate, there are no other options but to pursue God with absolute abandonment. It's either hope or give up. There is no in-between. And your only chance is in the relief that God is in control of the universe and can handle your life and the life of your teen.

Some parents have shared how difficult this can be. I know of a dad who nearly went spiritually bankrupt going through painful struggles with his teen sons for more than eleven years. He felt out of control and abandoned. He had so many questions for God as to why things hadn't gone better with them. Yet going through the hellacious experience forced him to grow in relationship with Christ. It taught him invaluable lessons of trusting and waiting on God. Things have turned around, and these parents are now thankful not because their teen suffered, but because the Lord brought them through the experience—and will continue to.

Coming to the end of yourself can actually become a good thing. By having no other options, you wrestle and pursue God in a deeper way. Your perseverance to find renewed hope in God is increased. In the original Greek and Hebrew, the word *hope* means "to expect, wait for, look for, trust, be patient, and remain in anticipation of God." The best way to hope and wait for the Lord in your life is to persistently expect His mercy and salvation. Then, while waiting, focus solely on what He is doing in you. Don't take matters into your own hands, but allow God to be your rescuer.

INCREASE YOUR LEVEL OF HAPPINESS

We all know parents who say that their children are their greatest source of joy and happiness. Yet a recent Time magazine poll seems to indicate this isn't the case with most people. When asked the question, "What one thing in life has brought you the greatest happiness?" only 35 percent of respondents said it was their children or grandchildren.4 When women were asked to rate their most positive activities, way down on the list was "taking care of my children." The study confirms that although parenting can be fulfilling and bring happiness and joy, the actual day-to-day experience of parenting can be filled with frustrations. Other studies reveal that parenting during the teen years are the most stressful. While your teen is in crisis it can become difficult to be thankful and joyful, much less happy.

The truth is, you can't depend on your primary happiness to be from your children. You will be disappointed. Teens can be a source of joy overall, but parents have to intentionally see the whole picture, the total sum of experiences, especially when teens are going through a hard time.

The Bible gives the wisest counsel on how to be happy in the here and now. A happy heart and positive emotions have been scientifically validated to be "like good medicine" (Prov. 17:22). A healthy outlook can help increase healing for heart patient, and is the best medicine for a hurting heart.

According to psychobiological research, we all have a "set point" of happiness that is determined partly by our personality, how we deal with stress, and other genetic factors. Some of us see the glass half-empty, and others see it half-full. Stress, anger, anxiety, and other strong emotions can all severely dampen our level of happiness. But after going through tragedy and hard times, we usually bounce back to our set range. Even better, we can intentionally increase our level of happiness. Following are some proven strategies that you can begin integrating into your life.

1. Release your teen to God.

For I know the plans You have for me (and my teen),
Lord—plans to prosper us and not to harm us,
plans to give us a hope and a future.
—Prayer based on Jeremiah 29:11

You are a steward whom God has appointed to raise your teen. It may take constant, conscious decisions for you to continually release your teen into His hands. And though this won't be the end of all the struggles, it will put you in your rightful place as a parent, leaving God in control and free to work in her life. When you deal with your desperate fears and worries that are fueled by a need to be in complete control, you can release your teen ultimately into God's hands. This not only relieves you of a mental burden, it allows you to focus solely on your partnership and role as a parent.

2. Trust in God's way and time.

As you continually release your teen to the Lord, putting your trust and hope in Him, you should not criticize, manipulate, and interfere with God's ways of dealing with her. If God can use a donkey to speak to His people as He did to Balaam in Numbers 22:26–30, then trust that He will use whatever means to reach your teen. It doesn't all depend on you. Even if she has to come to the end of herself, the Lord can use that as an opportunity to reach her heart in a profound way. You won't always be able to see the times when God is working in her life. Your job is to trust in the bigger picture of His master plan—and not interfere. This is a struggle for many parents.

When my husband, Rick, and I (Catherine) were first married, I had the hardest time releasing leadership and control. In marriage counseling, I complained that he wouldn't make the bed and help with the dishes. So he started to do these things, but I didn't like the way he did them. His organization of the dishwasher was very inefficient, and I'd have to go back behind him and redo what he'd done. The lackadaisical effort he put into making the bed was also unacceptable, so I offered lessons on how I would like it done—hotel style.

Eventually, Rick protested, "If you want me to share in these things, then you have to stop controlling how it's done. Let me do it my way, and learn to accept it." Although it still goes against my organizational skills, over the years I've had to just walk away, let it go, and accept that at least the job is getting done. And he's doing a great job!

We have to do the same thing in our parenting partnership with the Lord. Let go and let God. Trust in Him, and put your hope in the fact that He will finish what He started in His way, in His time.

3. Live one day at a time.

The Bible instructs us to "Be still before the LORD and wait patiently for Him" (Ps. 37:7 NIV). That means that we are to just be. Not stress out. Not worry. Just stand there. Just lie there. Listen. Live one day at a time. Be patient. Healing takes time. Growth and change take time.

Try telling that to a teenager who wants the pain and confusion gone now! And after months of wearying endurance with trials, try telling yourself. Waiting patiently and enduring hardship can feel like watching the grass grow.

Waiting and being patient takes hard work. It takes discipline. It is active and passive at the same time. When we are waiting—whether it is for the healing process to progress, for our prayers to be answered, or to get an appointment with a psychiatrist three months from now—we aren't just sitting in a heap, watching the time tick away. When we wait, we are actively anticipating and expecting what we are hoping for. But at the same time, we are not rushing ahead, manipulating, interfering, and fooling ourselves that busyness can substitute for the natural process of all things working out in God's time.

Everything I (Catherine) needed to learn about waiting during the last few years the Lord taught me through personal trials of parenting my teens, and from my dear therapist friend, Beth. She has endured years of horrific cancer treatments, miraculously experiencing God's grace and mercy with more days of life than she ever imagined. We found a kindred spirit through our similar journeys of adversity, although the specifics were completely different.

Over lunch one day, Beth shared how the Lord had given her deeper insight about waiting while lying helpless in a machine being scanned. There comes a place of surrender, she said, when we just have to "be"—to trust, hope, and allow the healing and growth process to happen naturally. True surrender involves relaxing and letting go of our frustrations, expectations, and restlessness with God's ways and timing. Only God in His almighty power can heal, draw our teens to Himself, and work inner growth and transformation. And the procedure is usually less painful, more swift, and thorough when we are cooperative, relaxed, and follow the program for self-care diligently.

WAYS TO DEAL WITH DIFFICULT EMOTIONS

These practical exercises will help you deal with the day-to-day frustrations of parenting a hurting teen.

HAPPINESS AND LIFE SATISFACTION

Here are some proven ways to raise your level of happiness.

1. *Get more pleasure out of the little things in life.* Savor life's positive emotions (such as joy, excitement, serenity, etc.) through your senses (such as the taste of your food, good smells, enjoyable music, the beauty of nature, etc.). Find humor and enjoyment in the simple things of life.

2. *Become more engaged in what you do.* Enjoy growing and learning in your family relationships, with friends, your work, recreational activities, and hobbies. Take up a new interest, or revive an old one that you can really get into to and take the next level.

3. *Find ways to make your life more meaningful.* Build on your personal strengths, and find ways to use these by giving and being involved with something that makes a difference. "Interpersonal virtues" like kindness, gratitude, and the capacity for love are more strongly tied to happiness than "cerebral virtues" such as learning.

4. *Incorporate your faith into everyday life.* The happiest people have a system of strong faith and beliefs. Faith in God produces change to our negative emotions. People who look beyond their present difficulty and put their trust in God's goodness cannot help but be joyful. Become part of a spiritual community by attending worship services, reading the Scriptures, praying, and finding social support. Studies show that the more you do this, the more frequently you will experience positive emotions and the higher your overall sense of life satisfaction. Strong believers are less depressed, less anxious, and less suicidal. They are also better able to cope with crises.

5. *Keep a gratitude journal.* Write down things for which you are thankful. Write a letter to someone who has positively impacted your life, and read it to that person.

6. *Count your blessings.* Be aware of what you do have, what God is doing in your life, and how blessed you are. Take time each day to write down a few things that went well and why they did. People who do this exercise daily for a month have reported being less depressed and happier for months afterward. A thankful and happy heart may prove to also be a remedy to help you through your struggles.5

7. *Learn to forgive.* Let go of anger, resentment, and other negative emotions. You will feel a physical difference.

8. *Invest time and energy with friends and family.* Studies show that strong ties to friends and family and commitment to spending time with them results in higher levels of happiness and fewer signs of depression. The biggest happiness factor appears to be strong personal relationships. When we are positively connected with other people, we feel happier.

9. *Develop strategies for coping with stress and becoming more resilient.* You can overcome stress-related anxiety by guarding your mind from negative patterns of thinking. Learn simple stress-reducing exercises, such as deep breathing, and apply them daily. Take care of your body. Get plenty of sleep. Eat well, exercise, smile, and laugh a lot. It will enhance your mood.

1. Get control over your stress and emotions.

When preparing to confront or interact with your teen, it is most effective to first get your anger under control. If you are confused, upset, and out of control, you will not be able to think clearly or communicate effectively. So first, get your mind and heart to calm down. An effective parent speaks calm and confidence into crisis.

The fear, stress, anxiety, or anger can be decreased by using interventions that are designed to reduce these physiological systems. Once you get your body calm, your emotional state will follow suit, and you will have a chance to think through the situation more clearly.

2. Be slow to speak.
Give yourself some time not just to react out of your anger but to respond in a productive way. In the heat of anger and other strong emotions, avoid spewing what comes to your mind. These thoughts are your secondary, surface emotions. They will seldom be productive but will usually wound and cause regret.

Words spoken in anger are never guided by the Holy Spirit, and they can never be taken back. They don't generate life-giving results. It might feel good for you to get it off your chest, but there are other more productive ways to do that. Instead, take time to get to the heart of the matter. Think through your primary deeper emotions. After processing your thoughts and feelings in more constructive ways, you will be more productive in communicating what you ultimately want to say, and you'll get better results by not wounding your teen or the relationship.

3. Sort out your thoughts and feelings before reacting.
Before you confront your teen, jot down your thoughts, beliefs, and feelings on paper. For example, if the school calls to tell you that your son has ten tardies, seven missing assignments, a D in biology, and they found cigarettes in his locker, it's crucial that you take a little time to sort through your thoughts and feelings. Catastrophic thoughts will run wild and generate feelings of fear, anxiety, sadness, and anger. A sense of "justice being served" will come over you, and your main thought will be to give your teen what he deserves. Nonetheless, it is important to sort out your feelings and gain a little perspective on how to best respond rather than react.

Don't destroy your relationship by lashing out in anger. You don't have all the details and information yet, so you'll need to be calm enough to ask questions and listen to his side before responding. Review the situation and become aware of your automatic beliefs and reactions.

4. Prepare a plan for how you will proceed with the conversation. Pray! and allow the Holy Spirit to minister His peace and wisdom to you. As you think about your conversation with your teen, break it down into two or three miniconversations. Don't unload all at once. Use parental self-control. Start with allowing him to respond, and then take time to digest the information and progressively respond.

EXPRESS YOUR THOUGHTS IN PRIVATE

You might not have anyone to talk to immediately to express your feelings. Find a safe, private place and have a good cry and meltdown if you have to. Write down what you feel and want to express immediately.

1. Journal your thoughts.
Many have discovered the healing power of opening up and expressing emotions through writing. In fact, journaling has been scientifically proven to be effective in reducing stress and is even instrumental in recovering from trauma and emotional upheaval.

2. Talk with a safe, close friend.
Although writing has a valued place in our lives to express ourselves completely and honestly, it is also nice to have a person to share with at times. This should be someone with whom you can feel safe, a person you can completely be yourself with, even if that means swearing or showing your darkest thoughts and feelings. You need to be assured that this person will be able to simply listen, contain their judgments, empathize with you, and still love you. There might only be one person like that in your life, or you might not have anyone at this time. Either way, what is most important is choosing someone who can be empathetic, compassionate, and, most of all, a good listener.

Your family and friends won't have all the answers for you. But they will be a source of comfort, encouragement, and maybe even a little medicine through some shared humor and fun. Even if you don't indulge all your deepest, darkest secrets, just knowing you are not alone and connecting with those who care for you is a source of refreshment.

3. Talk with a counselor.
At some point you might find it helpful to get professional counsel, especially if you are struggling with difficult emotions you aren't able to get breakthrough with, issues this situation has triggered from your childhood, a strained marriage, or a loss for what to do as a parent. It is always good to be able to share with a professional who can give you productive, effective input.

4. Take it to God to receive containment, direction, and hope.
Present your situation and specific needs to the Lord as you are diligent in prayer. If you have no words, pray through your tears. Find rest and comfort as you search for assurance from God. Look for and listen to words of encouragement from God. Pray the Scriptures. Use the encouraging stories, prayers, and scriptures in this book and from others. Read hymns, listen to praise music, and find that one sentence that will get you through the day. Meditate on it. Let it penetrate you to bring hope. Take a few hours or a day for a prayer retreat. Just get away to focus on time with the Lord.

5. Find ways to calm and comfort yourself.
Utilize some of the practical strategies for stress resilience, anxiety reduction, and overcoming depression in the other chapters. Do what seems to work for you at the time. Take good care of yourself by building your resilience, boosting happy hormones in your brain, and encouraging your spirit with hope in the Lord. If you are feeling hopeless and helpless, take action where you can, by taking care of yourself. Go for a walk. Turn on soft music and have a personal retreat. Do a spa day. Go out with some friends and laugh and have fun.

6. Keep a collection of helpful resources.

Develop resources you can refer to as reminders for containment and direction. This is especially helpful when you face setbacks and new challenges, which you will. Keep files of anything that is encouraging and helpful to you—sections from books, articles, notes from church teachings, radio programs, conversations with friends, what you learn in counseling. Then, when you find yourself discouraged or overwhelmed in another situation, you can be reminded, encouraged, and inspired on how to get through. We forget things easily when we are under stress or facing lengthy trials,

---

EXERCISE FOR CONTROLLED DEEP BREATHING

The easiest way to calm your emotions is to spend a few minutes doing controlled deep breathing.

1. Find a quiet place where there are no distractions. Go into a quiet room and close the door.
2. Sit comfortably in an upright position with your hands on your lap or on your belly to notice your breathing. Close your eyes.
3. Inhale softly, slowly, and evenly. Breathe deeply and normally through your nose with your mouth closed. Notice your breath and focus your attention on it. Become aware of expanding your chest and abdomen until they are filled. Keep the rest of your body relaxed. You can count to four in your mind while inhaling.
4. Now exhale slowly through your nose until you have exhaled completely, also counting to four if you want to keep a rhythm. Keep your eyes closed and your attention focused on breathing peacefully and evenly.
5. Do this repeatedly for a few minutes, clearing your mind of thoughts and focusing only on your breathing.

and when a new emotional upheaval hits, we need to be reminded and realigned with the truths God has already shown us to be helpful. This will also help you reevaluate your current situation and develop a new strategy for taking action.

7. Don't get lost and discouraged in a clouded perspective.

One of the great opportunities my teen daughter and I (Catherine) had last year during her semester of independent study was to travel extensively overseas with my dad. He had raved about Switzerland with the quaint little villages, the cows with fancy bells around their necks, and the spectacular scenic views. So we planned a full week to explore the area of Lake Thun. Since the rail system there is superb, we got tickets for unlimited travel for the week. We were so excited as we left Geneva on the train to head for Lake Thun because we were staying in an old house that had been converted to a bed-and-breakfast run by YWAM. My dad's description of his experience was almost dreamlike. Hillsides full of lush, green meadow grazing grass. Being woken up in the morning by the sound of cows slowly meandering nearby with their clanging cowbells. Fresh handmade yogurt from local milked cows and delicious Swiss muselix for breakfast.

In the other direction from the house was the glistening lake with a glimpse on the other side of France and with rambling hillside vineyards draping down to the waters edge. When we arrived it was raining hard, but as we rushed into the inn, it was everything and more than Dad had described. In the dinning room, there was an original scenic painting of cattle on a Swiss hillside, and the walls were covered in original damask silk fabric. The furniture was museumlike, as if out of a movie set. The beds were inviting, with just a bottom sheet and a big fluffy down comforter folded over at the end of the bed. In the bathroom, there was a huge bathtub raised on claws. And there was even a delicious Swiss chocolate on every pillow!

But when I woke up in the morning, it was still raining. I was so disappointed. No sound of cowbells. The herd was standing under the shelter of the trees. I couldn't see much past the end of the front porch, never mind to the "spectacular" view of the lake and beyond. The yogurt wasn't as he remembered it. It was sour and runny. And the whole week continued to be rainy off and on with mostly clouds. I did see a few cows and goats eventually, and partial views of the lake and hills. But no breathtaking views of the Alps or the scenes I had imagined. I bought many postcards capturing spectacular scenes, but I never got to see them for myself. We still had a great time, but I had to shift my expectations and simply enjoy the moment and memories we were making together.

From this experience, the Lord reminded me of how we are told of His wonderful goodness and His great works, yet we have to believe and have faith, because we don't necessarily get to see and taste it all everyday. We get glimpses of this in His Word and from what others share of what they have seen. But just because we don't see it for ourselves, or on an off day it tastes "sour," doesn't mean that God's goodness isn't a reality. Just because you can't see or taste the great work He is doing in your life and your teen's life, doesn't mean it's not happening. Trust and believe that as you pray to Him, He hears you. Know with assurance that He will complete the transforming work He is doing in each of you. And when you do see it and taste it, be grateful and thank Him.

TAKE GOOD CARE OF YOURSELF

Here are some practical strategies to keep in mind.

1. Be intentional with your lifestyle.

When flying on a commercial jet, the pre-flight demonstration always advises that we put our own oxygen mask on before trying to help anyone else. The same principle applies to your self-care as a parent. The better you take care of yourself, the better you will model this principle for your teen. Adapt this standard to all areas of your life. Eat well so there will be healthy food options in the house available for your teen. Exercise regularly and get to bed early so you can get enough sleep and rest to deal with the

SORTING OUT YOUR BELIEFS

Try the following exercise to put your beliefs in perspective.

1. Start by making a list of your beliefs and the emotional reactions they produce in you, given the situation and information you have so far. For example:

Situation: The school calls you regarding your son's tardies, missing assignments, and cigarettes in his locker.

Belief: What a liar. I ask him if he's done his homework and he says yes. If he gets a D, that means he has to repeat the class. What a hassle! He'll have to pay the price—-I'm certainly not helping him.
Reaction: Anger

Belief: Why is he late for classes? He'll be expelled if he gets two more tardies, and what am I going to do with him then? What an idiot. How can he be so late? What is he doing? I bet he's ditching class to smoke.
Reaction: Stress, anxiety, sadness

Belief: He's smoking. I bet he's drinking and using drugs. Great, now I have to deal with all that as well. That's all I need. More problems and expenses. I'm going to really let him have it for this.
Reaction: Anger, stress, anxiety, fear

2. Now break these down into three categories: the worst-case scenario, most-likely scenario, and best-case scenario. For example:

The worse case: He's a drug addict; he's going to fail his class and be expelled!

The most likely: He's smoking and not doing well at school

because he's hurting and struggling. This might all be due to stress and depression.

The best case: These problems that have surfaced will enable us to talk about what the underlying issues are behind these events and how we can work toward resolving these problems. The school will be helpful if I ask for their advice and show interest and involvement as we strategize together.

3. Finally, prepare a plan for how you are going to proceed with the conversation. And pray! Allow the Holy Spirit to minister His peace and wisdom to you. As you think about your conversation with your teen, break it down into two or three miniconversations. Don't unload all at once. Use parental self-control. Start with allowing him to respond, and then take time to digest the information and progressively respond.

challenges of parenting. (If you don't, you'll have a hard time facing all the emotional demands imposed on you and will tend to react rather than respond.) Take time for the people, events, and hobbies that you enjoy, as much as you can. Manage your own stress, anxiety, and depression. Because parenting hurting teens can be stressful and put you at risk for depression, be aware of triggers and symptoms, and get help before symptoms have a chance of arising.

2. Stay connected with support.

There will be times when you will feel all alone. But as much as possible, don't go the journey alone. Remember, for every one person on the battlefield, there is another there for support. Share your struggles in safe places where you can receive help, support, and encouragement. Get a lot of help from your family, friends, and community. Be sensitive to others, and be a source of comfort and hope to others, sharing what God has already done in your life.

WRITING EXERCISE

Try writing for twenty minutes straight (or longer) for four days. Follow the general guidelines of each day, though it's OK if you find yourself overlapping the given topics in your writing.

1. On the first day, write about your deepest thoughts and emotions regarding an emotional upheaval that is currently influencing your life. Really let go and explore how the event has affected you. Write about the event(s) and how you feel about it now.

2. On the second day, write whatever comes to you, but also write about how this emotional upheaval is affecting your life in general. Try to link the difficulty to other parts of your life—your relationships, friends, work, and even your past. Write about how you feel you may be responsible for some of the challenges you are experiencing.

3. On the third day, continue exploring your thoughts and feelings about the events that are impacting your life right now, but don't repeat what you have already written. Explore it from a different perspective and point of view. How has it shaped your life, and who are you becoming as a result of this?

4. In the last writing session, continue to explore your deepest emotions and thoughts about the issues in your life, but this time think about what you have written previously. Address anything that you haven't yet confronted. What are your emotions and thoughts at this point? What have you learned, lost, and gained as a result of this upheaval in your life? How will this guide your future?

Please note that if you are very depressed, you will not benefit from this exercise. Focusing only on negative feelings will create more problems. The more you use positive emotion in your writing, the more you will benefit. As you use words such as love, caring, funny, joy, beautiful, and warmth, you'll find that recognizing positive emotion in the midst of dealing with difficult events can help build an optimistic, hopeful spirit. While you can acknowledge the bad, you can look for the good as well.

(Adapted from *Writing to Heal* by James W. Pennebaker, Ph.D.)[6]

3. It's OK to take a break or have a minibreakdown.
My friend Beth recommends taking little retreats. She drives up to the Passionist Fathers Retreat Center, a little paradise nestled at the foot of the San Gabriel Mountains, and spends a few hours enjoying the beauty. At times, she'll do the stations of the cross, reading the Word and other meaningful resources. But her main thing is simply taking in refreshing and renewal with the Lord.

Other parents talk of favorite mindless escapes such as going up and down the isles of a store or taking to their beds for a few hours of time out, rest, and relaxation. Taking some space from your teen to occasionally recuperate is needed and appropriate. Don't feel guilty. Watch movies that are humorous or inspiring. Engage in whatever hits the spot for you at the time, as long as it is constructive in distracting your mind or giving you positive input.

TAKE GOOD CARE OF YOUR MARRIAGE

This point can't be stressed enough. The struggles of coping with a stressed or depressed teen can put a tremendous strain on your marriage—and often without you realizing it. Make your marriage a priority as much as you can. Your marriage is the foundation of your home and the emotional environment for your parenting. This nest or home base—the bedrock of which is your marriage—is one of the most important healing gifts and developmental examples you can give your teen. More importantly, it is your spouse whom you'll be spending the rest of your life with, not your kids. Although you do want to have a wonderful relationship and connection with your teen, you won't be sharing a bed or the daily rituals with her for the rest of your life.

This is difficult, because you might have to go through a season where your teen dominates your time and attention, even causing strain on your marriage. Research shows that parenting during the teen years can cause reduced life satisfaction and the most strain on a marriage. Evenings and weekends are full of driving the kids here and there, waiting up for them, and making your home an open house for activities. Most of your time and energy goes to the kids, running a household, and keeping up with school activities and other necessary events. With stressed or depressed teens, big chunks of time can be taken up by dealing with problems and solutions. You have to be intentional to spend some meaningful time with your spouse.

If your marriage is under strain anyway, spending time together might not be appealing. While you work on your marital issues separately, for the sake of your child, try to stay a unified front as you parent. In particular, avoid blaming each other for the problems. Differing personalities and parenting styles can cause severe conflict. Don't leave these unresolved.

The important thing is to take time together, no matter what. Even if it is brief, just be together alone, without the kids. Run errands. Go for lunch. Don't wait for a traditional date time, such as a Saturday night dinner. Chances are it won't happen. Make the most of spontaneous opportunities, such as when you know your teen is in a safe place for a while, or when she is at school, youth group, or at the movies.

One Saturday a while ago, my husband and I were holding hands as we went into Costco while running errands. I turned to him and asked, "Is this a date?" It occurred to both of us that we were going through a paradigm shift in what a "date" and "quality time together" looked like. He fondly replied, "Yes, Lovey, I suppose it is. Can I treat you to a Kosher dog?"

It is now over a year later, and my husband and I just took a walk on the beautiful beach of Laguna, California. We sat on the outdoor balcony of the Beach House restaurant overlooking the ocean, waves crashing below us. I had a great fish meal, wonderfully prepared and presented, with a garnish of banana leaves and a beautiful purple Hawaiian flower on top. As I sat watching the ebb and flow of the waves and staring at the glistening ocean, I could smell the fresh sea air. And I felt refreshed. Metaphorically, the constancy of the waves of God's love and faithfulness felt real and encouraging to me. As we watched the spectacular sunset slip over the edge of blue, red, and purple streaked clouds, I felt gentle closure and resolve. I caught a glimpse of the sunset flash and, in that moment, embraced a renewal in turning our hearts toward each other. This was especially a wonderful time for us because we are celebrating our anniversary (which was overlooked last year) and breakthrough of a long journey that has taken a toll on our relationship. Actually, we have had very little meaningful, enjoyable time alone in the last year, and some time by the seaside is absolutely wonderful. As life goes on, we will have more challenges. Yet God has brought us through.

I trust that He will do the same for you.

CAN ANY GOOD COME OUT OF THIS?

God has a purpose for you during this time of being refined like gold in the fire of adversity. He uses it to draw you closer to Him, transform your heart, and impact others. The Lord is full of mercy and comfort. He comforts us whenever we are in times of trouble, so that when others have trouble, we can comfort them with the same comfort He has given us (2 Cor. 1:3–5). Embrace His compassion and comfort during your times of trouble, so He can turn your brokenhearted misery into purpose-fulfilling ministry.

BECOMING USEFUL IN GOD'S HANDS

We each have a story to tell of God's love, grace, and mercy. We've been able to share some of ours with you, and some from other families. As we share what we have gone through and what the Lord has done for us, it encourages and inspires others. You, too, have your own stories to tell. Share them with others so they can find hope and help during life's stormy trials.

Oswald Chambers puts our role as storytellers in perspective in his devotional *My Utmost for His Highest*: "If you are going to be used of God, He will take you through a multitude of experiences that are not meant for you at all, they are meant to make you useful in His hands, and to enable you to understand what transpires in other souls, so that you will never be surprised at what you come across."[7]

As you become more sensitive to others who are struggling and hurting, offer to pray for them. Listen as they share, and empathize with them so they know that they are not alone in struggling. Write an encouraging note, sharing resources that the Lord has encouraged you with. Be a comfort and encouragement in any practical way. Remember what it was like for you in each phase of your journey, and try to meet others there. You don't have to have it all together for the Lord to use you to bring hope and encouragement-to be a hope giver. The human spirit can receive new hope just from an encouraging word or an act of loving-kindness. All you need is a heart of compassion.

In closing, we offer this prayer for you as you declare your purposefulness:

> *Lord, help me sense Your presence in my life as I go through this troubled time with my teen. Be close to me and comfort me when I feel brokenhearted. Free me from the oppression of negative emotions when I feel crushed in my spirit. Give me emotional stamina and spiritual strength for parenting my hurting teen. I love You and offer You my aching heart and my confused mind. I submit myself and accept whatever suffering*

is to be endured as a means to Your higher purposes. I honor You for ceaselessly working all things together for good in my life. I thank You and praise You that You are my God and Father who is full of mercy and comfort. I embrace Your compassion and comfort for me in these times of trouble. And I pray that I can be useful to You, passing on to others the compassion and comfort that I receive from You. Amen.

NOTES

CHAPTER 1

1. "Mysteries of The Teen Years," *U.S. News & World Report,* May 2005

2. Institute for American Values,. "A Report for the Nation from the Commission on Children at Risk," *Hardwired to Connect* (2003).

3. Dawson McAllister with Pat Springle, *Saving the Millennial Generation: New Ways to Reach the Kids You Care About in These Uncertain Times* (Nashville: Thomas Nelson, 1999).

4. Robert D. Putnam, *Bowling Alone: The Collapse and Revival of American Community* (New York: Simon & Schuster, 2000).

5. Robert D. Putnam and Lewis M. Feldstein, *Better Together: Restoring the American Community* (New York: Simon & Schuster, 2003).

6. Chap Clark, *Hurt: Inside the World of Today's Teenagers* (Grand Rapids: Baker, 2004).

7. M. Hallowell, M.D. *Connect* (New York: Pantheon, 1999).

CHAPTER 2

1. M. Hallowell, M.D. *Connect* (New York: Pantheon, 1999).

2. "The 2nd Annual *Teen People* Sex Survey," *Teen People* (October 2004): 116-119.

CHAPTER 3

1. Archibald D. Hart, *Adrenaline and Stress: The Exciting New Breakthrough That Helps You Overcome Stress Damage* (Dallas: Word Publishing, 1995).

2. Archibald D. Hart, *Stress and Your Child: The Hidden Reason Why*

Your Child May Be Moody, Resentful, or Insecure (Dallas: Word Publishing, 1992).

3. Archibald D. Hart, *The Anxiety Cure: A Proven Method for Dealing with Worry, Stress, and Panic Attacks* (Nashville: Word Publishing, 1999).

CHAPTER 4

1. U.S. Surgeon General Survey, 1999.
2. Archibald D. Hart and Catherine Hart Weber. *Unveiling Depression in Women: A Practical Guide to Understanding and Overcoming Depression* (Grand Rapids: Fleming H. Revell, 2002).
3. Institute for American Values, "A Report for the Nation from the Commission on Children at Risk," *Hardwired to Connect* (2003).

CHAPTER 5

1. Archibald D. Hart, *The Anxiety Cure: A Proven Method for Dealing with Worry, Stress, and Panic Attacks* (Nashville: Word Publishing, 1999).
2. http://www.cnn.com/2005/HEALTH/parenting/04/21/ drug.survey.ap/
   The 2004 Partnership Attitude Tracking Study surveyed more than 7,300 teens, the largest ongoing analysis of teen drug-related attitudes toward drugs in the country.
3. Violence and Traumatic Stress Research Branch, Division of Applied and Services Research, National Institute of Mental Health.
4. Robin Warshaw, *I Never Called It Rape: The Ms. Report on Recognizing, Fighting, and Surviving Date and Acquaintance Rape* (New York: Harper and Row, 1988).
5. http://www.nida.hih.gov/StressAlert/StressAlert.html
6. Adapted from excerpts of *It Happened to Me: A Teen's Guide to Overcoming Sexual Abuse*, Wm. Lee Carter, Ph.D).
7. Jeffrey Kluger, "The Cruelest Cut," *Time*, May 9, 2005.

CHAPTER 6

1. You can also learn more on this theory as it applies to marriage in the book *Safe Haven Marriage* by Archibald D. Hart and Sharon Hart Morris (Nashville: W Publishing Group, 2003).

CHAPTER 7

1. If you want to know more about a particular medication, ask your doctor or pharmacist. You can also visit www.WhatMeds.com, which provides information on the uses, precautions, and side effects for most commonly prescribed psychiatric medications.

2. Archibald D. Hart and Catherine Hart Weber, *Unveiling Depression in Women: A Practical Guide to Understanding and Overcoming Depression* (Grand Rapids: Fleming H. Revell, 2002).

CHAPTER 8

1. Daniel G. Amen, M.D., *Healing Anxiety and Depression* (New York: G. P. Putnam's Sons, 2003).

2. "Prevention That Works for Children and Youth," *American Psychologist* (June/July 2003): 458

CHAPTER 9

1. Pamela Paul, "Mind and Body Happiness: The Power to Uplift" *Time*, January 17, 2005.

2. Craig Steven Titus, "Resilience and Christian Virtues." Fribourg, 2002, Thesis presented to the faculty of theology at the University of Fribourg (Switzerland) to obtain a doctoral degree.

3. Bruce Wilkinson, *The Dream Giver* (Sisters: Multnomah Publishers, 2003).

4. Barbara Kantrowitz and Karen Springen, "Peaceful Adolescence," *Newsweek*, April 25, 2005. Results are from a 4-H study of positive youth development originally published in the February 2005 issue of the *Journal of Early Adolescence*.

CHAPTER 10

1. Viktor E. Frankl, *Man's Search for Meaning* (New York: Washington Square Press Publication, 1984).

2. Martin E. Seligman, *The Optimistic Child: A Proven Program to Safeguard Children Against Depression and Build Lifelong Resilience* (New York: Harper Perennial, 1995).

CHAPTER 11

1. Laurence Steinberg, "We Know Some Things: Parent-Adolescent Relationships in Retrospect and Prospect," *Journal of Research on Adolescence* 11, no. 1 (2001): 1–19.
2. Tim Kimmel, *Grace-Based Parenting* (Nashville: W Publishing Group, 2004).
3. John Gottman, *The Heart of Parenting: Raising an Emotionally Intelligent Child* (New York: Simon & Schuster, 1997).
4. Paul David Tripp, *Age of Opportunity: A Biblical Guide to Parenting Teens* (N.J.: Presbyterian and Reformed Publishing, 1997).

CHAPTER 12

1. www.spiritualityhealth.com/newsh/items/article/item_4301.html "Teen Care: Promoting Individuation, Not Separation"
2. www.fathers.com

CHAPTER 13

1. Henri Nouwen, *With Open Hand* (Ave Marie Press, 1995).

CHAPTER 14

1. Beth Moore, *Praying God's Word: Breaking Free from Spiritual Strongholds* (Nashville: Broadman & Holman Publishers, 2000).
2. Tim Kimmel, *Grace-Based Parenting* (Nashville: W Publishing Group, 2004).
3. Lewis B. Smedes, *Forgive and Forget: Healing the Hurts We Don't Deserve* (New York: HarperCollins Publishers, 1996).
4. "The New Science of Happiness," Time (January 17, 2005): 28.
5. www.reflectivehappiness.com
6. James W. Pennebaker, *Writing to Heal: A Guided Journal for Recovering from Trauma and Emotional Upheaval* (Oakland: New Harbinger Publications, 2004).
7. Oswald Chambers, *My Utmost for His Highest* (Grand Rapids: Discovery House Publishers, 1963).

ADDITIONAL
RESOURCES

LEARNING ABOUT TEENS

Clark, Chap. *Hurt: Inside the World of Today's Teenagers*. Grand Rapids: Baker Academic, 2004.

McAllister, Dawson with Pat Springle. Saving the Millennial Generation: New Ways to Reach the Kids You Care About in These Uncertain Times. Nashville: Thomas Nelson, 1999.

Rice, Wayne and David Veerman. *Understanding Your Teenager*. Nashville: W Publishing Group, 1999.

www.uyt.com—seminar information and resources by these authors

www.troublewith.com—Focus on the Family resource Web site for immediate help and long-term hope on a broad range of topics.

www.daretobelieve.org—Suzanne Eller's Real Issues, Real Teens books and resources for teens and parents.

STRESS

Colbert, Don, M.D. *Stress Less*. Lake Mary: Siloam Press, 2005

Hart, Archibald D. *The Hidden Link Between Adrenaline and Stress*. 1995.

Hart, Archibald D. *Stress and Your Child. The Hidden Reason Why Your Child May Be Moody, Resentful or Insecure*. Dallas: Word Publishing, 1992.

Swenson, Richard A. *Margin. Restoring Emotional, Physical, Financial, and time Reserves to Overloaded Lives*. Colorado Springs: NavPress, 1992.

www.focusas.com/Stress.html - Helping Teenagers with Stress

www.nctsnet.org - National Child Traumatic Stress Network.

RESILIENCE

MacDonald, Gordon. *A Resilient Life*. Nelson Books: Nashville, 2004.

Reivich, Karen and Andrew Shatte. *The Resilience Factor: How Changing the Way You Think Will Change Your Life for Good. 7 Essential Skills for Overcoming Life's Inevitable Obstacles*. New York: Broadway Books, 2002.

www.reflectivehappiness.com - Dr. Martin Seligman has created the Reflective Happiness Plan to accurately measure, improve, and sustain your emotional wellbeing for a more fulfilling and satisfying life.

DEPRESSION

Manassis, Katharina, Levac, Anne Marie. *Helping Your Teenager Beat Depression: A Problem-Solving Approach for Families*. Woodbine House, 2004.

Mondimore, Francis Mark, M.D. *Adolescent Depression: A Guide for Parents. A John Hopkins Press Health Book*. Baltimore: Johns Hpkins Press, 2002.

Seligman, Martin E. *The Optimistic Child: A Proven Program to Safeguard Children Against Depression and Build Lifelong Resilience*. New York: Harper Perennial, 1995

www.amenclinic.com - Daniel G. Amen, M.D., presents his breakthrough clinical research in Brain SPECT Imaging for depression, anxiety, ADD/ADHD.

WORKBOOK FOR TEENS

Copans, Stuart and Mary Ellen Copeland. *Recovering from Depression: A workbook for Teens*. Baltimore: Paul H. Brooks Publishing, 2002.

Cobain, Bev, R.N.C. *When Nothing Matters Anymore: A Survival Guide for Depressed Teens*. Minneapolis: Free Spirit Publishing, 1998.

SEXUAL ABUSE, RAPE

Carter, Lee Wm. *It Happened to Me: A Teen's Guide to Overcoming Sexual Abuse*. Oakland: New Harbinger Publications, 2002.

TEEN PREGNANCY

Schooler, Jayne E. *Mom, Dad, I'm Pregnant: When Your Daughter or Son Faces an Unplanned Pregnancy*. Colorado Springs: NavPress, 2004.

Goyer, Tricia. *Life Interrupted: The Scoop on Being a Young Mom.* Grand
Rapids: Zondervan, 2004.

www.living-well.org - LivingWell Medical Clinic is committed to serving
women, men, teens, parents, and all those involved in a circumstance where a pregnancy is unplanned or unwanted.

www.family.org/resources - This site offers a search engine where you can
buy books or videos about abortion, etc.

ANXIETY

Hart, Archibald D. *The Anxiety Cure. A Proven Method for Dealing with
Worry, Stress, and Panic Attacks.* Nashville: Word Publishing, 1999.

Amen, Daniel. *Healing Anxiety and Depression.* New York: Putnam's
Sons, 2003.

SUBSTANCE ABUSE

http://www.teenchallenge.com/includes/print/cfm?articleID=
7&centerID= 1021 - Teen Challenge, What Parents Can Do.

PARENTING TEENS

Larimore, Walt M.D. and Yorkey, Mike. *God's Design for the Highly
Healthy Teen.* Grand Rapids: Zondervan, 2005.

Thomas, Gary L. *Sacred Parenting: How Raising Children Shapes Our
Souls.* Grand Rapids: Zondervan, 2004.

Kimmel, Tim. *Grace-Based Parenting.* Nashville: W Publishing Group,
2004.

Tripp, Paul David. *Age of Opportunity: A Biblical Guide to Parenting
Teens.* NJ:Presbyterian and Reformed Publishing, 1997.

White, Joe, and Jim Weidmann, ed. *Parent's Guide to the Spiritual
Mentoring of Teens: Building Your Child's Faith Through the
Adolescent Years.* Wheaton: Tyndale, 2001.

Campbell, Ross. *How to Really Love Your Teen.* Colorado Springs: Life
Journey, 2003.

Gordon, Thomas. *Parent Effectiveness Training: The Proven Program for
Raising Responsible Children.* New York: Three Rivers Press, 2000.

Dockery, Karen. *Bold Parents, Positive Teens: Loving and Guiding Your
Child Through the Challenge of Adolescence.* Colorado Springs:
Waterbrook, 2002.

Riera, Michael. *Staying Connected to Your Teenager: How to Keep Them Talking to You and How to Hear What They Are Really Saying.* Cambridge: Perseus Publishing, 2003.

Seigel, Daniel J. and Mary Hartzelle. *Parenting from the Inside Out: How a Deeper Self-Understanding Can Help You Raise Children Who Thrive.* New York: Penguin Putman, 2003.

Clark, Chap and Clark, Dee. *Disconnected: Parenting Teens in a MySpace World.* Michigan: Baker Books, 2007.

PARENTING GIRLS

Shellenberger, Susie. *The Mother-Daughter Connection: Building a Lifelong Bond with Your Daughter.* Nashville: Word Publishing, 2000.

Hersh, Sharon A. *Mom, I Hate My Life! Becoming Your Daughter's Ally Through the Emotional Ups and Downs of Adolescence.* Colorado Springs: Shaw Books, 2004.

PARENTING BOYS

Dobson, James. *Bringing Up Boys.* Wheaton: Tyndale House Publishers, 2001.

Beausay, Bill. *Teenage Boys: Shaping the Man Inside.* Colorado Springs: Waterbrook Press, 1998.

Oliver, Gary J. and Carrie Oliver. *Raising Sons and Loving It!* Grand Rapids: Zondervan, 2000.

PRAYING FOR TEENS AND PRODIGALS

Sherrer, Quin and Ruth Garlock. *Praying Prodigals Home: Taking Back What the Enemy Has Stolen.* Ventura: Regal, 2000.

Larson, Scott. *When Teens Stray: Parenting for the Long Haul.* Ventura: Regal, 2002.

Kimmel, Tim. *Why Christians Rebel: Trading Heartache for Hope.* Nashville: W Publishing Group, 2004.

Gardner Littleton, Jeanette. *When Your Teen Goes Astray: Help and Hope From Parents Who Have Been There.* Beacon Hill Press, 2004

Yates, Susan Alexander. *31 Days of Prayer for My Teen.* Grand Rapids: Baker, 2004.

HELP FOR PARENTS

Hart, Archibald D. and Catherine Hart Weber. *Unveiling Depression in Women: A Practical Guide to Understanding and Overcoming Depression.* Grand Rapids: Fleming H. Revell, 2002.

Hart, Archibald. *Unmasking Male Depression.* Nashville: W Publishing Group, 2001.

Karp, David Allen. *The Burden of Sympathy: How Families Cope with Mental Illness.* New York: Oxford University Press, 2001.

Hart, Archibald & Sharon Hart Morris. *Safe Haven Marriage: Building a Relationship You Want to Come Home To.* Nashville: W Publishing Group, 2003.

Morris May, Sharon. *How to Argue So Your Spouse Will Listen.* Nashville: Thomas Nelson, 2007.

AUTHOR'S CONTACT INFORMATION
FOR SPEAKING, COUNSELING, AND COACHING

Dr. Archibald Hart
Dr. Catherine Hart Weber
www.hartinstitute.com
Hart Institute
P.O. Box 905
Sierra Madre, CA 91025